LUNAR NODES

DISCOVER YOUR SOUL'S KARMIC MISSION

ABOUT THE AUTHOR

Celeste Teal (Arizona) has been a passionate student of astrology for nearly thirty years. A graduate of the West Coast College of Astrology, Westminster, CA, in basic and advanced courses, she attained professional certification in 1986. Teal is a member of the American Federation of Astrologers and the Arizona Society of Astrologers. Besides hosting her popular astrology website, *The Moon Valley Astrologer*, she writes feature articles for popular astrology magazines, including *Dell Horoscope*, *American Astrology* (now called *Horoscope Guide*), and *Astrology: Your Daily Horoscope*. Celeste Teal has authored three previous books on astrological technique: *Predicting Events with Astrology* (1999), *Identifying Planetary Triggers* (2000), and *Eclipses* (2006), all published by Llewellyn Publications.

TO WRITE TO THE AUTHOR

If you wish to contact the author or would like more information about this book, please write to the author in care of Llewellyn Worldwide and we will forward your request. Both the author and publisher appreciate hearing from you and learning of your enjoyment of this book and how it has helped you. Llewellyn Worldwide cannot guarantee that every letter written to the author can be answered, but all will be forwarded. Please write to:

Celeste Teal
℅ Llewellyn Worldwide
2143 Wooddale Drive
Woodbury, MN 55125-2989

Please enclose a self-addressed stamped envelope for reply,
or $1.00 to cover costs. If outside U.S.A., enclose
international postal reply coupon.

Many of Llewellyn's authors have websites with additional information and resources. For more information, please visit our website at www.llewellyn.com.

LUNAR NODES

DISCOVER YOUR SOUL'S KARMIC MISSION

CELESTE TEAL

Llewellyn Publications
Woodbury, Minnesota

First Edition
Third Printing, 2012

Book design by Donna Burch
Cover art © 2008 by Image Source/PunchStock
Cover design by Gavin Dayton Duffy
Editing by Connie Hill
Illustration on page 2 redrawn with permission from Steven M. Johnson. Illustration on page 13 by Llewellyn Art Department. Illustration on page 201 redrawn with permission from Mohan Koparker, PhD (www .MOHANSTARS.com). Chart wheels were produced by the Kepler program by permission of Cosmic Patterns Software, Inc. (www.AstroSoftware.com)
Llewellyn is a registered trademark of Llewellyn Worldwide Ltd.

Library of Congress Cataloging-in-Publication Data:

Teal, Celeste, 1951–
  Lunar nodes : discover your soul's karmic mission / Celeste Teal.
     p.   cm.
  Includes bibliographical references and index.
  ISBN 978-0-7387-1337-3
  1. Astrology. 2. Moon--Miscellanea. 3. Human beings--Effect of the moon on. I. Title.
  BF1723.T43 2008
  133.5'32--dc22   2008037406

Llewellyn Publications
A Division of Llewellyn Worldwide Ltd.
2143 Woodgate Drive
Woodbury, Minnesota 55125-2989
www.llewellyn.com

Printed in the United States of America

OTHER BOOKS BY THIS AUTHOR

Identifying Planetary Triggers
(Llewellyn Publications, 2000)

Eclipses
(Llewellyn Publications, 2006)

Predicting Events with Astrology (New Edition)
(Llewellyn Publications)

CONTENTS

LIST OF FIGURES

INTRODUCTION

Out of all of the planets and all of the various parts of a horoscope, the lunar nodes have always held a special fascination for me. I've been drawn to them over and over again. When I was researching Solar Returns in the early 1990s, the lunar nodes really started to pop off the page, revealing a great deal of information about the trend and events of the year. I began making notes and writing articles about them. Not long ago, I realized that, in each of my books, the lunar nodes were given exclusive attention in the discussions in one form or another. My last book, *Eclipses*, included quite a bit about them, since eclipses are dependent on the lunar nodes and can only occur when a New or Full Moon aligns with them. By the time I finished that project I had pages of notes left over about the transiting nodes impacting the natal chart, about how the nodes function in relationship combinations, and more. My curiosity about the nodes was stronger than ever. I felt positive they held the keys to our soul's purpose and our spiritual mission in life. There was much convincing data to that effect.

I decided it would be worthwhile to compile everything I had and perhaps do more research to put together a book about these mysterious nodes. It seemed a great idea to create a complete lunar node book—all this information in one place for handy reference. I knew I could use such a book and felt that others would also find it valuable.

To complete this book I searched far and wide for information on the nodes that could either verify or add to my own findings. I even crossed over into Vedic astrology where the nodes are actually considered to be planets—not just planets, but really the most powerful indicators in the chart. This journey was well worth the effort.

I also felt it would be helpful to study large groups of people who had a particular nodal feature. In that way, if there were any outstanding themes behind the aspect, it should come to light when looking over a whole group of individuals. AstroDatabank lists, tight controls, and only the highest-rated data were used to cull through hundreds of public figures.

In these pages you will learn how to use the lunar nodes as a stand-alone tool for finding out many things about yourself, your friends, and loved ones. In thirty years of astrology study, I have learned more about myself and everyone I know through doing this work than from anything else up to this point. I am certain you are going to feel the same way. The nodes really do reveal our purpose and mission in life.

Sometimes a soul aborts his or her mission, or the mission is otherwise aborted. Most make it, although it may take most of the lifetime to complete the journey, make the contributions, and learn the lessons intended by that soul. This is basically accomplished by using the South Node talents to transition to North Node, gathering those new characteristics and then giving back to the South Node.

We can determine if a soul has taken an upward road in life or an easier road. Certain individuals have extra leeway, reaping benefits now for good deeds done in the past. Others have heavy dues to pay, or they have arranged to participate in a mission that requires a great amount of experience before they qualify. There are karmic implications in the nodes; they represent the small percentage of time that our free will appears to be operating at a minimal level. Karma is an objective-balancing mechanism existing in the universal spirit. There is heavenly guidance associated with the nodes, and sometimes that higher power takes over. Sometimes there are unanticipated benefits coming to us, while at other times there is a service requested of us. Much goes on according to arrangements we made that we no longer remember. Since karma and these divine universal designs are difficult to prove, it is through application of the principles presented that you can test them for yourself.

The nodes can even be used as timing devices. Whenever a nodal contact takes place, social encounters and connections occur with others who allow us to reap our good karma or pay some dues. This could be a transiting node contacting a natal planet, a transiting planet contacting a natal node, or even when an association comes about in which one person's node connects with the other person's planet.

The North Node is like a cup that is running over. Gifts from the higher powers are coming to us and good karma is rewarded. The South Node is an empty cup; we are expected to fill it up. We can provide a service that will contribute to another soul or to the growth and evolution of the planet. Much is happening as part of natural processes.

Right now I'm putting together this book—a direct result of all the data surrounding the nodes that I've taken in over the past few years. When I wrote *Eclipses*, it got me hooked on trying to solve that riddle. I studied some more, researched some more, and went through pages and pages of notes I'd made. In this summary I want to share with you what I've learned about the nodes that may help you as well. You take in so much and then you give out so much. The benefit for me is that I am finishing some work that frees me up to move on. I had South Node transiting over my Mars when I began the book, drawing me to put my energy into this large project.

The times of transiting contacts will be experienced as harmonious, uplifting, encouraging, and free flowing with the North Node contacts, or constricting, restraining, and sometimes complicated with the South Node contacts. These things can all be found in the nodes and utilized on a daily basis to complete the mission and move to a higher level on the soul's evolution. You will find complete chapters on any aspect of the nodes you are in search of.

While you will get the greatest good from this book if you have some astrology basics under your belt, it is designed to be easy for beginning astrologers to use. A glossary of terms is included at the end of the book.

Now, let's get down to some serious fun, exploring the lunar nodes. Before long, the nodes will be the first feature you'll examine when you begin any chart interpretation!

Chapter One

THE LUNAR NODES

The lunar nodes are among the most powerful influences we could observe in the horoscope, and yet they are invisible in the heavens. They are the unseen influences, representing the higher powers, or cosmic forces, at work. They represent karmic controls.

Ancient astrologers gave the lunar nodes tremendous importance, using them to forecast eclipses. Their knowledge and experience led the astrologers to believe that the nodes indicated special dealings with humankind by the higher universal forces—that they represented the higher power's interaction with humankind. Lunar nodes are currently given special karmic and spiritual significance, although there was a long period of time when they were disregarded by many astrologers because they are not real bodies in the heavens. Only Hindu astrologers have consistently held them to be the most potent influence in the affairs of humans and among the most important factors in a horoscope. In fact, in the Hindu system, where a belief in reincarnation is common, we are said to have four kinds of karma with each of the two lunar nodes ruling over two of them. Before we get into that discussion, a bit of explanation about these invisible points in the heavens is in order.

THE INVISIBLE NODES, ASTRONOMICALLY

Astronomically, the lunar nodes are the intersection points where the Moon crosses the plane of the ecliptic—that plane, passing through the center of the Sun, which contains the orbit of the earth. The orbit of the Moon around the earth defines another plane and these two planes are slightly inclined to one another. The intersections of the two orbital planes form an axis and the points of the intersections determine the lunar nodes. As the Moon circles the earth once a month, it spends half that time in the North Celestial Latitude and half the time in the South Celestial Latitude, crossing the ecliptic on two occasions. The North Node is where the Moon's path intercepts the ecliptic when

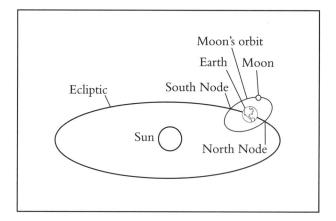

Figure 1: The Lunar Nodes

crossing from the South to the North Celestial Latitude, and the South Node is where the Moon crosses the ecliptic from the North back to the South Celestial Latitude two weeks later. The diagram below shows some simple basics.

The pair of nodes remain exactly opposite one another and, as the earth travels around the Sun, the nodal axis travels with it, so that there are two times a year that the nodal axis aligns with (points to) the Sun. Those are the times when conditions are right for an eclipse.

TRUE & MEAN NODES

The lunar nodes do not move at a fully predictable speed, but vary from day to day. Their position can be calculated one of two ways, termed True or Mean. Although there is only a slight difference in the two positions, you will likely want to know about this at some point. The true calculation gives the exact position of the nodes as the moon crosses the ecliptic, whereas the mean calculation gives the presumed position based on their average speed. The mean calculations were used before computers made it easy to calculate the true position, and now many astrologers have taken to using the true position. There is some debate as to which is best, although almost everything descriptive written about the nodes is based on their mean positions. The mean node is always presumed retrograde, whereas the true node may occasionally be direct, as if it is wobbling. The true node is only "true" twice a month—at the times the Moon crosses the ecliptic. Positions given between those times are a hypothesis based on an approximation of the celestial orbits, even though the Moon's orbit varies due to the pull of the Sun.

So, in both cases the positions of the nodes are generally somewhat of an approximation, and they are never far apart from one another, usually within a degree or so. Due to their consistent retrograde motion, the mean lunar nodes are most relevant for a study of karmic and spiritual implications in a natal chart. When used as a timing device in progressions, it is also the mean nodes that appear to be most accurate. If you are using software to calculate your charts, which is recommended, the best astrology programs will offer you a choice. You can check the default settings to be sure you're using the one you want.

THE NODES DEFINE OUR LIFE MISSION

Forming their axis, not unlike the Ascendant/Descendant and the Vertex/Anti-Vertex in a horoscope, there is an alliance or a partnership formed between the two ends. The lunar nodal axis is likened to a dragon or a serpent, representative of experiences and happenings that bestow special wisdom upon an individual. Such wisdom comes as the result of our efforts to utilize our experience and knowledge from the past in order to move higher on the ladder of evolution.

The lunar nodes move backward through the zodiac—in the horoscope, this means they are always going in a clockwise direction around the wheel, while the other planets progress counterclockwise. The nodes regress slowly, about nineteen degrees per year, spending about a year and a half in each zodiac sign.

In the spiritual sense, as an Axis of Fate—as more modern astrologers describe the nodes—their retrograde motion suggests that happenings in the present have roots in the past. Right now the life pattern is being affected by legacy. We have certain birthrights and certain responsibilities. The nodes could be viewed as portals through which the higher universal force merges forces and has interplay with humankind. They symbolize cause-and-effect developments in life. They represent a meeting ground for issues that have a bearing on fate or free will. No one has total free will (except perhaps enlightened yogis and saints) and the nodes mark the spot where karma is a factor. Karma is not a punishment. It is the fulfilling of responsibilities that results in expanded spiritual growth. The nodes represent these compelling forces of destiny. Experiences that unfold when the nodes are activating the chart often defy or seem to operate independently of free will, reason, or judgment. Whether this is experienced as a wanted or an unwanted event, it may be seen as the manner in which the higher forces are intervening or giving you a boost, helping you stay on your intended path of personal destiny.

There are things to be learned through the nodes that are not to be found through any other chart factors. They explain the "why" behind our very existence. They explain our purpose. They bring light to why other chart features manifest as they do, as the nodes represent special influences that may act independently of others, or can actually counteract others. They define our karmic lessons and our destined missions. They prove that our lives are strongly influenced by karma and that we had specific intentions before arriving in the present life.

When I was nearly eight years old, an incident occurred that I experienced as extremely traumatic. The nature of the event is not as important as the result of it. The incident and the trauma was so acute that in the midst of it I guess I simply exited my body and left this earth plane. There is a long gap in my memory and I have no recall of the real events going on for a period of several hours, only learning much later what had transpired. However, soon after the incident I became aware of a vivid memory of a pre-birth experience. I've often wondered if this visitation took place during that gap in my memory, or if a pre-birth memory was partially restored at that time:

I was on another plane, a heavenly place, getting ready to come to earth, and I was standing before an illuminated form—it was really more of an energy than a form. We were going over everything that was required of me to come and do the things I wanted to do. Our communication took place telepathically. I was reminded that by coming now, I'd chosen a life that would be very hard in the beginning—lots of pain and emotional hurts. This would continue for a long time. The one thing I had to promise was that I would keep my enthusiasm for life and not let the hurts get me down, because there were to be rewards later on for me. I vividly recall that I was so excited about coming that it felt like my heart might just explode right out of me. I felt like the spirit part of me was jumping up and down in anticipation. I was full of joy and couldn't wait. From that vantage point, everything seemed so easy. I made my promise with hardly a moment of hesitation.

There was also some instruction about a time when I would be called upon to carry out my special service, beginning around the turn of the century, and that there would be a group of us doing similar work. I was to be part of an important group mission—that was the most thrilling part. From my peripheral vision, I was aware of other souls standing toward my right. I felt that these others were waiting for their individual interviews. These others who were coming around the same time as me were not necessarily part of my group's mission. They had their own missions and their own promises to make—but we were all working for the same ultimate goal, and it felt like an honor and privilege to do work for this amazingly pure energy source.

I told no one of this for many years; actually I couldn't. It was vivid and yet other-worldly, and my young mind couldn't grasp the totality of what it was all about. I sort of grew into it and things made more sense as time went by. I have always wondered if this memory clicked in when it did or if the visitation occurred because I needed that heavenly guidance so badly right then. I can tell you that it did help me get through a lot of bumps, hardships, losses and sad occasions. I was resilient because I remembered the promise.

Then, right on cue, my life took a seemingly destined turn and the pace of events accelerated. In late 1994 I met my wonderful husband through a remarkable series of synchronicities. It was love at first sight and a feeling of instant recognition. Largely because of him, and improving circumstances, within two years I was doing my beloved astrology full time and writing books for astrologers, the first two being published right around the turn of the century. In the last decade I have realized that everything revealed to me in that vision/visitation has occurred. From whatever source, the revelation proved to be genuine. Notice, though, that what I would be doing wasn't revealed to me at that time—that my calling would be in the field of astrology. I had to discover that for myself when the time was right.

Anyway, in large part it is this experience that convinces me that we do have our special missions and karmic services to provide, and that we actually had some say-so in designing the whole plan. Our soul does not perish. I feel sure that many of you have also had similar visitations or communications and likely hold similar views about there being a purpose for each of us, even if you have no conscious recall of such otherworldly instructions.

This explains so many things about our differences; even starting with physical differences at birth, described largely by the nodes, and why some people seem to have easy lives while others have it so tough. Those having it tough may have actually requested a life in which they could take on more lessons, pay a lot of karmic debts, and make a big leap in their evolution. Or, it might have been the desire of the spirit to accomplish some purpose at a certain time that necessitates hardships for the soul—like working one's way up to be worthy of the honor to participate in certain causes. There's a lot of experience that is needed first.

It may be that the everlasting soul acquires a newly animated spirit each lifetime and then takes up a physical body, the vehicle required to accomplish the preset mission during our short time on earth. In esoteric astrology, the Moon is symbolic of the soul, while the Sun represents the spirit. The nodes are the keys to unlocking these secrets. They provide information about all three: the soul, the spirit, and the physical body. This is logical, since the nodes are the result of the relationship between the Moon, Sun, and Earth.

As far as defining our intended mission, the node positions in the natal chart begin to tell this story from birth. This axis shows our link to the past and points to the future. The south end of the axis reveals what we came into this life with: our assets and liabilities, our accumulated good and bad karma. The South Node represents the suitcase we brought with us. This is all the stuff we owned. By sign, the South Node indicates our nature and inborn character traits that are clearly visible through our behavior and actions. They are automatic, based on prior successes and past fears. We have lifetimes of experience under our belt of the nature of the South Node sign. It's easier to continue doing works and deeds that utilize those qualities. Like an old pair of pajamas, we find a certain amount of comfort wearing these old clothes, even though there are some less desirable features about them. They are fading, the elastic is weakening, and the fabric is no longer crisp. We certainly don't make our best impression in them. The inborn tendencies are so habitual that, unfortunately, we tend to express some of the less appealing traits of the sign holding the South Node, and that is the worst thing to do. To strongly act out the negative sign traits of the South Node may mean a person is headed toward great unhappiness, setbacks, and remorse. The South Node could be viewed as a weak spot. It has been compared to quicksand, as it shows the footsteps we left behind us that we may be tempted to retrace, maybe only to fall into a black hole.

Our goal and plan now was to acquire the positive traits symbolized by the exact opposite sign, where the North Node lies. It represents the future, and those attributes to be acquired next on our continuing journey. The highest qualities symbolized by the North Node are those that we aimed to claim, that we actually were excited to make claim to: to do works and deeds that exemplify that sign. While the South Node symbolizes a comfort zone, the North Node symbolizes the new and novel—therefore it takes some courage to venture into the new territory. There is challenge, like starting school that first day. There is guidance for us at the North Node, but we must put forth a conscious personal effort in that direction to draw on all the blessings the universe has in store for us. Moving forward brings the greatest happiness.

We do not actually demonstrate our North Node traits until we cultivate and develop them. Throughout our life, events and circumstances push us toward this end. Life experiences encourage us to develop those new faculties. Life rewards us with unhappiness when we try to continue on the old path, to remind us of our intents and purposes. We can utilize all the many talents we brought with us to accomplish the task by redistributing that energy. A knack associated with the South Node may be just what is needed to carry out the mission symbolized by the North Node. Some make the transition more rapidly than others. Most are working through some facet of this personal challenge for the entire lifetime and possibly into the next. If you are very aware, you may find you still have some hang-up associated with your South Node, even if you have managed to develop many of your North Node traits. Some South Node traits may linger, as they are so habitual. Sadly, some individuals make little progress or don't make it, but they will get the chance again. Eventually, gradually, we all make it. There's really no such thing as failure when it comes to meeting our spiritual destiny.

FOUR KINDS OF KARMA

Anything left unresolved from previous incarnations was brought in our luggage.

I mentioned earlier that, according to the Hindu system of astrology, there are said to be four kinds of karmas. The first, called Sanchita karma, is the total accumulated karma we each carry from all our previous lives. The second, called Prarabdha, is the small portion of the total karma that we are ready to experience and which must be fulfilled in this lifetime. The third kind, called Kriyamana, is what we are creating right now by our actions and our exercise of free will. The fourth kind, called Agama, is the karma we are creating for our future through the use of visualization and our intentions for the future.

In the Vedic astrology system, the South Node is called Ketu, and is considered to rule the first two kinds of karma. It presides over the past and our karmic inheritance. The North Node, Rahu, rules the latter two kinds of karma, and presides over the future.

These simple concepts help us grasp the function of the nodes, and enable us to work along the best path for enlightenment. The South Node is especially significant in that small percentage of time that our free will is negligible. Sometimes things happen as the result of free will exercised in the past. On the positive side, how we deal with events occurring right now has everything to do with our future karma. Obviously, anyone could begin to create positive karma for the future through the practice of creative visualization and by having pure intentions. We are actually carving out our future with our present thoughts! If we are doing great at the latter two types of karma that we are creating, it could actually offset or limit the amount of loss we suffer during the times we are burning off old negative karma (periods that can be identified). Rewards are due to us for positive works as well, and even these kinds of events and developments, traceable to the North Node, may take us by surprise or are seemingly unconnected to our free will. The cosmic forces shower us with blessings at certain times (also identifiable) for past good deeds.

Both nodes and the events stemming from them commonly involve other people and our interactions with them. It is through associations and meetings with other people that we pay debts, provide services, or accrue dividends, and enjoy our good karma. In fact, the very people that cause us upsets are often the ones that push us to learn our karmic lessons and move forward. When we recognize this, we are starting to get it.

No one makes it here without having some unpaid debts, and some of these will have to be paid this time around, along with certain new debts that are accumulated.

Maybe you are one of those people, or you know someone, who says that they no more than commit some small crime, and within days they are paying retribution for it. They say their karma comes back on them immediately. It is true, I believe, that if one is conscious that an action or an intention is wrong, it likely takes much less time to suffer the consequences. Crimes committed unintentionally or without awareness that a wrongdoing was committed may not ripen to be repaid until that soul has further evolved. The more aware and conscious one becomes, the more responsibility one must take.

Some have more debts than others. When called upon to pay a debt, we may resist, but then we face the likelihood of a hard lesson about what we call fate. The free will factor here is in how we choose to respond to a seemingly fateful experience.

The North and South Nodes have been given many names and associations.

The North Node symbol is ☊. It is associated with a hilltop, a place of elevation. The North Node is called Rahu by Hindu astrologers. It has also been called Caput by Western astrologers, but is best known as the Dragon's Head, generally considered the more positive end of the dragon. It represents a place of incoming cosmic energy. It is like a cup that overflows, and its symbol reminds us of this. Gains, especially material and worldly acquisitions, are made possible by an infusion of the God force, but one must be willing to reach out and grasp the opportunity. The North Node embodies our capacity to respond to new experiences. There is anticipation here, and this node represents a place of intake, of new substance and sustenance, like new foodstuff provided to us. Inwardly, we have a sense of this, of what it is we're supposed to do, but there is no guarantee that we'll actually move in that direction. This is where new karma can be created.

The South Node symbol is ☋. It is associated with a valley. Hindu astrologers call it Ketu, while in the West it has been called Cauda, but it is most popularly known as the Dragon's Tail, the more vulnerable end of the dragon. There are sacrifices and restrictions associated with it. It has been linked with a swampland, as it indicates where waste products are shed. The South Node represents our capacity to liberate ourselves from the power of the past. There may be a sense of responsibility and knowingness regarding debts owed or some timeless service to be performed. The South Node symbolizes the need for release or evacuation. As suggested by its symbol, it represents an empty cup that must be filled. The universe expects something from you. Through this node we contribute to effects that are everlasting.

Together the pair of nodes function as a two-way flow, complementing one another. Like a seesaw in action, they work together. We are given new materials to assimilate by the North Node. We make sacrifices and give of ourselves to something greater than ourselves at the South Node. We reach within to draw from our accumulated experience and knowledge to share and give back to the greater whole. This is quite an instinctual and natural process in large part, and when individuals have mastered their nodes and this natural rhythm, abundant fulfillment is the result.

Together, they reveal our interactions with others and our connections in the big picture.

In the next chapter you'll learn what the nodes reveal about your mission, your looks, and your demeanor, based on their general position in your natal chart.

Chapter Two

NATAL NODES CHART POSITIONS

One of the nodes will exert the most obvious, or dominant, influence throughout your life. To learn about your mission, you must first locate the position of your nodes in your chart. Most readers likely have their natal horoscope calculated already—and if not there are resources listed in the appendix for this. Feel free to link to one of the websites listed there, where you can get a free copy of your horoscope by entering your birth data.

YOUR MISSION & THE LINE OF ADVANTAGE

As I said, one of your nodes will appear to exert a more noticeable influence in your life. If the South Node appears in the uppermost portion of the chart, or in the First House, this indicates that you have chosen an uphill road in this life. Your desire, mission, and driving force to contribute is greater than your desire to assimilate, accumulate, or amass. You have already amassed a great deal of experience in the past and now it is your plan to utilize all the wealth of knowledge you've acquired to make a lasting contribution to the world. Even so, you'll still have enough new raw material coming in at appropriate intervals and in the appropriate departments of life to sustain you on your mission. If you've ever felt that you are an old soul, you may very well be right. Additional features of your nodes will help determine this as we go along.

If the North Node is dominant, by being in the First House or overhead, you're here to take in and assimilate new material, amass new experiences. It is an easier road to travel in many respects. Circumstances are in your favor to make a speedy rise in life. You'll still have opportunities to make personal contributions, as timed by the nodal contacts. Others may see you as having a life of many advantages or of being especially blessed, but you've somehow earned this. In fact, while others might not see it, you may have your own struggles in taking advantage of your position. On the other hand, if you abuse having so much power and abundance, the last part of this lifetime and the next may be spent paying oodles of karmic debts. There's a good chance that you are a younger soul; however, other features of your nodes will help determine this as we go along.

In studying and doing research for this book, I came across some findings set forth by George White in 1927, which was republished in a small book, *The Moon's Nodes*, by the AFA (American Federation of Astrologers) in 2004. I was excited to learn that Mr. White's assessment of these nodal positions in the natal chart was a very close match to my own findings from their positions in the annual solar return chart. Instead of having a clear-cut line running from the Ascendant to the Descendant in which to divide the map, this division line appears to run through the Second and Eighth Houses, close to the cusps of the Third and Ninth Houses. Mr. White called it the Line of Advantage, whereby having the North Node above that line was the preferred placement inasmuch as it indicated a greater degree of help and assistance extended by the higher forces during one's lifetime. Actually, neither position can be said to be the "preferred" position. We each have the one that is right for us, the natural result of previous involvements, experiences, choices, and decisions. In fact, as we become more spiritually evolved, having the South Node uppermost may eventually be the preferred placement, but on the surface, there appear to be certain material and worldly benefits when the North Node is above the line of advantage.

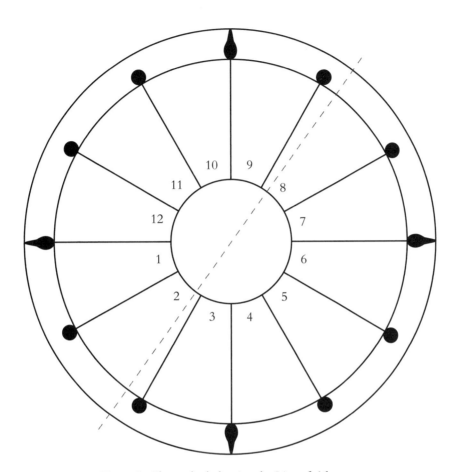

Figure 2: Chart wheel showing the Line of Advantage

NODES ON THE MIDHEAVEN OR OVERHEAD

One of the most prominent places to have one of the nodes is on the Midheaven, the cusp leading into the Tenth House. It represents the public status. The Eleventh House position also reflects strong nodal influences throughout the life. The reason for this will become clearer when we talk about progressions. The Ninth House is also a strong position, and much of the following descriptions can be applied generally in those cases when one of the nodes falls in any of these three houses—nine, ten, or eleven. The closer the node is to the Tenth House cusp, the stronger its influence.

Having the North Node situated uppermost gives many assets and opportunities for success. It may appear to work as a luck factor and brings these individuals to prominence. Money comes easily; there is promotion and recognition for accomplishments, mingling with or having contacts and relationships with important people. Often, one is born into a well-to-do family of good background, in which the parents assist in catapulting the individual upward. There is usually a good amount of confidence and extroversion displayed.

Some famous personalities with North Node on the Midheaven are Meryl Streep, actor; Sydney Omarr, astrologer; Mark McGwire, baseball player; Celine Dion, singer; Carl Sagan, astronomer/NASA consultant; Padre Pio, Italian healer, monk, and stigmatic; and Paula Abdul, the beautiful, multitalented judge on American Idol.

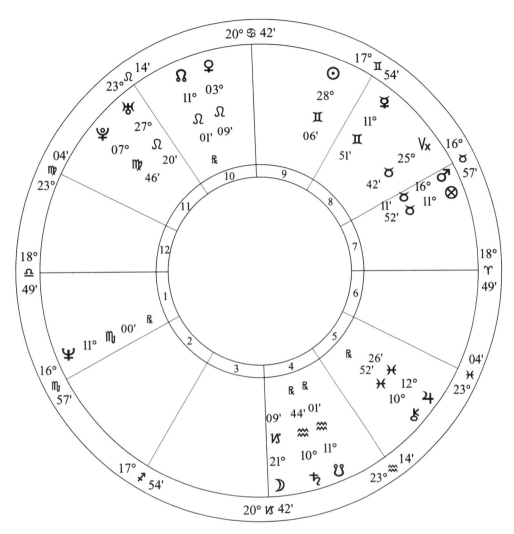

Figure 3: Paula Abdul birth chart: June 19, 1962, 2:32 PM, Los Angeles, CA

Besides athletes, actors, and entertainers—including child stars—there are many politicians and royalty with this position. Many are born into a role of leadership or groomed for such a role from an early age. There may be a distinct image to live up to or to protect. These individuals appeal to the people and the masses, especially women, and easily assume a role of authority. They come across as sympathetic to the needs of their public and have a comforting, reassuring manner about them. They have grace, style, and a natural sort of dignity. Whether physician, magician, musician, or the very occasional notorious criminal, these individuals usually become outstanding in their field.

When it is the South Node nearest the Midheaven, there are obstacles in early childhood that necessitate a lot of hard work to make a mark in the world. The individual struggles and nothing is handed over on a silver platter. The parents may be poor or uneducated and their straitened circumstances or situations impinge or bring heavy responsibilities. It is only through diligent efforts and staying resolutely on track that these individuals can experience dividends.

A couple of them that did are Denzel Washington, actor; and Gloria Steinem, editor, writer, feminist, and founder of Ms. magazine. Raised in a disciplined home to parents who divorced in his youth, Washington was working part-time jobs by the time he was in his early teens. (He also had a mitigating influence showing in his chart, however, with the Sun conjunct his North Node, which would have propelled him toward success more easily.) Ms. Steinem was born to a mentally ill mother and a father who left the family when she was young. In a role reversal she became her mother's caretaker for many years, dispensing her meds for her mental condition, which included hallucinations. Steinem's earliest years were a gypsy-like existence, as they moved so frequently that she attended each school for only a short period.

There are fewer easily recognizable names of people with South Node nearest the Midheaven than in the previous example of North Node overhead. These people may be carrying heavy burdens and it isn't so easy to appear before the public. Of the ones who do, it seems these individuals are not so overwhelmingly popular or so easily loved by the public. They often promote causes or take up activities that are unpopular, distasteful, or somehow unacceptable to the majority. The movements they get behind may be controversial in some way. This could be wrapped up in their mission. But, as a group, they appear to be less charming, sophisticated, or refined. Many are a little rough around the edges. Even Prince Alfred, Queen Victoria's fourth child, who had this position, was

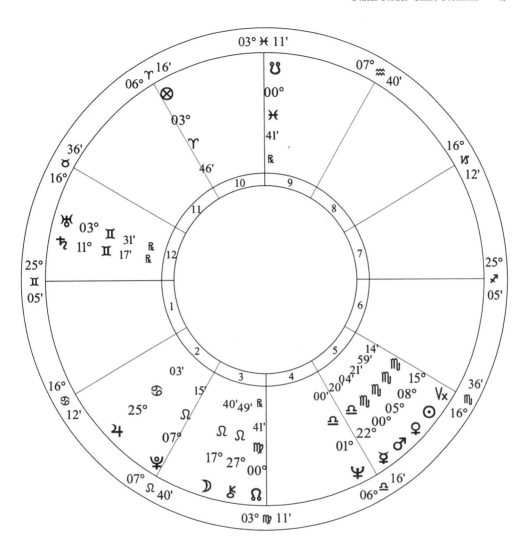

Figure 4: Larry Flynt birth chart: Nov. 1, 1942, 9:10 PM, Salyersville, KY

known for a bad temper and lack of tact. Others come across as if they are angry, unsettled, or have an ax to grind.

Keep in mind that many of these people may be old souls, and besides having harder trials and heavier responsibilities, some may become even more set in their old ways, demonstrating negative tendencies of the past.

This is a more introverted group overall. In many cases, their self-confidence is low and these individuals appear more prone to stress.

Many among this group are gaining more in a spiritual way than in a material sense, as they are working on refinement. This was certainly the plan, and making spiritual progress is an opportunity for all of them. Of course, there are many fine people among this group who make valuable contributions. Kevin Costner, Betty Ford, Louis Pasteur, and George Lucas all have their South Node in the Tenth House.

However, it does seem there is often some inherited sadness or tragedy through the family line that lies beneath and may have an important motivating influence upon these individuals in whatever line of activity they take up (Ethel Kennedy, for example).

Individuals with South Node overhead usually exhibit a more solemn outlook than the lightheartedness of North Node people. When the South Node is the most dominant influence, the individual has a very strong pull to the past, often looking backward for understanding, whereas the North Node individual is more interested in forgetting the past and forging into the future. Whenever one leaves present time to dwell on the past, it drains the energy to a degree—since South Node people tend to do this, it may have a more or less weakening impact on their efforts. Being older souls, they have more to reflect upon, whereas North Node people may have fewer of these distractions, often being younger souls.

One thing to be aware of is that if there happens to be a planet conjoined with either node, it will create a more complex story. A planet near one of the nodes may give it more influence, or change its influence in some way. It puts more weight on one end of the seesaw. More on this and the additional layers of details about the life mission will be discussed in coming chapters, but if there is no planet near either node, it is usually the one above the line of advantage that holds prominence and influence.

There are more notorious people with South Node sitting right on the Midheaven. For instance, Zacharias Moussaoui and David Berkowitz, also known as the Son of Sam, appear in this group. Those with South Node conjunct the Midheaven do not exhibit the same quality of wholesomeness or "loveableness" as those with North Node on the

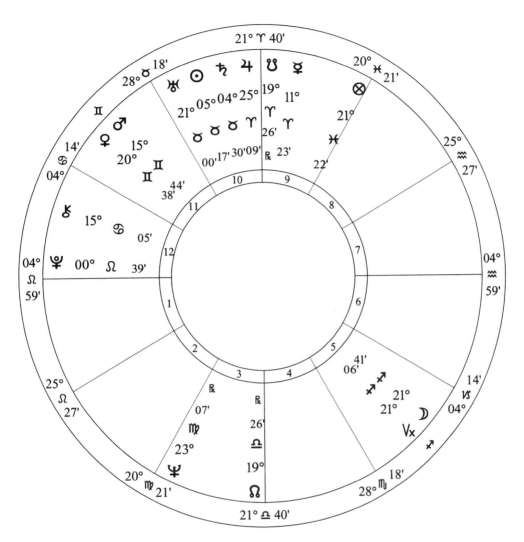

Figure 5: Al Pacino birth chart: Apr. 25, 1940, 11:02 AM, Manhattan, NY

Midheaven when looking at the overall groups. They may have some trait of sinfulness or decadence about them, such as are seen in madams, those involved with pornography, or other divisive lines of endeavor. I'm thinking of Linda Lovelace, Larry Flynt, and Heidi Fleiss, to name a few. Even Denzel Washington played the role of Malcolm X, the angry leader—and Al Pacino, who has that slightly sinful, magnetic attraction, has played many licentious or corrupt roles in his acting career. However, in his chart, it is noticed that Jupiter is not far from his South Node, which does much to sweeten its influence and neutralize the ill effects.

If not actually on the Midheaven, it is beneficial to have the North Node in good aspect (relationship) to the Midheaven. This will improve the circumstances for a North Node falling in the lower part of the chart. Check to see if it forms a trine aspect to the Midheaven by falling four signs away. There may still be hardships and responsibilities to accept. Circumstances force this, but there is more assistance (from the higher powers) to meet the task, and a lot is learned at a young age. Strength and confidence is acquired.

The aspects to be acquainted with are the conjunction—♂, which means the two are sitting right next to each other; the sextile—✶, which is two signs or 60 degrees apart; the square—□, which is three signs or 90 degrees apart; and the trine—△, four signs or 120 degrees away. The horoscope wheel contains 360 degrees and each of the twelve signs contains 30 degrees. A conjunction is strongest, the trine and sextile are friendly relationships, while the square produces challenge. An orb is the amount of leeway allowed from the exact aspect. For this discussion, you can give this a fairly wide orb. I am using a three- to five-degree orb for aspects of the nodes to the Midheaven, less for a sextile.

If the North Node is uppermost in the chart and in close sextile aspect to the Midheaven, two signs away, this is like a second helping of benefits, gaining first by the North Node position up top, and second through the nice aspect. Teresa Heinz Kerry's North Node is in the Eighth House (of joint resources and inheritances), actually slightly below the line of advantage, but sextile her Midheaven. She is the heiress to the Heinz fortune.

NODES ON THE ASCENDANT

The Ascendant is the start of the First House, symbolizing the self and the physical body. Along with the Midheaven, it is sometimes referred to as an angle as these points and their opposite points form a cross in the horoscope and are personally sensitive areas in the chart.

When the nodes lie across the Ascendant and Descendant (the First and Seventh House cusps), the life appears particularly fateful or predestined. These individuals live a life of providence. In other words, the higher cosmic forces have great influence over that life. Events and circumstances are sometimes ascribable to divine intervention. The life seems controlled by these higher forces to the point where the individual is mostly caught up and moved along by these powerful cosmic currents. The soul undergoes many learning experiences and is just waiting for the time to be reunited with the all that is or the oneness.

Some individuals with this nodal position include JFK Jr., Jim Morrison, Queen Elizabeth, and Jackie Kennedy Onassis. JFK Jr. had the North Node on the Ascendant; the last three had the South Node there. All lived lives that seemed destiny driven or touched by fate. For the last two ladies, with North Node on the cusp of the Seventh house of "others," their mission in large part was to sacrifice themselves for their partner, which they did gracefully. The South Node on the Ascendant can be extremely self-limiting. Excessive compromises may be made for the partner or for other people.

Due to the fateful quality, one must be careful when reading the chart of an infant especially, since there is occasionally a physical complication—or of anyone having the nodes lying across these angles. It is as if fate and destiny could intervene at any moment, as with JFK Jr., whose life and death appeared to be particularly fated.

The life of Jim Morrison of the Doors ended tragically at his own hands, and this seems to reflect the more negative connotations of having South Node on the Ascendant. He gave all of himself. Remember the empty cup? He submerged himself completely back into the sea of the everlasting. Perhaps his mission was aborted by actions of self-sabotage. While no autopsy was done and his death was officially declared to be from heart failure, mystique has followed his death, with speculation that it was the result of an overdose of heroin combined with alcohol. Suicide may be one of the best indicators of a mission cut short. Janis Joplin, who also died an untimely death due to drugs, had the same position with South Node on her Ascendant.

Those with South Node conjunct the Ascendant are very soulful people. This trait is almost tangible. They have a sense of how ephemeral life really is. Still closely connected with the past and possibly to past states of consciousness, they have interests in dualisms: life and death, dark and light, good and evil, etc.

In positive works they show others how to live happier, healthier, more fulfilling lives. They are often involved in fairness issues and may be active advocates in movements they believe in. There are many who bring healing to others through some avenue. There are

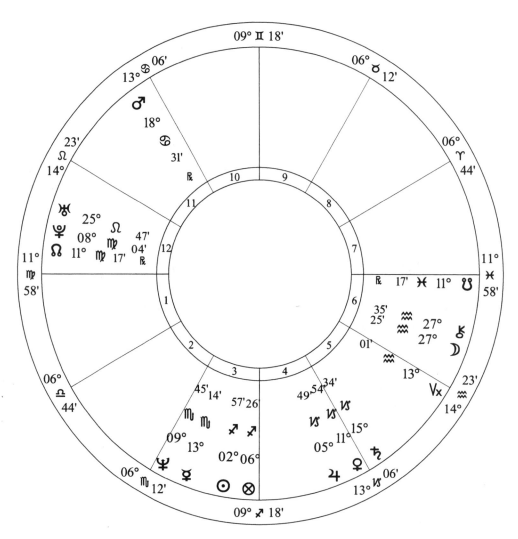

Figure 6: JFK Jr. birth chart: Nov. 25, 1960, 12:22 AM, Washington, DC

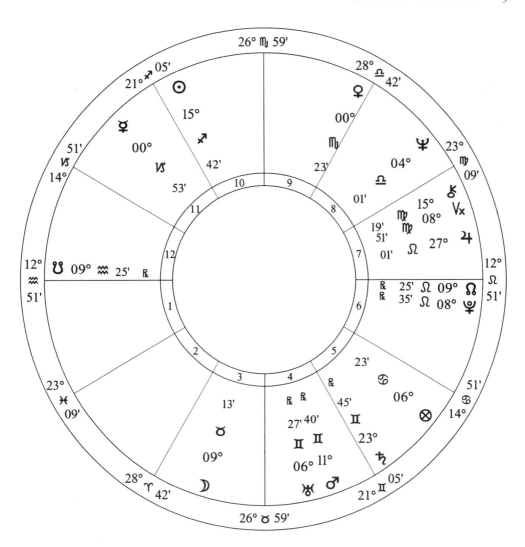

Figure 7: Jim Morrison birth chart: Dec. 8, 1943, 11:55 AM, Melbourne, FL

occultists, scientists, and appreciators of incredible phenomena; writers and film directors, actors, and singers among this group. Dick Clark has brought healing to many others through music venues. He has South Node at the Ascendant and North Node on his Descendant with Chiron, and in Taurus, the sign of music.

In many cases with South Node on the Ascendant, it may take a lot of trials or a long time to be accepted; those with this position may be shunned in their early years. South Node conjunct the Ascendant may have multiple marriages, or it may be a case of "you can't live with them and you can't live without them."

Those with North Node conjunct the Ascendant make a name for themselves, often becoming sudden or overnight sensations. They may be given a nickname for some unforgettable or distinctive trait or style. They may do precise or exacting work in any one of a number of areas such as science, astrology, design, art, literature, illustration, or along the lines of entertainment. Perhaps the most distinctive difference about North Node rising (at the Ascendant or nearby) is that these individuals are not advocating on behalf of others—they are advocating for themselves, and this is as it is supposed to be. They are learning to promote themselves and develop their personal power.

Again, for those with the North Node nearest the Ascendant, there is a more extroverted demeanor and self-confidence, while South Node nearest the Ascendant causes introversion and the person is more apt to be stressed, intimidated, or to suffer from low self-esteem.

If not actually on the Ascendant, a nice aspect to the Ascendant by the nodes is a favorable feature. This may give more than the ordinary amount of spunk and stamina to face life and any obstacles that arise. The personality is a definite assist. Angelina Jolie has her North Node trine her Ascendant from the Fifth House position. So did Pablo Picasso. Tiger Woods has a sextile to his Ascendant from North Node on his Third House cusp.

The benefits of having North Node overhead are reduced when square the Ascendant, which is a stressful 90-degree angle, or three signs away, and things may worsen if South Node is overhead, with the individual having to go through heavy trials. Judy Garland, the multitalented but ill-fated actress/singer who starred as Dorothy in the original Wizard of Oz, had this latter configuration.

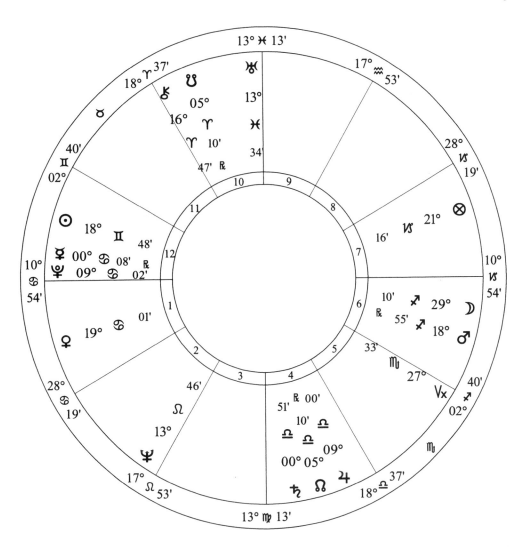

Figure 8: Judy Garland birth chart: June 10, 1922, 6:00 AM, Grand Rapids, MN

NODAL INFLUENCE ON STATURE & APPEARANCE

The nodes may also exert an influence on stature. Generally speaking, the height tends to be increased with the North Node in the First House, near the Ascendant or overhead in the chart. This is especially true if falling on the Ascendant along with another planet. The person tends to be long-limbed and lanky, like JFK Jr., who had Pluto conjunct North Node on the Ascendant. If the North Node is overhead and in good aspect to the Ascendant, this also tends to increase height, whereas it will have a neutralizing or reverse effect if the upper North Node squares the Ascendant. Even a half square, 45 degrees, from an upper North Node to the Ascendant can mean a significant reduction of height. An overhead North Node that is obstructed by planets in square also limits potential height, and if there are multiple squares by strong planets, it can reverse the usual effects entirely.

Height may be decreased if it is the South Node in the First House, or on the Ascendant and unaccompanied by a planet. If a planet joins the South Node on the Ascendant, this may give more height than if the planet were not assisting. The height is generally decreased also by having the South Node uppermost in the chart, more especially so if it squares the Ascendant. A good aspect from the overhead South Node to the Ascendant may neutralize some of the effects of shortness of stature. An overhead South Node sextile the Ascendant may increase the height, for example. Also, if a planet joins the North Node, even with the South Node uppermost, this tends to increase height. RuPaul, popular American transvestite, is 6'5" with Pluto conjunct his North Node, even with having South Node overhead. Pluto is the planet of extremes and the North Node is the giver of height. Clint Eastwood, at 6'4", has Mars conjunct his North Node, so that even with having his South Node uppermost, the aspect gave him height.

The Moon appears to have some special influence in the matter as well. Usually, if the Moon accompanies either node, height and size may be increased.

The line of advantage that runs through the Second and Eighth Houses, explained in the beginning of this chapter, is something to consider when making these judgments.

Of course, these are general guidelines, and the rising sign and particulars of the First House must also be accounted for in judging stature and appearance. Having a preponderance of planets in the upper portion of the chart generally reflects increased height, while having most of the planets in the lower half of the chart shows decreased height, so that one could have emphasizing factors or a neutralizing balancing-out of factors. For

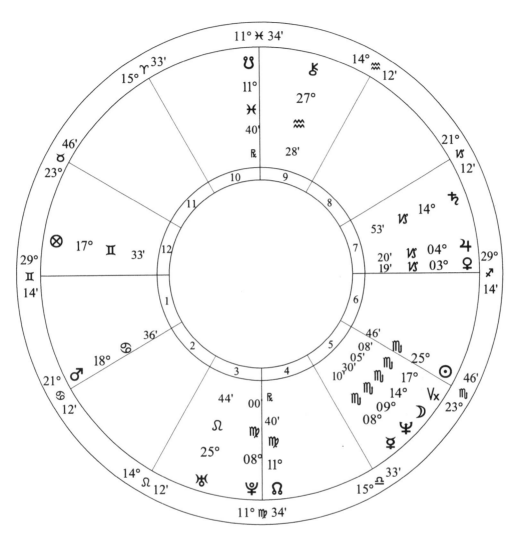

Figure 9: RuPaul birth chart: Nov. 17, 1960, 6:52 PM, San Diego, CA

instance, height would be increased if the North Node were overhead, along with many planets also overhead. If South Node is overhead, along with most of the planets, this will add height, just not to the same degree as the former.

Jason Alexander, who played short and pudgy George Costanza on Seinfeld, has South Node rising in Aries, giving a double emphasis for short stature by having South Node in the First House and also in the sign Aries, the sign naturally corresponding with the First House and Ascendant. He is short in spite of having planets conjunct his North Node. He might've been shorter if not for that assistance to his North Node. Pablo Picasso was just 5'4", having South Node overhead and half his planets in the lower portion of the chart. Television star Ed Asner is also short and stout, having South Node near the Ascendant and a majority of planets in the lower portion of his chart.

Umberto Pelizzari, the record-setting Italian scuba diver, actually has South Node conjunct his Ascendant, but it is in Sagittarius, ruled by our largest planet, Jupiter, known for its expanding influence. Also, with his South Node sextile Venus, a Fortune planet, and most of his planets overhead, he is 6'2". So, we see that a good aspect from a Fortune planet (Sun, Jupiter, or Venus) to South Node on the Ascendant has this mitigating effect, especially when combined with the additional features.

Just remember that the North Node tends toward tall and lean while South Node tends toward short and stocky, and the nearer the node to the Ascendant, the stronger its influence.

Think also of the planetary nature, such as Jupiter would expand the physique if on the Ascendant with North Node. Saturn, the other extreme, would be more restricting of the build if found on the Ascendant with South Node or if Saturn is on the Ascendant and the South Node is uppermost in the chart, especially if many planets fall in the lower portion of the map.

There is one more way to judge the natural body shape and size, and this comes from the Moon itself. The phase of the Moon at birth may give an inclination as to slenderness or heaviness. If the Moon is closely approaching the Sun, which is a New Moon when exact, the body tends toward slenderness, reflected by the ideal crescent shape of the Moon. Just following a New Moon, the Moon is still showing only a sliver, so this stage also inclines toward slenderness, but with more susceptibility to weight gain due to the increasing stage of the Moon. As the Moon nears the Full Moon, it becomes more rounded and so the potential for a fuller figure increases. The Full Moon is plump and round so that might be the natural tendency if born at this Moon stage. Just after the Full

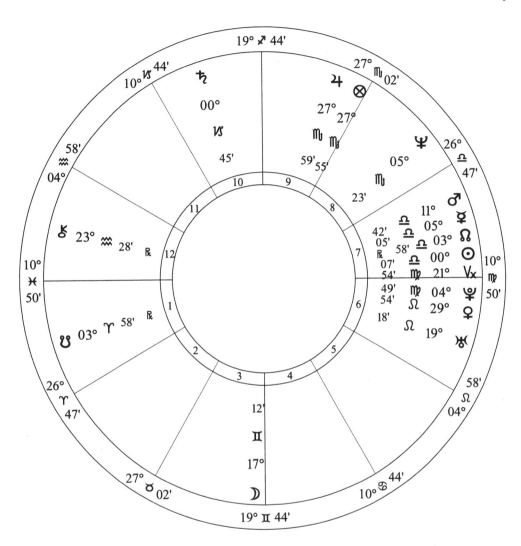

Figure 10: Jason Alexander birth chart: Sept. 23, 1959, 6:04 PM, Newark, NJ

Moon, the Moon is still quite rounded, but is now decreasing in light so that attention to diet and exercise would make it easier to manage weight.

If you combine this lunar factor with the nodal features, you may make some astonishing discoveries about those who may struggle with their weight. The nodes may indicate one thing while the Moon phase says something quite the contrary, so these individuals are always trying to bring out the inner slender person but having a difficult time of it. Oprah Winfrey comes to mind. Her North Node is in her First House and she has planets on both ends of her nodal axis, which gives a healthy appetite and increases her potential size, but she was born at the waning Moon, normally inclining to slenderness. Her Moon and Ascendant are in Sagittarius however, ruled by our largest planet, Jupiter, so this adds to the number of factors inclining to heaviness. All of this helps account for her up and down weight history, making it difficult to keep the pounds off. She may be dealing with what could be a life-long battle, and this may be part of her mission, to inspire others to never give up. Then, there are those who can't gain weight no matter how hard they try. The chart may reveal the reason if the Moon and the nodes agree that being on the slim side is a product of destiny.

Other ways that the nodes define appearance is that birth defects, physical problems, or accident-prone tendencies may be found with the South Node conjunct Ascendant. Other additional chart factors would concur. We have already seen several examples of a propensity for drug addictions and accident-prone tendencies with South Node conjunct the Ascendant. It is helpful to keep in mind that the Ascendant and First House describe the physical body and the South Node is the empty cup, so there are sometimes losses or sacrifices of a physical sort, even occasional cases in which a body part might be missing at birth.

Those with South Node near the Ascendant often have hypnotic or penetrating eyes, a trait observable in Jim Morrison and Janis Joplin. These individuals may have a very mesmerizing effect on other people, and there is a mystique about them.

Great beauty or good looks are given if the North Node is in the First House, or if the North Node forms a beneficial aspect to the Ascendant. Again we can see this reflected in JFK Jr., Angelina Jolie, and Tiger Woods.

It is said by Vedic astrologers that the North Node glance is downward—a way to identify a strong North Node influence, such as falling near the Ascendant or otherwise pronounced. The South Node glance is upward. These glances obviously reflect something about the influence of the nodes, such that the downward glance of the North

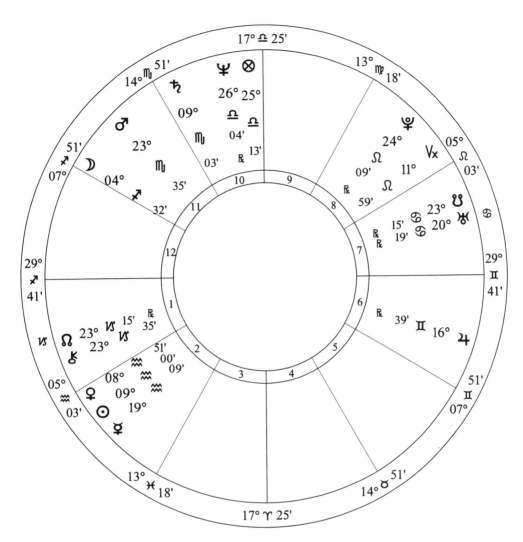

Figure 11: Oprah Winfrey birth chart: Jan. 29, 1954, 4:30 AM, Kosciusko, MS

Node comes from increased height or from an attitude of assurance, while the South Node upward glance stems from a lower position height-wise, or from self-consciousness. It is likely that both factors contribute to these glances. Remember the associations of the North Node with a hilltop and the South Node with a valley?

In Vedic teachings, having one of the nodes in either the First or Second House gives a very strong influence on appearance. Thus, Vedic astrologers include the Second House as a prominent position, the same as suggested by our line of advantage.

The more prominent node even tells something about the appetite. The appetite is increased if the North Node is most prominent, and is decreased with the South Node dominant.

If there is no other planet conjoined with either node, it is pretty safe to consider the one above the line of advantage to be prominent, thus describing the appetite, demeanor, and other physical features.

In the next chapter we will look at some special aspects that reflect the highest cosmic blessings bestowed on a person, and those requiring the greatest karmic sacrifices.

Chapter Three

EXTRA PUSH BY THE HIGHER POWERS

Besides the Ascendant/Descendant axis and the Midheaven/IC axis, there are two other points in the horoscope derived from angles that are very important in determining a soul's mission and karmic responsibilities, based on aspects they form to the lunar nodes. These are the Part of Fortune and the Vertex. The Part of Fortune is quite self-descriptive, while the Vertex is associated with destiny.

NODES IN ASPECT TO THE PART OF FORTUNE

Okay, this should be really good stuff! This should be more true if it is the North Node with the Part of Fortune or in good aspect to it. Right?

Take a look at your chart to find your Part of Fortune—⊗.

Evel Knievel had the North Node conjunct his Part of Fortune and overhead in the chart. Maybe this gave him greater amounts of protection during his daring stunts. Not many people could get away with what he did.

His easily recognizable name gives a first clue to what it means to have North Node conjunct the Part of Fortune. These are award winners. They win medals, accolades, and honors. They are champions and shining stars. If acting, they play starring roles. They are especially gifted and talented, and capture attention. Nat King Cole, Ted Turner, and Fred Astaire have the aspect, as well as David and Frederick Barclay, British millionaire twins.

Sometimes these individuals are born into nobility or a well-known or well-to-do family, and the family name precedes them. They usually have plenty of material abundance.

These people are highly creative and inspired in their work, even passionate in their undertakings, but they are also original, inventive, or somehow different. This aspect of North Node conjunct the Part of Fortune absolutely appears to hold many special blessings that bestow heaps of joy and fortune in a life.

It may be that this is a soul that has earned valuable karmic credits, including the possibility that this is a soul who, through no fault of his or her own, failed to accomplish the previous mission or it was aborted last time around, and they are now given special aid. There are occasions when the larger world karma and events can overpower our own. This can happen through wars or epidemics, or similar calamities. In such cases, the soul is then offered special protection or assistance.

On the opposite side of the spectrum are those who have South Node conjunct the Part of Fortune. Martha Stewart has South Node conjunct the Part of Fortune in the Fifth House. This seems relevant—a sign perhaps that she could lose fortunes by speculating in the stock market (ruled by the Fifth House).

But, look at this: James Van Praagh has his South Node conjunct Fortuna, and so does Angelina Jolie. In these cases, they dispense of their fortunes or give of it freely and willingly to help others, Van Praagh through his abilities as a medium and Jolie by expending her time, money, and energy to adopt children and to support worthy causes across the world. The South Node represents an obligation. These people can share their joy and fortune to make a difference in the lives of others.

These individuals with South Node conjunct the Part of Fortune are willing to get their hands dirty and really dig in to do work that others may find distasteful. There may be some connection to some sinister character or dealings, though. Gerald R. Ford, our thirty-eighth president, who stepped in when Nixon was forced to resign, had this aspect. So did Otto Dietrich, chief publicity agent and constant companion to Hitler, as well as American murderer Eric Menendez.

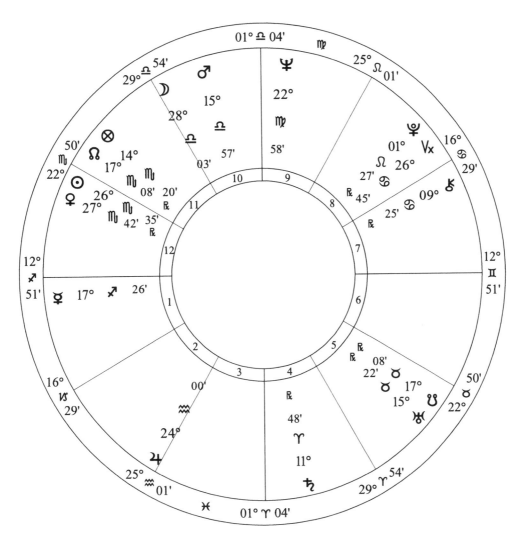

Figure 12: Ted Turner birth chart: Nov. 19, 1938, 8:50 AM, Cincinnati, OH

Of the overall group, they appear to be less well-off materially than with North Node conjunct Fortuna—perhaps tougher, hard-nosed, a little quirky, offbeat, or weird. They may adhere to different perspectives than the norm. They do not always command the same high respect or public support and popularity. Even with the names mentioned thus far, we can see that the characters can attract a bit of controversy or at times provoke unpopular opinions.

There are scientists, astrologers, entertainers, and politicians in this group. Quite a mix of characters have this aspect, including well-respected individuals such as Giorgio Armani and Jacques Cousteau, and this appears to be a particularly delicate condition with little room for error. The individual must find a way to share his or her joy and fortune and give back in some way to the greater good, or the road can be quite difficult. Getting passionately behind a worthy cause appears to be a common denominator for the most successful among this group.

Look in the chart for assistance. If a planet is conjunct the North Node, this will help pull the individual to find a way forward. Chevy Chase of Saturday Night Live fun and familiarity has South Node conjunct Fortuna in the Fourth House, while his North Node joins Pluto and Jupiter in the Tenth House. If there's a good aspect from this South Node/Fortuna pairing to the Ascendant or Midheaven, this will help. A Fortune planet joining the South Node and Fortuna may be a big help. Model Claudia Schiffer has the Sun tucked between her South Node and Part of Fortune, near her Midheaven. Of course, check to see if this conjunction falls high or low in the chart. Unless squared by planets, it helps to have the overhead North Node and this conjunction of South Node with the Part of Fortune in the lower portion. It gives greater difficulty if overhead and with no assistance anywhere. So much frustration may come of it that resentment, retaliation, or other self-defeating actions could follow. The aspect may even manifest in disease. There are some potential dangers during infancy so that the greatest care and caution should be taken with regard to a child born with this aspect.

A trine from the North Node to Fortuna also exerts an influence. The trine is quite favorable for success, and this is a resilient aspect. It provides extraordinary help, regardless of which node is uppermost. It fairly assures that an individual will easily make the nodal transition as it was intended. Take note of the house position of Fortuna to find where the fortunes lie.

As a group, these people are respectable and doing good works. Not much bad can come from this aspect unless there are extremely problematic planetary conditions. Having

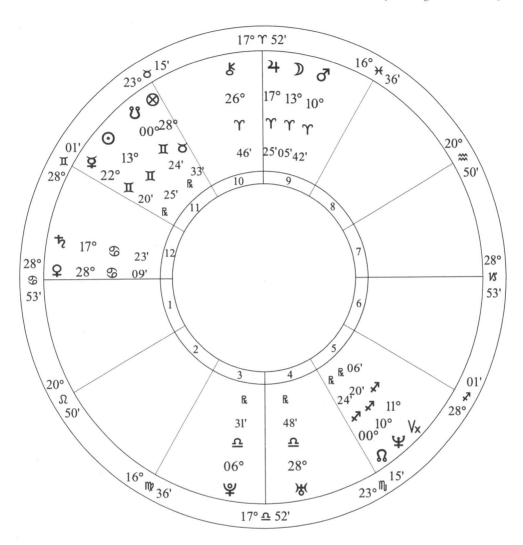

Figure 13: Angelina Jolie birth chart: June 4, 1975, 9:09 AM, Los Angeles, CA

the Part of Fortune or node in the sign of Scorpio or the Eighth House may tend to lesson the benefits of the aspect, or it works in unusual ways. Hope Cooke has Part of Fortune in the Eighth House, trine North Node on the Ascendant. Raised by wealthy grandparents after her parents split and her mother died in a Nevada air crash while solo piloting a small plane (a suspected suicide), Hope became Queen of Sikkim after meeting and marrying a prince. He was later overthrown and the marriage ended after nearly twenty years and two children. Others with Fortuna trine to the North Node are Pierre Cardin, Mark Hamill (Luke Skywalker of the *Star Wars* trilogy), and Jesse Ventura.

An even greater number of easily recognizable names comes from the group with Fortuna trine South Node, an indication that this aspect assists in utilizing the old methods and talents in such a way that achievements immediately begin to manifest in the area of the North Node. The suggestion is also made that this soul has earned some karmic credits that can now be drawn. Some individuals with this aspect include Albert Einstein, Louis Pasteur, Mark Spitz, Barbara Hutton (heiress to the Woolworth fortunes), Carmen Electra, Doris Day, Isaac Hayes, and Jayne Mansfield. Even Patricia Krenwinkel has this aspect with South Node near the Ascendant and with several stressful planetary aspects to her nodes. Her death sentence, for the murders she helped carry out for Charles Manson, was commuted to life in prison and she now comes up regularly for parole.

More benefits can be expected if the North Node is uppermost. Again, having the nodes or the Part of Fortune in Scorpio or the Eighth House may be more problematic, and in a general way this sign or house position of the nodes can potentially give more difficulty than any others.

Squares of the nodes to the Part of Fortune have been found in the charts of cancer victims, those with severe psychological disorders or incurable diseases (schizophrenia, epilepsy), or those having to endure sudden negative events, including traumatic experiences, exile, torture, accidents, or even death. There may certainly be extra struggles, but problems associated with squares of the nodes to the Part of Fortune are more easily mitigated according to other favorable contacts made by the nodes. There is notable talent here such as Pablo Picasso, Sally Field, Oprah Winfrey, Ginger Rogers, and Bruce Springsteen. All of these subjects, except Picasso, had the mitigating help of North Node above the line of advantage, along with assistance from planets like Pluto or Mars forming an empowering aspect to the nodes.

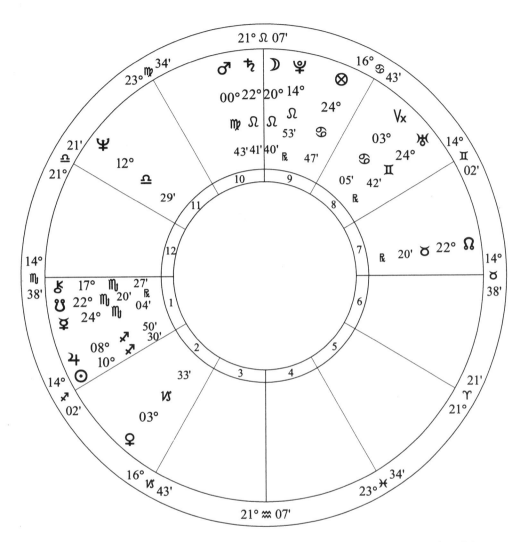

Figure 14: Patricia Krenwinkel birth chart: Dec. 3, 1947, 4:41 AM, Los Angeles, CA

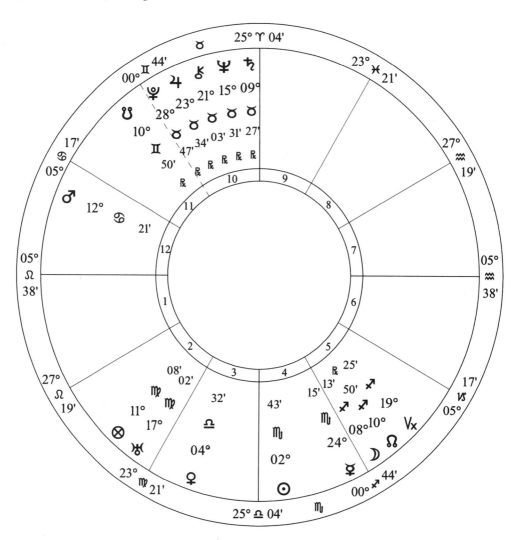

Figure 15: Pablo Picasso birth chart: Oct. 25, 1881, 11:15 PM, Malaga, Spain

These individuals with nodes square the Part of Fortune may be making extraordinary leaps in their evolution provided they overcome some challenges.

If you check the house position of the Part of Fortune, it is sometimes found that there is difficulty collecting all of the fortunes associated with that house. Sacrifices are made relevant to this house position or some of those benefits are denied. For example, Picasso had his Part of Fortune in his Second House. With the square from the nodes, even with his extraordinary talent, he suffered severe poverty.

It is likely because of the severe trials and liabilities put upon these souls that a large number of them shun or rebel against social norms, or in extreme cases turn to a life of crime. Alas, this doesn't turn out well in this lifetime, and only results in greater tribulations later.

We will talk more about these aspects involving the nodes to the Part of Fortune when we discuss progressions, where the contact also proves to be quite significant.

I'm using the traditional Part of Fortune: Ascendant plus Moon, minus Sun, the Arabian part representative of joy and fortune. This should not be confused with the Part of Spirit, which is the reverse formula: Ascendant plus Sun, minus Moon. The Part of Fortune shows where the Moon would be if the Sun was exactly in the Ascendant position in the chart, representing an ideal alignment between the inner person and their outer vehicle, with Fortuna indicating the kind of personal adjustment needed in order to bring about such ideal conditions and illumination.

NODES IN ASPECT TO THE VERTEX

In order to understand what an aspect of the nodes to the Vertex might mean, we must first review some general understanding of this point. The Vertex, which is the west end of the true east-west axis through the birthplace, is associated with encounters with others and experiences over which one has little or no control. The Vertex is somewhat comparable to the Descendant. This is where we attract others to fill in missing parts of ourselves or to play those parts of ourselves that we disown.

The degree opposite the Vertex is called the Anti-Vertex. It is like an auxiliary Ascendant, where we personally identify. Edward Johndro, who pioneered research to these points, set out to prove the Anti-Vertex to be the most important end of this axis, noting the quality of destiny to these points. Similar to the Ascendant, Johndro called the Anti-

Vertex the Electric Ascendant and observed that while the Ascendant shows free choice and volitional life, the Electric Ascendant showed no choice and involuntary actions.

Later, Charles Jayne convinced Johndro that it was really the Vertex that produced the best evidence and it showed the greater emphasis as a point of fate. Not only encounters with others, but experiential encounters are noted with the Vertex; it represents appointments with destiny. Besides the nodes themselves, the Vertex is the most "fateful" indicator in the chart.

The Anti-Vertex/Vertex is basically a self/other polarity. The Vertex symbol is **Vtx**. The Anti-Vertex has no symbol. It is directly opposite the Vertex. Astrology software programs calculate the Vertex for you.

With the North Node conjunct the Vertex then, this is somewhat the same nature as having North Node conjunct the Seventh House cusp. This equates to giving a lot of control to the partner or to others in general. The destiny or calling involves another for whom we may be doing a service.

These individuals do work as part of a group, in a partnership, or as a member of a larger team. The spouse or a parent may be important and has much pull in the life of this individual. He or she may carry on with work started by someone else or follow in the footsteps of a parent. Ties to others appear significant as to the amount of success, acclaim, achievements, or recognition received. These individuals are from all walks of life, and are most likely married or at least involved in a close partnership, where the partner may act to complete them in some way. Thus, in these aspects the life of the individual may appear to be running less under the personal control and more under the direction or control of others. Partnerships are everything. The destiny is very much influenced through associations. Abigale Folger, heiress to the Folgers Coffee fortune had this aspect, as does Cheech Marin, member of the Cheech and Chong comedy team. Gladys Knight, leader of the long-lasting rhythm and blues pop group, has this connection. Kato Kaelin, best known as a friend to Nicole Simpson, also has this feature.

There may be connections to victims, working on behalf of victims—and these individuals are vulnerable to being hurt through close association, or as a result of one.

With South Node conjunct the Vertex then, this would give a greater opportunity for taking decisive action, similar to having North Node on the Ascendant, and yet we know, according to Johndro, that the Anti-Vertex allows little choice, and that actions are more or less involuntary—the result of developments over which one has little control. These folks respond to opportunities afforded them, which may be reduced in number by the efforts or actions of other people or outer elements. There may end up being only one choice, and they must take the only course of action or the only option open.

Whatever it may involve, these individuals may still wind up taking a central role, or are thrown into the limelight. They are often more or less forced into new experiences.

Neil Armstrong has South Node conjunct the Vertex, and his life was full of actions of last resort during his flight training and as he moved up to astronaut, many times due to unusual malfunctions during flights. His participation in the space missions was largely under the control of others. It was even someone else's decision that he would be the first of the Apollo 11 crew to set foot on the Moon, due to the fact of his having "no large ego."

These folks start things. They lead the way, they are pioneers and firsts in a field. They are heads, directors, and founders, introducing new things. They live on the edge. They forge new territory, often as the result of developments that they did not originally initiate or prepare for. They may become well known for initiating something. Peter Hurkos, with South Node conjunct the Vertex, claimed to have gained ESP abilities after a fall from a ladder and blow to the head that left him unconscious for three days.

Another thing we know is that for all these folks, there are very specific karmic developments in life. Events may seem fated or destined, and they may feel there is a special mission to carry out. They make the best of things from what they have to work with, often making a name for themselves or earning a title. George W. Bush has South Node conjunct his Vertex. What we know of this aspect suggests that Mr. Bush was forced into new experiences and had to start things as the result of developments outside his control—yet he was allowed few options by other people who were pulling the strings. This gives an interesting and plausible interpretation to many of the actions he initiated during his presidency.

South Node trine the Vertex produces individuals possessing multiple talents. They come into this life well equipped with various gifts, and may need only some self-teaching to brush up on several skills. They achieve in multiple areas, sometimes starting in one vocation and branching out to include similar related fields. They can do this and that, and this and that. They earn multiple diplomas. They are known for multiple creations, multiple works, and multiples of anything. For example, Whitney Houston, with enviable singing talents, has a range of three octaves. These individuals are especially active in the various arts. This may include expertise in the occult fields. I've found few

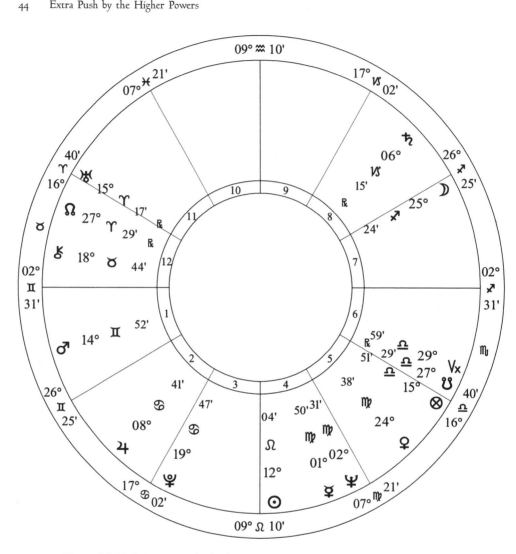

Figure 16: Neil Armstrong birth chart: Aug. 5, 1930, 12:31 AM, Washington, OH

criminals with this placement, but even among those, the criminal is known for multiple works—such as John Wayne Gacy, who committed thirty-three murders, and Henri Désiré Landru, with a record of having killed ten women. Generally this appears to be a very helpful and beneficial configuration, an extra push from the universe to go far. South Node trine the Vertex is an additional helpful feature in Al Pacino's chart. There are ample opportunities for meeting helpful people and forming connections. These individuals are particularly capable of creating harmony easily in their lives—maintaining a nice, even balance.

The North Node trine the Vertex is similar.

These people have definite missions with roots in the past and may also feel a sense of some special calling. Consider Celine Dion, for instance. In all of these subjects, connections to groups, doing group works, or working in partnerships seem to play a role in meeting the destiny.

I have kept these orbs narrow, allowing just three degrees in most cases.

North Node square the Vertex does seem to give certain disadvantages and sometimes extreme challenges or run-ins with life. There is a cross to bear. This can be a health issue, a trauma, tragedy, or strange mishaps or circumstances in life. Something occurring in the life can cause them to go the unpopular route; their whole outlook in an area may have been damaged or corrupted.

Battles with drugs are a fairly common theme. Natalie Cole, Althea Flynt, John Barrymore Jr., and musician/singer Bon Scott all had North Node square the Vertex and all had problems related to drug abuse, the latter dying after an all-night drinking binge.

Many times, their relationship area is notably unusual. Either there are multiple marriages, or no marriage, or else something stands out as extreme about the marriage or partnership. In a lot of cases, there is an underlying disharmony in the family heritage or a turbulent early family history that lies at the source for later problematic situations. With an aim to somehow come to grips, understanding, or finding meaning for the domestic dysfunction, this may be a motivating factor behind both successes and failures. There are difficulties balancing out the self/other, along with problems establishing a secure footing in the world. In an extreme example, Althea Flynt's father went on a homicidal rampage, killing her mother, her grandparents, and then committing suicide while she watched the entire horror at just eight years of age. The end of Althea's life was no less tragic, an addict with AIDS who drowned in the bathtub from an overdose.

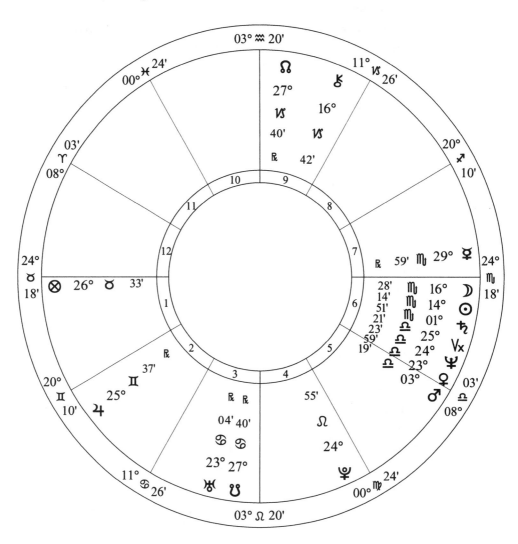

Figure 17: Althea Flynt birth chart: Nov. 6, 1953, 5:45 PM, Marietta, OH

Individuals with the nodes square Vertex may feel very limited by their options in life. Silvia Baraldini, an activist with the Black Panthers in the late 1960s, became a political prisoner in the United States. Mata Hari, prostitute and exotic dancer, had this feature. She was put to death by a firing squad for espionage during World War I. Premature death is a possibility, sometimes in infancy.

With the nodes square the Vertex, there could be a hereditary health disorder, as with Princess Alice, Queen Victoria's third child, who carried the hemophilia gene—the bleeding disorder. There may be a handicap to overcome, or some unusual event that impacts the well-being, as was the case with Thomas Dickson Armour, who was blinded by a mustard gas explosion while serving in World War I. He later regained some of his sight and took up golf. John Ogonowski, the airline pilot of the plane that crashed into the north tower on September 11, 2001, in New York, had this aspect, and this may be an example of a mission cut short through no fault of his own. Even in such instances, the nodal features in the chart appear to reflect such possibilities. Therefore it cannot be ruled out that it was part of a mission he opted for. It seems that the nodes help explain why bad things sometimes happen to good people. Pat Tillman, killed by friendly fire in Afghanistan, also had the feature.

Overall, there appears to be some burden, perhaps burning off of karmic debt, or building reserves of karmic credits for future utilization when these two most fateful indicators square one another.

Of course there are many famous and successful people with this position, although there may still be private matters or circumstances of these sorts that the public is not aware of. Jon Bon Jovi, Mary Tyler Moore, and Robert Redford have the feature, but each of these individuals has strong mitigating influences showing in their natal chart. Jon Bon Jovi has an upper North Node in sextile to his Ascendant, while Redford has North Node right on his Midheaven with Part of Fortune in his First House. Moore has an upper North Node in sextile to Venus, a Fortune planet.

With a square of the nodes to any of the angles, including the Vertex or the Part of Fortune, there does seem to be this huge factor of karma at play, so take the time to examine the aspects between these points and the nodal axis. We can assume that with nice aspects an individual is reaping some karmic credits and favors, while with squares there is a need to fulfill some prior commitment or burn off some debt. Also, check right here to see if the planetary ruler of either node squares the Vertex. This can be hampering, restricting, or crippling as well. Aspects between the angles and the

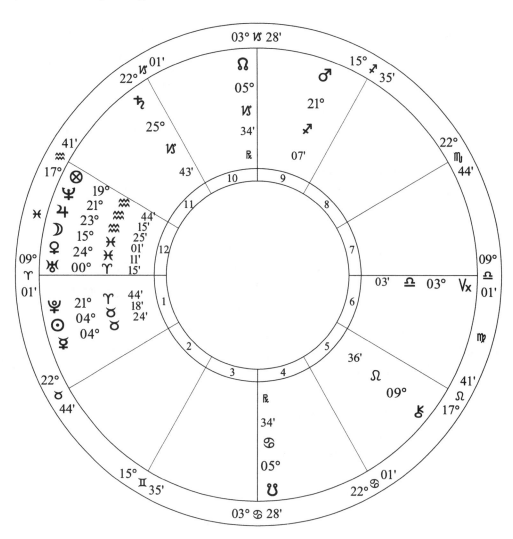

Figure 18: Princess Alice birth chart: Apr. 25, 1843, 4:05 AM, London, England

nodal rulers indicate assistance or trials in taking advantage of the constructive role of the nodal axis, designed to move us forward on the path to final enlightenment. When personal sacrifices or hardships can somehow be brought to benefit humankind, the positive action earns credits now and later.

In the coming chapter we'll talk about the nodal influences according to their specific house positions in your chart.

Chapter Four

NATAL NODES BY HOUSE POSITION

The North Node house represents an area of potential power. People who follow the path indicated by the North Node are the happiest and most fulfilled. The South Node is more like a drain and is often a symbol of self-dissipation. By house, it shows where past-life residue puts pressure on the current life. The South Node house represents past achievements—those things we've already learned and mastered. It has been called the point of least resistance, because it is easy to fall back into the same old groove, but it is a dead end that way, retarding growth toward the North Node end, which represents new faculties to be developed. That is the next step on the divine path and what we came to do. Cultivating the new faculties brings balance to the range of our experience, and rounds us out spiritually. The North Node symbolizes potential gifts from divine sources, which easily results from conscious application of efforts toward that end. Conditions and circumstances throughout life will (must) encourage us to evolve toward the North Node end, even though it makes us nervous as we give up the old habits and behaviors of the past.

Together, the nodes serve as our personal guiding lights, showing what we've accomplished and what challenges are yet to be mastered. To transcend completely to the North Node takes most of a lifetime, or even beyond. Ultimately, a person reaps the greatest growth and satisfaction by utilizing the North Node potential in such a way that contributions result in the area of the South Node. Balance and reciprocation must be established between the two ends.

The influence of the nodes is not always easy to detect in a person, depending upon how close your acquaintance is with the individual. We become good at covering up the fact that to a greater or lesser extent we do choose the line of least resistance. When things get scary, at the North Node end especially, we tend to hide behind our South Node—but over time we do begin to pick up more of the positive traits of the sign and house of the North Node as we shed the less desirable traits that came with the South Node package. You might say, oh yes I *used* to be like that, referring to one of those old less desirables. Or, I used to be more like that—not so much anymore. The South Node is in reference to the past—not just past lifetimes, but including earlier years of this life. Over time, most people make the transition as intended.

We'll take a surface look and a look beneath the surface, including some archetype associations, to see what we can discover about the meaning of the nodes in the various houses. Remember, there is no need to pass judgments. I've not glamorized these descriptions, but have written them in a way that will, I hope, maximize understanding. We all have some old skeletons in the closet or we wouldn't be here. We're all working toward perfection, but it takes many lifetimes to reach the perfection we're intended for. Many thousands of years are required to evolve to the highest potential. In the big picture, we're making this journey together.

FIRST HOUSE NORTH NODE

On the Surface: This position promises popularity and appeal. The personality, which may be described as lordly, is effectively projected to the outside world. Self-centeredness or self-absorption may result, and there is a lot of introspection. These individuals find a creative way to express themselves and are passionate about doing so. There may be a special knack for intuiting future trends that proves to be an asset. Relationships may be entered too easily, or without discretion, which can be costly in the long run. Married life may go through ups and downs and the partner is often unique in some way. Mutual benefits are the result of cooperative efforts although individuals are attracted to competition and should never make compromises too eagerly. These people are generally respected, action oriented, attract attention, have good vitality, and are moving up in life. Often on the tall side, they have a healthy appetite.

Below the Surface: This individual is learning to assume a role of leadership and develop personal power. In the past, it was the desire to please that caused her or him to submerge their individual identity in meeting the needs of others. On too many occasions, undependable people were counted upon and sacrifices made in their behalf. Now, there is an awareness of the lost identity and a necessity to come out from living in the shadow of others. The challenge is to be assertive and independent without becoming overly aggressive or too much of a loner, and to establish a good balance between personal needs and the needs of others. There may be an understanding of the secret workings of the universe that must be shared. This is the *Entrepreneur*, the *Pioneer, Innovator, Explorer*, or *Athlete*. The sign of the North Node shows the avenue by which to establish their unique identity.

Famous personalities with this position include Oprah Winfrey, who has maintained a long-term relationship without marriage, and who has obviously made tremendous progress on her destined path. She, in her life work that is so much in public view, demonstrates many of the First House North Node traits. Muhammad Ali, JFK Jr., and Carlos Santana also have this position.

SECOND HOUSE NORTH NODE

On the Surface: The earning powers are good and this person easily attracts resources and credit. High debt is a hazard however, because the desire to accumulate material things may be never-ending. Talent for financial management and utilizing material resources gives excellent potential in business. A job offering security and stability leads to contentment and happiness. Owning collectibles may be an interest and is favored, although investment presents some risks, and there may be trouble with an inheritance, or no inheritance at all. With beneficial aspects, this may give access to others' resources, although such fortune may come late in life. With stressful aspects, there may be elevated expectations that are never fulfilled, or a period of plenty is followed by a period of deprivation. Eventually he or she learns to get by on personal resources rather than depending on others. Wise about managing spiritual resources, they are skillful at making fresh starts from scratch and for helping others discover their self-worth.

Below the Surface: The individual is working to establish personal values. This may be through studying the standards of others, especially to understand what makes people treasure the things they do. Early on, envy may be displayed, a wish to trade places with those living a rich life, or blaming others for personal bad luck. In the past, money may have been earned through questionable activities or in extreme cases, through deceptive means. Sexuality or subtle manipulative powers may have been used to secure the possessions of others or to test the boundaries of their values. As a result, sexually transmitted diseases may be a danger. The individual now finds it impossible to grow through the labors of others, and there is a necessity to develop principles that have personal value. Too much interest in the business of others no longer works. Happiness is found by focusing on personal security, enjoying the material and sensual pleasures of earthly life, but with regard to the worldly games of profit and loss. This is the *Artisan,* the *Craftsperson,* the *Trader, Engineer, Architect, Builder,* or *Midas.* The sign of the North Node shows the manner by which personal values can be established and built up.

Famous personalities with this position are Walt Disney, Jimmy Hoffa, and MC Hammer.

THIRD HOUSE NORTH NODE

On the Surface: A gifted seller in the marketplace, active in the close community, this person has a persuasive personality with an unusual communicating style. Absorbing information easily, he or she learns most by applying facts and logic and through first-hand experience rather than following the dictates of others. There is a healthy skepticism with regard to theories or metaphysics—a need to find positive proof before endorsing anything. Self-undoing comes through a tendency to generalize based on superficial knowledge. This may be a lifelong student. Excellent for intellectual pursuits, the mental energies are boosted. Vocations using a pen are especially favored and offer lucrative paths. There is curiosity about distant places mixed with fearfulness of foreign places and people—an instinct to avoid them. This is a dreamer. There is some nervousness, and a need for variety. These individuals are dexterous and good with their hands.

Below the Surface: He or she is learning to interact with people but feels somewhat restricted, for in the past there was a great amount of freedom, and time was spent developing great stores of wisdom. This person did a lot of philosophizing in earlier lifetimes, taken up with theories, religion, higher studies, following gurus, and such. To do so, sacrifices were made in the area of enjoyable relationships. Now, fearful of losing the old freedoms, there is a complex network of people to interact with. Life presents one test after another in communicating and relating. This may cause friction in the marriage and a feeling of being caged in by the current life relationships, which are there to force them to stop being vague and to master the art of clear communication. This allows a practical means for spreading their vast knowledge learned previously. This is the *Networker, Messenger, Teacher, Scribe,* or *Apprentice*, dispensing precise bits of information needed by each person contacted and having an immense impact on the awareness of each. A streak of wanderlust sets in from time to time, a wish to visit far away places, a reflection of their cosmic mental journeying. The sign of the North Node indicates the manner by which she or he can share their knowledge in a way others will most appreciate.

Famous people with this position includes Bill Maher, TV talk show host; Richard Bach, author of *Jonathan Livingston Seagull*; artist Salvador Dali; and Leonardo DiCaprio.

FOURTH HOUSE NORTH NODE

On the Surface: A strong supportive foundation is anchored in the home and family. There's a close involvement with the mother and deep-seated domestic tendencies and sensitivities, although the father may be absent, somehow lost, or disregarded. This individual doesn't care much for travel and gravitates toward a permanent home and quiet life. Real estate, farming, the food industry, handyman, or interior design are areas of potential. Tradition and customs are important. Fault or possible undoing comes from clannishness or resisting new blood. Parenthood may be denied, or issues may surround parenthood. There are changes in the profession. Career is of lesser importance than the private family life, although there is administrative talent. The reputation must be protected; if the individual becomes overly ambitious in vocation there is an impending fall. The demands of a career must not override the family needs.

Below the Surface: This person came into this life with a strong sense of pride and dignity, where in the past he or she held absolute authority. Now it may be difficult to settle for less. Resentment stirs if forced to take a rear seat or deal with situations they feel are beneath them. The early relationship with the parents is significant and any defiant streak is to mask a need for their unconditional love. One parent may have built up such elevated expectations of the subject that whatever she or he achieves falls short of the mark. Life may hardly feel worth living unless they are achieving something outstanding. Supporting unpopular causes or attracting weaker persons in order to play a protective or authoritative role may be a distraction from the real work of getting personal affairs in order. Whereas in the past they sought success for recognition, now their achievements are to be their own reward, cultivating soul growth as they develop their instincts, send down roots, and build a secure foundation for themselves and their descendants. This is the *Mother, Parent, Protector,* or *Caregiver.* Meditation, contemplation, and spending time in seclusion bring benefits. Fulfillment comes through spiritual activities that elevate the consciousness of others. The sign of the North Node shows the ways to grow toward emotional fulfillment and happiness.

Famous personalities with this position are John Lennon's son Julian, Roy Orbison, RuPaul, Judy Garland, Kevin Costner, and Pope Benedict XVI.

FIFTH HOUSE NORTH NODE

On the Surface: Highly creative, the personality factor is important in achieving success. Charm is evident and this person possesses plenty of mental energy and self-expressiveness. He or she is striving toward individuality and developing the ego. There could be artificiality, and if North Node becomes over-exuberant, signs of megalomania. They follow their personal desires rather than the opinions or dictates of others. Highly imaginative, but rather impractical, their far-out fantasies or futuristic ideas may be hard to achieve. Still, they contemplate much about the value of their work. Attracting friends easily, their need for friendships and group involvements could distract them from seeking their own acclaim. A vocational, rather than a traditional, education works best, although there may be a break in education. There are excellent relations with young people but concerns about the development of children. Major crossroads in life may revolve around children. Through their eyes, she or he realizes their own self-worth. Romances have a past-life connection.

Below the Surface: In the past life, where time was devoted to furthering group efforts, every wish was granted and now this person lives in an expectant fairy tale land, trying to discover why reality is different than they remembered. The karma is to learn about the power of dreams and be careful what is wished for, because now they have the power to truly create their destiny. Always in search of symbols as substance to build upon their dreams, people are studied to find the why behind their actions. Finally they realize that their life experiences have resulted from acting out their imaginings. This is all very well, provided they have created on behalf of the greater good and not for self-ish purposes. Realizing they will always have new dreams to pursue, they begin to focus on one at a time. Some with these nodes have a recollection of past cosmic conscious-ness and are here to share the information. This is the *Lover* (passionate about creative *work)*, the *Prince, Princess (Cinderella), King, Queen, Flirt, Enchantress,* or *Entertainer.* The sign of the North Node shows the manner in which to focus the creative talents to make dreams a reality.

Famous people with this position include Marie Antoinette, Pablo Picasso, Whitney Houston, Demi Moore, Robert Blake, Maurice Gibb, and Angelina Jolie.

SIXTH HOUSE NORTH NODE

On the Surface: A hard worker. There is excellent capacity for dealing in the practical side of life as he or she is developing faculties for managing earthly matters and is will-ing to take on tasks others would not. While career conscious, dedication to service may override ambitions of a personal nature. They may take a back seat willingly. A problem-solver, there is the capacity for handling details and restoring order. This person often takes a clinical approach to life and tends to worry. There is a great deal of introspection, but sometimes a suspicious or fearful nature that can be crippling. While this individual usually wins out over enemies, learning to forgive those who've wronged him or her in the past is a must. Success and recognition often comes after a struggle. Although dem-onstrating gutsy qualities, this person can sometimes be a crybaby.

Below the Surface: This person has chosen a life of service and a focus on practical matters as in the past she or he was caught up in a spiritual life. In fact, these people may feel caught between two worlds, as they almost achieved final enlightenment. Barely missing it, they may not want to get overly involved in life now. Something valuable they learned was how physical disharmony is the result of mental disharmony. There's an interest in diet, nutrition, and health, with talents to develop healing powers, including healing methods based on faith. Their health is usually robust, although a health or con-fining issue may develop for them or someone close that has a definite purpose, putting them in touch with their untapped talents. They tend to reminisce—people and life are scrutinized intensely, with expectations of being likewise scrutinized. Unaware of it, they may drift back in time, remaining inside the self, dredging up imagined or real past fears to the point that they become the basis for the present life, causing a lack of confidence. While periods of isolation favor spiritual growth, coming out of the self, interacting with others, and maintaining a positive outlook provides enjoyment from helping others, especially by using discriminatory and analytical talents to do so. Here to be of service rather than a savior, this is the *Samaritan, Worker, Service Provider, Doctor, Nurse, Nutritionist,* or *Nun.* The sign of the North Node shows the manner in which dedication to service can be most productive, bringing fulfillment.

Famous people with this position are Erma Bombeck, Barbra Streisand, Clint Eastwood, Anne Heche, Tyra Banks, Giorgio Armani, Drew Barrymore, and astrologer Evangeline Adams.

SEVENTH HOUSE NORTH NODE

On the Surface: The individuality and personality is well developed, although this individual carries a great deal of self-consciousness and may be a loner. There is something otherworldly about him or her—they may seem to be operating on another plane. He or she is developing charm and diplomacy, as there are untapped gifts in the art of compromise. Partnerships are extremely important and must be carefully chosen because sacrifice for the other is a prominent theme. There are magnetic attracting qualities and the one attracted may be powerful, worldly, or demanding, but may also provide a rise in fortune. This individual does attract attention and may possess a good amount of self-importance but may struggle to gain position. They are ambitious, but may overlook areas needing self-improvement.

Below the Surface: In past lives, he or she only had to worry about personal thoughts and actions. Now, there are lessons to learn about devotion, cooperation, and partnerships, although there is remembrance of so much freedom in the past. All of the inborn confidence and strength accumulated in the past must now be utilized on behalf of others. Though the tendency is to focus on the self, such focus only brings unhappiness. In extreme cases, a physical or emotional impairment is used to gain sympathy. Eventually the person learns that the greatest fulfillment comes from dedicating his or her focus and energy to helping others, especially the spouse. Moving away from self-absorption is necessary to realize their true capabilities. They must take care not to become overly dependent on others as the only way to derive a sense of self. It takes a special partner to pull off a happy matrimonial state, someone who doesn't restrict the other's spirit of independence. Often there is something unique about the relationship—perhaps the marriage is never legalized, or the couple is separated, either by location or in consciousness. This position gives tremendous opportunity to make spiritual progress in this lifetime as this is truly a special mission, when contacts are made with those individuals most in need of this person's ability to inspire them with confidence and courage. This is the *Judge, Mediator, Avenger, Arbitrator, Critic, Peacemaker,* or *Diplomat.* The sign of the North Node shows the manner by which making sacrifices for others brings greatest fulfillment.

Famous personalities with this position include Jackie O., Prince William, Queen Elizabeth I, General Wesley Clark, Calista Flockhart, Elizabeth Dole, and Barack Obama.

EIGHTH HOUSE NORTH NODE

On the Surface: This position gives talent in business, working with figures, doing research, or work that deals with old things. Material protection is often excellent as this person attracts generous partners, although the life partner extends much control over their life. Many avenues support the material needs—however, there are periods of personal financial drains, dissipation of assets, and the necessity to accept financial help at least once in the life. A curious handling of money is noticed; neglectful, or perhaps demonstrating both miserly and carefree spending habits, depending on the situation. There is usually little luck in speculation. Happiness lies in occult and metaphysical realms, seeking the spiritual meaning of life. One should open up to all types of experiences as power, passion, and self-control is developed. This individual may be an extremist or resistant to social niceties and norms.

Below the Surface: In the past, these individuals led a physical, material life, possessive and self-indulgent. Now, they want it all. Striving for status, only temporary satisfaction comes from each new possession, as no matter the gratification that comes to them, there is yet another possession just out of reach. Financial clashes arise until they learn to be content with what they can actually use right now. The values of others may have been unappreciated in the past. Wastefulness of inherited property might have contributed to some family hostilities. Insatiable sexual desires also create problems. Unless checked, the self-indulgent and possessive tendencies of the past could cause the current life to be an ordeal until they allow their old value system to be transformed. The karma is to overcome the need to profit through the physical universe and attune to the values of others, especially to help others discover their unique personal worth. There are talents for dealing effectively and constructively with the subconscious of others and an inner reliance that is unequalled, a gift for overcoming setbacks and an ability to create new conditions; learned by being forced to find the strength to undergo a rebirth. Rigidity about having things the old way and refusing to listen to those who love them are the main blocks. This is the *Therapist, Psychologist, Investigator, Researcher, Analyst, Scientist, Wizard, Magician,* or *Politician.* The sign of the North Node shows the manner by which their personal rebirth can be set in motion.

Famous people with this position are Albert Einstein, Jimi Hendrix, Ricky Martin, Barbara Walters, and Senator John Edwards. Stripper Candy Barr had this position, with Pluto conjunct her South Node.

NINTH HOUSE NORTH NODE

On the Surface: Those with this position may take up a lifelong study, pursuing philosophical fields and higher knowledge. Intellectual fields are open and there is thirst for knowledge. Involvement in publications is common. Mental skills are apparent in writing or along artistic lines. There is an ease of expression, overly so, to the point that giving too much information can become a fault. This individual becomes scattered by the many intrusions of others, especially siblings, relatives, or neighbors. Lack of mental focus and direction may be a downfall. There may be periods of fruitless wandering, although such an individual may profit from travel. It broadens her or his perspective and they may ultimately find fortune and destiny by relocating at a long distance. An auspicious placement, benefits are greater in the last half of life. This person may be a twin—affairs involving siblings are a product of destiny.

Below the Surface: There is excessive curiosity and such a need for people left over from the past lives that there are many connections and relationships, which become complicated. Trying to solve everyone's problems, this person feels that more knowledge could only help. A love for trivia from the past carries over, and he or she seeks information to have on hand whenever a problem needs to be solved. Fear of being misunderstood and an overly active mentality causes drainage of true capacity, preventing progress. The individual loves giving advice and solving puzzles, but spends much time rehashing in their mind what they have said. They want to say it again, but better. Attachment to these small details and past analytical ways blocks a larger perspective, which would allow them to let the small things slide and concentrate on the larger possibilities. They must cultivate faith; seek enlightenment and a spiritual life, expanding their wisdom about the truth of existence. Material comforts are less important. This is the *Seeker, Preacher, Traveler, Mentor, Guide, Tutor, Philosopher,* or *Storyteller.* The sign of the North Node shows the manner by which he or she can seek and succeed in opening up to new possibilities and freeing their higher mind.

Famous personalities with this position include Johnny Carson, Bob Dylan, Barry Gibb, Bill Clinton, twins Mary Kate and Ashley Olsen, and Robbie Krieger of the Doors, who had a twin brother Ronald, also with this position.

TENTH HOUSE NORTH NODE

On the Surface: With leadership qualities, this is a life of prominence. There is executive and management ability that promises a rise in life. This often happens early in life, as the person has a strong sense of purpose and is courageous about pursuing his or her destiny. They demonstrate an emotional side that has a certain appeal. There are affiliations with prominent and successful people. The reputation is good, with many honors and an enjoyment of respect. This is an auspicious placement for fame. This creation of the professional family and workaholic tendencies may be in conflict with a happy home life. Pressed into playing a dominant role, there are heavy demands from family, and parenthood is a difficult role; the spouse may be absent at some point, forcing him or her to play the role of both parents and being the sole supporter. The health or development of a child may cause concerns. There may be problems with family over real estate.

Below the Surface: The person may be caught in a web between things that need to be done for the family versus things done for the self. There is karma owed to the family—in the previous life the family and parents may not have been well appreciated. Now, very sensitive and with deep ties to the mother, which doesn't guarantee a smooth relationship, his or her own family burden becomes so heavy that resentment stirs. They don't feel appreciated for all that they do. They would like to break free, but with a strong attachment to their roots there are tangled family relations that keep them emotionally involved, for better or worse. Fulfillment comes from directing the efforts outward into society and toward large-scale organizational efforts without neglecting the needs of the immediate family. Balancing the two brings happiness and contentment. Self-respect comes from the outer work, and joy comes from the ability to provide shelter and nurturing to others. This is the *Father, Patriarch, Provider, Lawmaker, Authority, Executive, Chief, Dignitary, Organizer,* or *Role Model.* The sign of the North Node indicates the manner in which concentrated efforts lead to achieving the highest potential.

Famous people with this position include Julia Roberts, Prince Charles, Celine Dion, Jane Fonda, Paula Abdul, Tony Blair, Christian Dior, and Ron Howard.

ELEVENTH HOUSE NORTH NODE

On the Surface: These individuals are young at heart. It is easy to make friends and they are intent about joining the right groups and associations that will aid in realizing their ambitions. Being seen in the right places and with the right people to advance social prestige is important. They gain popularity and enjoy speculation, sports, glamour, and easy romantic conquests (often a detriment). There is an imbalance between the love given and the love received in friendships and romance. He or she possesses a sharp intellect, although learning is internalized. Formal education is sought more as a social responsibility than a true liking for it, and there may be a break in schooling. Sacrifices are made to further the career of another. There is some problem with having or raising children. It's an auspicious placement in which material gains and the fulfilling of desires occurs in middle age.

Below the Surface: This is a romantic dreamer who likes being seen as a hero or heroine. The need to be seen as sacrificial, combined with a desire to play the lead character in an adventurous romance, is so compelling that there are times the chosen avenue forces them to give everything up for someone else. Having someone to love them is a carryover need, fulfilling the past sense of ego and need for appreciation. This strong attachment to their former ego must be released. With a forceful will, their excessive pride and wanting to be the boss brings the greatest self-undoing, ensuring the ego will be sacrificed at some point, either in fairness to another or by being forced to lean on someone stronger than themselves. The more they hang on to their pride, the more their real power is denied to them. The karma is to learn the value of friendship and to become a servant to humanity, growing beyond physical possessiveness and the passionately involved interactions of the past in favor of more impersonal interactions. It is through this association with friends that they come to see themselves from a detached perspective and learn their true identity. A life of ease with this position is repayment for a previous life of seeking spirituality. This is the *Hero/Heroine, Soldier, Warrior, Knight, Rescuer, Liberator,* or *Messiah.* The sign of the North Node indicates the ways in which developing detachment ensures that he or she can focus their energy on shared causes.

Famous personalities with this position include Edgar Winter, Robert Downey Jr., Roberta Flack, Naomi Judd, Gary Busey, and George W. Bush.

TWELFTH HOUSE NORTH NODE

On the Surface: Possessing a strong willpower, a hint of fate may attach to the riches or power achieved. There are gifts of insight and intuition, which open up unique solutions to problems—this person's own or those of others. He or she can see beyond material realms and may find that drugs or alcohol offer an escape from the material world, enabling them to take a dip in the sea of the nonmaterial—thus it is easy to become addicted to substances. There are interests in research and in carrying out work behind the scenes, sometimes in institutions for those in need of rehabilitation. A healing touch is noticed. Adaptable to changing tides, too great a focus on small details or doing menial tasks can keep this individual overly busy. They are easily imposed upon and may overextend their strength and energy. The price may be never getting anywhere of consequence, or life in the physical world may seem exhausting. They do better working on independent projects than under someone's orders. There are periods of isolation. Health issues conflict with work.

Below the Surface: In the past life, he or she was used to having control and orderly conditions. Now, seeing chaotic conditions everywhere, there are critical tendencies, often looking down on others and judging them. They expect a lot from anyone working for them. Disliking work that is beneath their dignity, circumstances may force the necessity for it. Deeply introspective, a need for inner serenity causes self-absorption. This can lead to dwelling on unpleasant subjects, like health problems or enemies, which can lead to disease or paranoia. Internalizing anger causes health problems that are usually blamed on work conditions. The physical state is dependent on purity of the mind. The karma is to learn compassion, transitioning from a life of pigeonholing every aspect of life to a new consciousness of spirit, seeing the self as part of the larger whole rather than separate from it. This individual must focus on idealistic callings and activities that uplift others, cultivating faith and spirituality. This is the *Mystic, Hermit, Visionary,* and *Intuitive.* The sign of the North Node indicates the ways that transformation allows their pure essence of spirit to flow.

Famous people with this position are Marilyn Monroe, Kirk Douglas, Roy Horn, and Neil Armstrong.

NORTH NODE HOUSE TRINITY

In his book *Lunar Nodes*, Mohan Koparker points out that the karmic energy from past incarnations, which comes in from the South Node end of the nodal axis, is processed by an individual and then redistributed into the present life according to the house network established by the location of the North Node. This network consists of the houses that form a Grand Trine, and includes the house of the North Node. The areas covered by this network are quite significant in the life of an individual in terms of karmic growth during the lifetime. Each of the four networks establishes a specific group.

If your North Node is in houses 1, 5, or 9, your redistribution network for processing past life influences falls in these three houses. Koparker says that this group is responsible for intellectual and creative growth in society. In the Western system, this is known as the Trinity of Life.

If your North Node is in houses 2, 6, or 10, your network comprises these three houses in which to redistribute and utilize your stores of energy from the past. As Koparker explains, this is the group responsible for material structure and business growth in society. In Western astrology, this is called the Trinity of Wealth.

If your North Node lies in houses 3, 7, or 11, these houses make up your networking system in which to redistribute the past karmic influences. This group is in charge of maintaining peace and harmony in society. It is known as the Trinity of Association in Western astrology.

If your North Node is in houses 4, 8, or 12, these houses comprise your special network. With considerable experience, this group fulfills the most karmic balancing in this lifetime, as they do whatever is needed and ordered by the other groups. This is called the Trinity of Psychism in Western systems.

Review the houses comprising your Trinity, noting the associated archetypes to see if you identify with any of them and whether your work reflects karmic growth.

In the next chapter we will take a look at the spiritual implications linked to the nodes in the signs, where you can discover whether you are a prisoner of the past or are advancing forward on your destined path.

Chapter Five

NATAL NODES BY SIGN POSITION

The sign positions of the nodes are somewhat less personal than house placement, due to the fact that the nodes remain in the same sign for about eighteen months at a stretch. The sign placements have implications that resemble the house associations in the previous descriptions. In other words, the First House North Node is similar to having the North Node in Aries; the Second House North Node is similar to having North Node in Taurus, etc. Still, there is much valuable information available from a study of the node's sign position. Between the house position and the sign placement, the nodes provide a good glimpse of the "why" behind our lives.

In your horoscope, it is the nodes that tell of the spiritual vibration under which you made your entry. These points reveal the continuous threads running from lifetime to lifetime. They tell the story of your evolving soul. The North Node shows where you're going and the South Node shows from where you've come. Always directly opposite one another in your horoscope, they work together, with the endowments from your previous experience furnishing a foundation, offering a gift, in exchange for the new experiential realms you've chosen to conquer.

Because we're more comfortable doing things we're familiar with, it's easy to become entrapped at the South Node. It shows the talents and things we could almost do with our eyes closed because our accumulated experiences in past lifetimes have made us experts in the things represented by the zodiac sign containing the South Node. The planet that rules the sign of this node reveals a lot about our observable traits and talents according to its nature. The South Node sign and its ruler reveal our most ingrained patterns of behavior; this is what we've learned through lifetimes of experience. However, in the bigger scheme, it's crucial to move on to our destiny that is reflected at the North Node and the attributes of that zodiac sign. This is where we feel somewhat uncomfortable, a bit nervous or as if what we feel called to do is too risky to do. While we feel very comfortable at the South Node, we are sometimes frightened to tread into the new territory symbolized by the North Node, yet we must gradually relinquish the old comforts and move on, for that was our plan. Even though it is all new territory, with experiences yet untried, the North Node sign and the planet ruling it shows the kinds of experiences we were excitedly anticipating when we made our entry this lifetime.

You may feel this sense of calling and instinctive guidance as follows.

ARIES NORTH NODE

If your North Node is in Aries, then your South Node is in Libra. This position suggests that in the past you estimated your own happiness according to the happiness of those around you. Keeping others happy ensured your own survival and happiness. Now you must find your own identity rather than one that is an extension of others, learn to take a stand on your own, and give up the need to please all the people all the time.

Assets and Liabilities: You came from a life of considerable luxury. You led an easy-going existence, enjoying the good things in life, pursuing mental activities. This is noticeable in your love of books, and you may have been a bookworm, even in your early years. Past-life talents include tact and diplomacy and the ability to see both sides of any issue, with Venus ruling your South Node. There is also a knack for handling money. You are involved in many kinds of relationships, often attracting individuals who are naïve, self-interested, or childlike. You recognize that their particular imbalance relates to issues of giving and receiving. You may also attract those who are undependable, which forces you to learn self-sufficiency. These encounters enable you to gather much experience and knowledge, but you may make compromises too easily, allowing partners or other people to sway your thoughts. Carried to extremes, with concern about your social image, you become unable to make up your mind on any issue and incapable of taking a decisive stand. You are working now to develop your ability to initiate actions and demonstrate a more assertive side of your nature. You must become more decisive and trust your impulses, for the more you take chances, the more successful you become. If you find that others are manipulating you, or that you never say no, giving beyond what is comfortable due to a feeling of incompleteness unless connected to another, you may be operating at the wrong end of your nodes. Use your inborn aptitudes to move toward the new possibilities. Instead of looking to how others can complete and define you, bringing you a sense of inner harmony, look to how you can achieve this for yourself. It's okay to be a little more self-serving as long as the Aries North Node doesn't grow into selfishness. Ultimately you'll become independent—a pioneer, an adventurer, or entrepreneur—unafraid to try new things, signified by Mars as your North Node ruler. The house position of the North Node indicates where a new birth and a sense of identity can be achieved.

A few individuals with North Node in Aries are Tarzan (the fictional character), Paloma Picasso (daughter of Pablo, and herself a designer), Theodorus van Gogh (brother to Vincent, and an art dealer), James Dean, Celine Dion, Meryl Streep, Rachael Ray, Julia Roberts, and Neil Armstrong.

TAURUS NORTH NODE

If your North Node is in Taurus, then your South Node is in Scorpio. These positions suggest that having been through many emergencies and crises dealing with loss and separation, you must let go of old anxieties about picking up the pieces, learn moderation, and have faith that the material abundance of the world will meet your needs.

Assets and Liabilities: You see the hidden sides of things. You understand power exchanges in situations and sense when something is afoul. But you can become overly suspicious of the motives of others, thus a part of you may be out to stay one-up on them. This comes from Pluto, ruling your South Node. You may have lost a lot in the former life and now you just want to get along and protect yourself from any further losses. You might have compromised your values or integrity in exchange for being taken care of financially or materially; consequently, you may start out being careless with money, expecting someone else will assume the responsibility. You seek material security now with Venus ruling your North Node, and there are potential talents for handling money. As you are learning about building new value systems, new banking and security systems, you encounter people with whom there are battles dealing with sex, money, or power. Themes of trading sex for money, or money for emotional security, or similar trades, are those you may be faced with to resolve these issues of "what's yours and what's mine," and to connect with your inner values. Comparing yourself to someone else always results in a feeling of insecurity, and then a tremendous need for validation causes you to say what you must in order to remind others of your power, hopefully getting their agreement. This residual need for validation may even cause you to do what you think will gain you the most approval, rather than what you really want to do. If keeping up appearances is your main consideration, or if money and material security overrides your sense of morality, you may be stuck, still operating under old value systems that were forced upon you in the past. Getting involved in dishonest schemes would definitely have severe consequences. You are a builder, and must have faith in your ability to attract fortunes and win achievements by doing what makes you feel good—otherwise, all the applause in the world will never be enough. The house of the North Node shows where opening up to a new awareness about trust and security can replace the residual struggles.

Public figures with this position include Prince Charles, Jackie O., Dick Clark, Kenny Loggins, Carlos Santana, Stevie Nicks, James Taylor, Hillary Clinton, Clint Eastwood, and Al Gore.

GEMINI NORTH NODE

If your North Node is in Gemini, your South Node is in Sagittarius. This position suggests that in the past you were a free spirit, perhaps a wanderer, used to going it alone and unaccustomed to social responsibilities during those philosophy-seeking days. Now, you must get intimately involved and connected with society, even though you start out feeling clumsy in such unfamiliar territory.

Assets and Liabilities: You become an excellent communicator but must first be forced to intermingle with others and get proficient at expressing yourself. You are constructing new educational systems by acquiring hands-on experience. Any tendency to get caught up in old beliefs will stunt your growth. You must let go of a reliance on your earlier gurus and books. If you find yourself insisting that your philosophy is the only right one, you may be operating at the wrong end of your nodes. Or, if you are afraid to challenge an idea just because it is in print, again you may be stuck in the past. You are meant to explore possibilities. There are many encounters with others who need to disentangle themselves from old doctrines that were enforced by someone of a powerful persuasion. You can assist them as you are learning to test and challenge the common mind-set. You exude energy for life and have amazingly fast thought processes. Mercury is your North Node ruler, offering youthfulness and a gift of gab. You are a messenger and there is no one more versatile and interesting to listen to. Life sets you up to be constantly involved with others on a daily basis—there's not much time alone. You are especially good at teaching teamwork and full of original thoughts and ideas. You could be a gifted writer, a teacher, lecturer, or any one of a wide range of fields. You have much to share from your past adventures and experiences. With Jupiter showing the gifts you brought, you are meant to widely distribute joy and hope. Just watch a tendency to over-expand, especially in material pursuits. The house of the North Node shows where active participation brings advantages.

Some individuals with North Node in Gemini are George W. Bush, Bill Clinton, Patty Duke, Sally Field, Calista Flockhart, Jessica Lynch, and David Letterman.

CANCER NORTH NODE

If your North Node is in Cancer, then your South Node is in Capricorn. This position suggests that in the past you were of a business mind, cool, calculating, and proud of the public status you held. You were immersed in worldly affairs. Now, the challenge is to open up and experience the feeling of nurturance, both from the receiving end and through the giving end, even though it is difficult to let down your guard about your privacy.

Assets and Liabilities: Especially in your younger years, people found you to be cool and distant, though willing to take on a lot of responsibility. You came across as conservative, slow to act and perhaps a little on the pessimistic side. You may have left the family initially to go out and have new experiences, as there is still a lot of material ambition and a need to be on center stage. You are highly practical and especially skilled in organization. You attract people to you who are in search of recognition. From your earlier experience, you show them that in order to attain success they must behave as if they are under constant observation. In the past you were one of the authorities making the laws, with Saturn ruling your South Node, and now you must follow them to the letter. It isn't easy to get away with even the smallest of crimes. If you find that you are suspicious of others, self-serving, using others for personal aims, or often depressed due to a lack of material success, it is likely you are operating at the wrong end of your nodes. The more you concentrate on your career, to the exclusion of your family, the more insecurity and unhappiness you find. You must learn about nurturing and turn your attention to the home and family. Family security was lacking in your earlier life, but now you can establish a solid home base, with the Moon ruling your North Node. Eventually, you can become an excellent cook with a happy family life, and enjoy an appreciation for assuming a central position. If you can deal with sensitive issues, this is a sign you are on the right track as you are balancing these areas of home and career. The house of the North Node shows where others are waiting to be nourished.

Some of those with these nodes include Erma Bombeck, Whitney Houston, Nicolas Cage, Johnny Carson, Queen Elizabeth II, Alan Greenspan, Hugh Hefner, and Mark McGwire.

LEO NORTH NODE

If your North Node is in Leo, then your South Node is in Aquarius. These positions suggest that in the past you worked with many friends to achieve goals that were common to a larger group. Now, you must learn to stand on your own, overcome self-doubt, and build strength within yourself, for you are ready to be a strong leader. Your longing for friendship only dissipates your energy and undermines your ability to build self-confidence.

Assets and Liabilities: In the past, you worked to achieve things for other people and were involved in unusual activities and projects, possibly a bit eccentric with Uranus ruling your South Node. In fact, you like it that others see you as unique. As a youth, you came across as somewhat shy, but always ready to pitch in and do things for other people, rarely saying no. You may have taken on responsibilities in organizing group efforts that you didn't get credit for. Now it is imperative for you to get credit for your work and make a name for yourself. You are working to develop self-confidence and kingliness. In this life, circumstances will force you to stand on your own—during certain periods there may be no one for you to lean on—but it is these periods of isolation that are necessary in order for you to gather your strength. You've gained a lot of experience and wisdom in the past and now you are to relay all of that through your creative efforts. You attract people who are domineering, possessive, or jealous—who need to break free from rigid habit patterns. This is your forte, and you teach them through your example and from your innate sense of fairness. The ability to be flexible that you learned in the past is an asset to becoming an admirable leader with an ability to oversee others. You have the capacity to instill confidence, poise, and kindness in others. As you get older you demonstrate more self-absorption, which is as it is supposed to be. However, this position is one in which the North Node needs to develop the sense of self. This can lead to overexuberance, creating an enormous sense of ego and pride. You must learn to lead without letting your sense of yourself go to your head. Enjoy all the admiration, but don't lose your regard for others, because that would spoil even your most noble intentions. Ruling your North Node, the Sun provides you with good vital forces and energy, along with your leadership potential. The house of the North Node shows where to direct your unique creative energy to bring a gift to the world.

Some of the people with this nodal axis are Barack Obama, Princess Diana, MC Hammer, George Harrison, Jimi Hendrix, Paula Abdul, and Demi Moore.

VIRGO NORTH NODE

If your North Node is in Virgo and your South Node in Pisces, emotional sensitivity could impede your good judgment, leaving you lackadaisical about managing your life. You've known the sorrows of others and have become used to putting others ahead of yourself, creating co-dependencies and relying upon favorite fantasies and superstitions to get you through life. Now, you must learn discrimination about those you choose to help, learn practical planning, and how to clearly define goals for yourself.

Assets and Liabilities: You've come from a life of luxury and seclusion, likely pursuing spiritual experiences. It may be hard to leave behind such a dreamy life. This is to be a life of finding an ideal balance between heavenly pursuits and practical duties, as now you are called to tend to details of the everyday world and learn about logic and reason. With Mercury ruling your North Node you are encouraged to learn better management skills. You possess great sensitivity and can feel the pain and misery of others. You attract those who are suffering in some way, or who are hypercritical of themselves.

There may be connections to alcoholics or the homeless. It hurts you to see others suffering. Understanding that negative influences and thoughts must go somewhere, you absorb these for others, sending them love and compassion in return, but you must be careful of letting these sad cases drain you of your own strength. Be sure the people you choose to help are worthy of your efforts. You could end up spreading yourself thin, or fall into depression. You are learning to be less swayed by your emotions and more experienced in making judgments based on your critical faculties. You must learn when to say no. You are quite health conscious, likely learning about diet, herbs, and natural remedies. Others come to you with questions about their health issues, for which you often have an answer. You are developing your critical abilities, where you become aware of flaws and can teach people how to live life more efficiently. Dieticians, nutritionists, healers, doctors, and nurses fall in this group. If you find that you are full of self-pity, fearful of life, or addicted to drugs, you are operating at the wrong end of your nodes. You must cross over to where you appreciate work and use your gift of insight to help others live a better quality life. With Neptune ruling your South Node, you must resist daydreaming and escapist tendencies. For you, there is power in logic and reason, not in dreaming. Dedicating yourself to service brings happiness. The house position of the North Node shows where bringing structure and form will enable you to realize the material reality of your past cosmic understanding.

A few individuals with these placements are Christian Dior, Martha Stewart, Bob Dylan, Michael J. Fox, JFK Jr., and George Clooney.

LIBRA NORTH NODE

If your North Node is in Libra and the South Node in Aries, you have achieved a great deal of self-confidence from past experience. With a competitive drive, you've learned to make swift and critical decisions, concerned mainly with self-interests and self-love in the past. Now you must take all that self-esteem and spirit of competition and put it to work on behalf of others. Sharing and cooperation are keynotes as you learn to be sensitive to the needs of others.

Assets and Liabilities: You have come from a life in which you learned to protect yourself. With Mars ruling your South Node, you have dealt in combat and have learned courage and self-sufficiency. In fact, you are so aware of your individuality that you may try to hide it in order to appear more pleasing and approachable to others. You are learning the art of compromise through your experiences in close relationships and partnerships. Some of these won't go well as you are brought into contact with aggressive or angry people. You have the capacity to absorb their negativity—at the same time you are a good role model, demonstrating a healthy sense of self-identity. You learn that you are to be neither totally self-sufficient nor totally dependent as you are establishing a balance between the two. You become ever more pleasing in tone and demeanor as you learn that working in union with another has advantages. You learn you can get things without fighting. With such a strong magnetism, others will even surrender to you. You develop diplomatic skills and learn about law and order, maybe becoming a judge or a counselor. Diplomacy will become your forte. You expend a lot of mental energy as you study how to establish peaceful relations. You have excellent insights into the motivations of others and can point out flaws as a way to achieve fairness and harmony. A gift of this placement is a high degree of inventiveness. Venus rules your North Node, generally a good placement, often bringing riches. If you find you are dictatorial, self-centered, or still involved in tussles where diplomacy doesn't achieve peaceful ends, you have more work to do before you find true contentment. The house of the North Node shows where cooperation brings fulfillment.

Some of the people with this placement include Richard Cheney, Judy Garland, John Lennon, Chandra Levy, Tina Turner, Nancy Sinatra, and Madonna.

SCORPIO NORTH NODE

If your North Node is in Scorpio and your South Node in Taurus, you've come to expect a great deal of stability and settled conditions in life that have been secured through accumulated possessions and hard work. Now, unable to let go of anything or anybody, you trap yourself with excess baggage that hinders you from seeing new possibilities or experiencing change of any kind. Eventually, you'll find yourself by letting go of those things that are now only decayed remnants of the past.

Assets and Liabilities: With your South Node ruled by Venus, you've brought over artistic talents and you are refined in nature, with an appreciation for aesthetics. You were likely surrounded by fine art and considerable material security and were very resistant to any change or disturbance to your lifestyle and routine. Now, there are early struggles as you are brought into contact with people who do not know how to handle their finances or how to properly prioritize their values. This is an area where you have plenty of experience, so you are a good influence and teacher. But you may experience some financial losses yourself as you are learning to be less attached to material things, instead turning your attention to the more spiritual realms, which brings the material world into a healthier perspective. There may be extreme changes in your living situation in this one lifetime. This is an intense placement, as you must confront deep realms encompassing passion, sexuality, obsessions, and the fight between good and evil. There is a revolution involving your value systems and this is an ongoing process. It favors research as you have the potential to develop deep insight. You come to understand the phases of the cosmos, cycles relating to life and death, and the laws of the universe. Possessing magnetism, you are developing a strong will with Pluto ruling your North Node, and you must learn to move toward your desired goals without compromise or hesitation. If you rarely feel envy over the material possessions of others, and if you've learned that money can't buy the truly important things in life, you are operating on the appropriate end of your nodes. If not, the house position of the North Node shows where to focus your energies in order to experience a rebirth.

A few famous people with this nodal axis are Abraham Lincoln, romance writer Barbara Cartland, Walt Disney, Clark Gable, and Evel Knievel.

SAGITTARIUS NORTH NODE

If your North Node is in Sagittarius and the South Node in Gemini, you have learned the gift of the chameleon, ever flexible and able to maneuver splendidly without ever having to take a decisive stand about your personal beliefs. Now you must move beyond the wealth of superficial knowledge and follow the target marked for higher knowledge as you seek wisdom, truth, and allegiance to one committed belief.

Assets and Liabilities: You've come from a life where you were always in the company of others, usually pursuing intellectual activities. As a result of all the daily communications, solving others' problems, your intellectual capacity was often drained and you were denied the time to pursue philosophy. Now you have the opportunity to enjoy more seclusion as you explore spiritual and esoteric realms, developing a longer attention span and your independent thought processes. You have the potential to be an excellent communicator and may become a gifted writer, although you may start out as a jack-of-all-trades, due to your need to be a free spirit—not tied down in too many earthly encumbrances. You may even get the chance to travel the world. There is some residual indecisiveness and fearfulness about committing yourself to one side or one idea. You'd prefer to keep both sides open, which doubles your future choices. Overcoming these tendencies and learning to speak the truth that comes from your higher mind is your task. Those who are caught up in outdated ways are attracted to you—with a talent for seeing both sides of any issue, you are able to show them new ideas, new methods, and beliefs. With Mercury ruling your South Node, don't let your tendency to talk too much and listen too little be a rut you can't get out of. Still, you have a wonderful sense of humor. You are a truth seeker and not much interested in material things, although with Jupiter ruling your North Node there's usually no lack. You can be a spiritual teacher or a philosopher who helps others understand that we can live together without prejudice. You come to recognize the common thread that lies at the root of all belief systems. You understand that we are all on this journey together, looking for our connection back to the source. The house of the North Node shows where developing higher consciousness is your channel to ascend above all discord.

Some individuals with this placement are Swami Vivekananda, Leonardo DiCaprio, Drew Barrymore, Jane Fonda, Bill Gates, Angelina Jolie, and publisher William Randolph Hearst.

CAPRICORN NORTH NODE

If your North Node is in Capricorn and the South Node in Cancer, you have such attachments to the past that you constantly look there to analyze today, immersed in the child side of your nature and tending to become absorbed in the emotional ordeals of others. Now, you must look outside yourself to find a larger ideal with which you can identify, enabling you to grow up and become a model of competency, self-sufficiency, and maturity.

Assets and Liabilities: While great achievement and success will come to you, possibly far superior to that of your peers, it will usually come later in life, with Saturn ruling your North Node. You may start out as overly shy, reclusive, afraid of responsibility and easily depressed, perhaps prone to ulcers from over-worry, a tendency carried over by the Moon ruling your South Node. You are a leader of the future, but you must first overcome strains in your family life. In the past you were immersed in family and domestic life, having your needs met by the family, which prevented you from going out and trying new things. Now, you are born into a family with problems, especially emotional problems, which you feel a responsibility to deal with. With a sense of trepidation about going out in the world and making it on your own, you may even use the excuse that family obligations prevent you from doing so. This will delay the inevitable as you are to learn self-competency. You may attract people into your life that can be of no material help, which pushes you to make it on your own. Those who don't understand their own emotional problems gravitate to you and you provide a shoulder to cry on, with a knack for healing their souls by absorbing their emotional problems. But you can get bogged down unless you strive for a good degree of detachment. At the same time, you are usually not allowed to express your emotions or show your sensitive side, so people may feel they don't really know you. Eventually you come out of your shell, rising above your dependence on your family and friends. You toughen up and present a good image, making a fine reputation for yourself as you learn to be self-sufficient. Self-discipline and persistence are among your strong points. You become a business owner, an architect or organizer, respected and responsible. Anything is possible if you set your goals and then work toward them. After considerable experience and struggles, balance is achieved between family and career responsibilities. While there may be family troubles, you can never completely break away, as then you would only find yourself attracting a new family situation to deal with. The house of the North Node indicates where to align your life with values based on honor, respect, and tradition in order to realize your highest potential.

Among those with these nodes are John McCain, Woody Allen, Sonny Bono, Roy Orbison, Kris Kristofferson, Johnny Mathis, Kevin Costner, John Travolta, and Althea Flynt.

AQUARIUS NORTH NODE

If your North Node is in Aquarius and your South Node in Leo, you've developed pride and dignity, and have enjoyed respect and admiration, as in the past you were used to being in the spotlight. While forming relationships with those who made you look good, you tended to look down on those of lesser status. Now you will choose to be more dedicated to the greater humanity as you work to further the objective of a larger order, rather than for self-aggrandizement.

Assets and Liabilities: In the past life you were highly respected, doing individualized work. Because of that, self-image is extremely important to you. You are quite aware of your individuality, and what others think of you means everything. Protecting your reputation is most important. With a strong sense of decency and right and wrong, you uphold the laws. Due to your prior authority status, you want to be taken seriously, and you like to set the rules. Because it comes naturally with the Sun ruling your South Node, you tend to be bossy, or at times arrogant and self-important, so you must practice being humble. Marriage entails difficulties as you are used to taking the dominant role. You may seek and gain recognition, but this time it isn't all about you. In fact, fame will become psychologically unimportant. There is much to learn about the world and its woes before you can do your greatest work. You learn much from those people you attract who are cool, distant, unable to receive love, or are trapped in self-pity. Carry out your mission to infuse others with the warmth of your spirit, spreading the radiance of the Sun to spark creativity in others, and use your wisdom to better the world. By nurturing your hopes, desires, and wishes, they have every chance of becoming a reality. Because you have the voice of authority behind you, it gives you the power of persuasion. You have potential to teach others why diversity makes the world a better place, and that there is no need to judge or fear those who hold views different than their own. If you still exhibit bursts of explosive anger, or display an ego-centered need for admiration, you must begin to see yourself more as part of the greater humanity and share the burden of our collective evolution. With Uranus ruling your North Node, you have potential ingenuity, especially when you plan your strategies based on self-objectivity. Then you find happiness. You can make friends who are especially helpful, opening you up to new vistas. The house of the North Node shows where to work on a mission for humanity that will release you from the chains of your past-life ego.

Some public figures with an Aquarius North Node are Giorgio Armani, Albert Einstein, Tony Blair, and Robert Blake.

PISCES NORTH NODE

If your North Node is in Pisces and South Node in Virgo, in the past you regimented everything according to material and finite principles, seeking perfect order through detail and fearing contamination. A perfectionist? Yes. An analyst? Yes. Now, you realize there's more to life than meets the eye or can be measured—yet it's difficult to let go and dive into the uncharted seas of faith where you'll learn that all is one, that you cannot separate yourself from others forever and that it isn't up to you make judgment calls on anyone.

Assets and Liabilities: In the past you were methodical and regimented. You were critical, detail oriented, attracted to solving puzzles by applying facts, far from being led by any instincts. Now, you are developing your intuition, becoming more trusting and guided by your feelings as life progresses. Moving away from purely practical considerations, you enjoy an exchange of feelings with others as you become receptive to dealing with emotions. In order to learn about compassion, someone close to you deals with suffering or misfortune and you discover ways to ease their misery. You come in contact with healers and learn about healing. From this and prior knowledge you bring healing methods and vital information to others. Just be careful that you don't absorb others' negativity and hold it in, taking on the whole burden. You must learn to replace negative vibrations with love, and then release them; otherwise you risk becoming a victim or a martyr. Do try to avoid being a know-it-all, a tendency coming from Mercury ruling your South Node. Others may see you as having hypochondria tendencies, but you are sensitive to pollution, absorbing chemicals and environmental elements and then releasing them. There may also be residual memories of physical limitations, or an inability to release stiffness and rigidity (due to the old need for regimentation) that causes stress on the organs. Yoga poses may help and while you do need to be aware of environmental hazards, becoming fanatical about diet and cleanliness only worsens things. You are perhaps so fearful that everything outside yourself poses a health threat you can attract disease by your resistance to it, a signal that you are operating too much on the wrong end of your nodes. Relax, and rise above the small details. You are spiritually gifted, with a creativity that is rare and unique. You can lift others out of the ordinary with your imagination, instilling in them the faith to trust their instincts and putting them in touch with their spiritual side. You appreciate beauty and you're dreamy and mystical. There is potential to develop your intuition to the point of prophecy. While the liabilities seem heavy, the rewards for making this nodal transition are of the highest order with Neptune ruling your North Node. The house of the North Node reveals where to relinquish your grasp of all rigid definitions, mindsets, and structures.

Some folks with this axis are Edgar Cayce, Dale Earnhardt Sr., Anne Heche, and Robin Williams.

Throughout life, opportunities and circumstances allow for you to make this transition from the old, familiar ways of the Dragon's Tail toward the new realms and adventures of the Dragon's Head. Events happen that pull you toward your destiny. The nodes work together and you could view the nodal axis as a seesaw in motion. As you draw on your prior gifts and utilize them in their highest capacity, the past is gradually resolved, releasing you to explore more of the new territory and the new direction you're meant to move toward. Your previous gifts contribute to your onward journey. The South Node signifies the capacity to release the past and its control over you. The North Node represents the ability to respond to new experiences and move into them. We take in at the North Node and give back at the South Node. The new substance that is provided to us through the North Node must be assimilated and then utilized in a way that benefits are channeled back through the South Node. If you find that life is unfulfilling or your dreams are nowhere in sight, it may be that you are stuck, operating on the wrong end of your nodes, and so you must strive to move forward.

If you have a planet near the Dragon's Head, it will help propel you more easily in the new direction as it urges you to leave the past behind. In fact, circumstances would tend to dissuade you from falling back too heavily on your South Node if you are tempted to do so. You are meant to have new experiences and you may be a youthful soul. With a planet near the Dragon's Tail, you have a particular tie to the past that requires culmination this lifetime. In this scenario, you've brought with you special knowledge or talents that you wanted just one more lifetime to perfect. There may be a need for your special skills (of the nature of that planet) by one or more persons on your destined path. You likely made a pledge with the higher cosmic forces that you could be relied upon to demonstrate and utilize these skills when called upon, in trade for some opportunity to further your evolution and spiritual progress. You may be an old soul, with considerable experience, and making extra efforts now to attain final enlightenment. With planets on both ends of your nodal axis, you are at a critical point on your long journey. We will discuss all of this fully in a coming chapter.

Whether or not you have a planet bringing a specific influence though, your nodes still hold the key to the various activities you should pursue, and identifying those skills you've already mastered. These keys are found in your controlling planets, the rulers of your North and South Nodes, which we'll discuss next.

Chapter Six

YOUR KARMIC CONTROL PLANETS

The Karmic Control planets are the pair of planets that rule the signs containing the North and South nodes. Eastern astrologers call the South Node ruler the Karmic Suction Control (what you're bringing over) and the North Node ruler they refer to as the Karmic Distribution Control (how and where to distribute your energy in this lifetime).

The planetary ruler of the sign in which the North Node falls is indicative of the traits, faculties, and talents in need of development, as compared to those strengths that have already been developed, signified by the ruler of the sign holding the South Node, which must now be utilized constructively to move into the destined future.

Not only are these planets descriptive of these traits by their very nature, but also by their house and sign placements these two controlling planets have strong implications in the life.

The placement and condition of the planet ruling the South Node shows where dues will be paid for past life actions, and where work will be done that utilizes the past life talents. Together with the South Node sign and placement, this planet identifies one's basic nature and aptitude. The placement and condition of the North Node ruler indicates that place where special help is received in furthering the cause of the soul in the current life. Together with the North Node sign and house position, this planet helps identify the intended mission for this lifetime.

You will find this all to be very interesting because these planets furnish a second way to assess your previous talents and to further define your intended path. They provide an inside look at what it is you are all about.

WHERE THE RESULT OF YOUR PAST IS MANIFESTING

What happens is that the past assets and liabilities come out in the house occupied by the planet that rules the South Node. You can see these things in action as they are manifesting in this house. Talents show up here as well as old bad habits. In a way, this is where you show your true colors. While the sign of this planet is also informative, it is best to use the sign for refinement, and focus mainly on the house position to start. Think of the sign of your South Node and the associated traits given for your placements in the previous chapter, and then study how they are showing up in the activities of the house holding this control planet. There are way too many combinations to give all the possible descriptions, so I will give some examples instead:

Mercury in the Third House ruling a Virgo South Node may indicate a tendency to be critical in speech, or talk too much about trivial matters, especially of a worrying sort—about health concerns, advising on nutrition, and so forth—without noticing that one's audience is bored or tired of it. It might also manifest as a knack for writing about subjects that require great attention to detail, utilizing the analytical capabilities. If this Mercury was in Sagittarius, ruled by expansive Jupiter, this could be a prolific writer or one who embellishes or exaggerates the worries. You see, the South Node tendencies and traits could be utilized in either a positive or a negative way in this Third House area, or some of each will show.

Now, let's say it is still Mercury ruling the Virgo South Node but now falling in the Ninth House. This could show real talent as a teacher or professor or in some communication field that requires precision, such as a webmaster on the Internet for instance, or it could come out in a critical attitude toward religious and spiritual beliefs—a dogmatic refusal to go along with a belief in God or a higher power due to a need for absolute proof brought over from the Virgo South Node. With North Node in Pisces, calling for a need to transcend such self-imposed boundaries in order to attain enlightenment, this could stand in the way of potential spiritual progress.

What about Pluto in the Third House ruling a Scorpio South Node? This could come out in an abrasive or confrontational conversational tone whenever the individual's power is slightly challenged, but it might also come out in talents dealing with mass communications or transportation systems; for instance, a technician installing underground communication cables for the phone company, roadway construction work, or aptitude for working in mail delivery. The negative traits and the better qualities may even both show up.

Moon in the Second House ruling the Cancer South Node could show an excellent business sense or it might show up as an irresponsible handling of money, leaning too much on others—a woman, perhaps—to make up for the lack of one's own earnings, unless and until he or she feels like it. If this Moon was forming nice aspects, this help might be available from time to time, which could slow this person down in making the full use of their Capricorn North Node potential.

You see, there are many and varied ways for this to come out so that it will be to your advantage to explore these things for yourself. You'll also be amazed at what you can learn about the people in your life. The closer your association, the more you will be able to account for little quirks, mysteries, or admirable qualities that escaped your understanding in the past. In many cases you will verify that both positive and negative traits are exposing themselves in this same house. That is actually not so bad because it means progress is being made.

There are also sacrifices attaching to the house holding the South Node ruler, however, relating to the nature of the planet and sign. These may be more or less problematic, but there are always some. There may be less than ideal relationships or losses connecting to this house. For instance, there might be the loss of a child, or no children, if it is the South Node ruler in the Fifth House, difficult relationships with siblings if in the Third House, the loss of pets if in the Sixth House, and so on. There is some unhappiness, block, or situation that is more or less out of the hands of the individual to control or do anything about. Such blocks, losses, sacrifices, or situations may come up sporadically on numerous occasions throughout life. Vulnerabilities attach to the house containing the ruler of the South Node.

While an examination of the aspects to the control planet, especially between the control planet and the nodal axis itself, will reveal whether there are more positive or negative traits coming out, or the difficulties involved in bringing out the best, the more one can emphasize the positive and gracefully deal with sacrifices, the more it will help move forward on the journey.

In severe cases, usually identifiable when the nodes themselves or this control planet form stressful aspects, it is sometimes found that none of the positive traits are showing up and, in fact, there are not only negative traits coming out but also the karma is apparently causing a heavy repayment in the affairs of the house where the South Node ruler falls. There is severe denial of the substance of the house, such as continual financial drains if in the Second House, lack of opportunity for higher education if in the Ninth House, or continuous struggles attaining the ambitions if in the Tenth House.

WHERE TO FIND YOUR POT OF GOLD

When it comes to the planet ruling the North Node, this planet suggests by its nature the traits to strive for, and according to its house position, it shows where there are opportunities for new growth and development. By directing the efforts to the activities associated with that house and consciously tapping into the potential, results rapidly come forth. There is a measure of luck or fortune available. This is where you have the opportunity to create future karma. The cosmic forces reward you for applying yourself in the manner and location signified by the planet ruling the North Node. In fact you will likely find that you are already quite involved in the associated affairs. This is what you came to do. This house defines much about the path, the mission, the purpose intended in making the decision to come back now.

Of course these benefits attaching to the ruler of the North Node and its house position can also be misused or distorted in some way, and much of this will be found according to the aspects to the nodes and the control planets. It is important to be aware that the North Node or its ruler could go overboard or get carried away, exemplifying the negative traits of that sign in the house in which it falls, and thus becoming just as detrimental to happiness and fulfillment as if one remained stuck at the South Node.

Here are some keywords for the houses to start you on your interpretations:

First House: personality, demeanor, confidence, independence, sensitivity, physical body

Second House: money, earnings, possessions, resources, spending, values, priorities

Third House: communications, transport, intellect, ideas, publications, siblings, neighbors

Fourth House: family, home, roots, heritage, parents, private life, real estate

Fifth House: children, creativity, romance, speculation, hobbies, sports

Sixth House: health, hygiene, work, service, pets, employees, co-workers

Seventh House: partnerships, marriage, other people, competition, professional advisors

Eighth House: joint finances, support, gains or losses through others, occult, death

Ninth House: education, religion, philosophy, spirituality, journeys, publishing

Tenth House: profession, recognition, ambitions, public life, organization, authorities

Eleventh House: friends, groups, social circle, humanitarian efforts, hopes, wishes

Twelfth House: charity, sympathy, seclusion, places of rehab, behind-the-scenes activities

Check the house of your South Node ruler to find if you are experiencing losses connecting to this house, or if your inborn talents are showing through. Check the house of your North Node ruler to see if you are tapping into the potential, working to capitalize on the associated gifts.

You can also refer to coming chapters for more about house associations, as well as descriptions of the influence of the planets to assist you in your interpretation efforts.

Once in a while there's a situation in which both the controlling planets are in the same house. The individual is all wrapped up in those affairs and activities. There are inborn talents, karmic debts, and residue, and while it is a place to contribute, there is also new growth potential from further broadening the experiences in the activities reflected by the house. It is something of a win-win situation, although there could be the feeling that certain doors are closed. Though individuals might like to branch out, they know instinctively that they would be hurting themselves to divert the focus too far away, or to quit working in this area. In such cases, check the house trinity to see if you are contributing to the intellectual and creative growth in society, to business and trade, to peace and harmony, or in service to humanity. Al Pacino has such an arrangement in his Eleventh House. With his North Node in the Third House, and the same trinity, he is devoted to work that furthers the peace and harmony of society.

If the planet ruling either node is in the sign of the opposite node, there is a mutual reception. The past and future are so connected that the individual will need to draw on past knowledge to get where the soul needs to go. An awareness of the past makes it easy to retrieve just the right bit of prior experience needed now. If a planet joins the

South Node, something from the past may need to be repeated. Again, however, there is enough remembrance or glimpses into the past situation to successfully make it through and on to meet the future. A couple of individuals having a mutual reception are Paula Abdul and Ted Turner.

Perhaps a most difficult nodal axis to come to terms with is when the nodes fall in houses that are precisely counter to their sign positions, such as a Capricorn North Node falling in the Fourth House (must be mother and father, protector and authority, emotionally detached and sensitive, etc., making it strenuous to achieve either family harmony or vocational success). In such cases, unless there is a mutual reception or a planet conjunct one of the nodes to give it the greater influence, or helpful aspects to the nodes or their rulers, it is imperative to establish and maintain as harmonious a balance as possible regarding the matters signified by the houses and signs. One could not give too much weight to one end and neglect the other end for long. The rhythm of the seesaw must be regulated.

I have also found many cases where this nodal reversal doesn't appear to be so problematic. However, in each case there has been some special assistance to the node or its ruler, such as: North or South Node trine the Vertex; North Node trine Midheaven; North Node trine Part of Fortune; South Node ruler trine South Node; ruler of South Node in favorable aspect to nodes; and nodes in harmonious aspect to the Midheaven. It is more difficult if the node squares the Vertex or an angle. Planetary aspects to the nodes also offer input and we will cover these in the next two chapters.

HELPFUL ASPECTS TO THE NODAL RULERS

- When the ruler of the South Node is well supported by aspects, there is facility for working with the old methods.

- When the ruler of the South Node is in good aspect to the South Node, this provides good functioning.

- A good aspect of Jupiter to the South Node or its ruler is an asset, especially by conjunction. Bringing over enthusiasm and optimism is helpful throughout life.

- A conjunction of the Sun to either node ruler is very helpful, as this is a Fortune planet.

- If the ruler of the North Node and the Sun are the same, this increases the chances to make an easy transition, provided that stressful aspects do not seriously handicap the ruler.

- When the North and South Node rulers are in favorable aspect to one another, the natural rhythm and flow of transitioning is easily established.

- When the North Node and its ruling planet are in the same trinity, this is fortunate.

Now, let's take a look at how each of the planets can influence the nodes by falling in close alignment or in aspect to either of them.

Chapter Seven

NODAL ASPECTS TO INNER PLANETS
IN THE NATAL CHART

A planet with one of the nodes is a planet of special significance. This gives more weight to one node, like placing another body on one end of a seesaw. The conjunction of the node with a natal planet will noticeably intensify the planet and bring out its nature in the way an individual goes about handling life. The functions of the planet are easily traced in the life. Actually, when it comes to orbs, these conjunctions can be given a pretty wide leeway, up to seven degrees or more, although I am using tighter orbs (three degrees in most cases), for the groups studied and individuals cited. Obviously, the closer the aspect, the stronger the influence would be.

Planets conjunct the North Node show qualities to be consciously developed in the current lifetime. If there are multiple planets or a dynamic planet involved, there is a particular sense of urgency about this and the individual is somewhat compelled to develop the qualities attributed to the planet. Life propels them toward the future, and life experiences urge them to leave the past behind. New knowledge and experience is accumulated and traits indicated by the North Node sign show up earlier in life. There are opportunities to influence others for material gains and special dividends; if this is a planet of fortune—Sun, Venus, or Jupiter—repayment from the cosmos for past good deeds. There may be some over-eager tendencies displayed in youth as far as taking advantage of the North Node blessings until this soul comes to appreciate the true potential in it for him or her in this lifetime.

A planet near the South Node indicates qualities developed previously. They are habitual and it takes little effort to call them into play. In this scenario, something has been brought over to this lifetime for more perfecting. Talents associated with the planet can be further developed or utilized more fully, more positively, and with more consciousness. The sooner these talents are put to constructive use, the better. This soul may have extraordinary recall of their purpose, which establishes the need to live certain lessons over again. The past may be repeated in some way because sometimes the karmic lesson, signified by the planet, is taking more than one lifetime to finish. South Node conjunct a planet often represents a degree of reckoning for past mistakes or failures. An individual comes knowing of this in his or her heart and soul, and has opted to set things right in this lifetime. In this grand universal design of which we are all a part, it is the only way to evolve. The past has a hold over this person. He or she is chained to it, especially to resolving issues of the nature of the planet. Until the past is resolved, the fruits of the North Node can be of little reward. In this situation it may take a longer portion of life to get off the old track and move toward the future potential. If debts are indicated, the price to pay may be steeper if the planet and node are progressing toward the conjunction rather than separating. (More on this in chapter 9.)

If a planet is conjunct the North Node, look to the house the planet rules. The affairs of that house are usually provided a boost. Progress and benefits from that house may require little effort. Gains or favors attach to the matters or people ruled by a planet conjunct the North Node. If a planet is conjoined with the South Node, the matters of the house the planet rules may suffer or present struggles. There may be unfulfilled expectations, trials, or old issues to be resolved. Losses or obligations attach to the matters or people ruled by a planet conjunct the South Node.

If there are planets on both ends of the nodal axis, there are past lessons to work through, but also enticements to make the effort and have a successful mission. This is like a special crossroads in a soul's evolution, and ensures a busy life. There are chances to make both material and spiritual progress in the current life. North Node is auspicious for material prosperity and worldly influence while South Node favors spiritual advancement. Donald Trump has such a chart. So does Jennifer Aniston. In his book *Karmic Astrology: The Moon's Nodes and Reincarnation*, Martin Schulman suggests that in such a scenario the soul is confronted with the need to resolve an intense conflict in the present life and that by focusing on the energies of the more beneficial planet, the soul is enabled to evolve to the point of reaping benefits from even the most stressful conditions.

Another configuration that reflects upon a special crossroads situation occurs when there is emphasis on both ends of the nodal axis, even though a planet is not involved in both. For instance, having North Node conjunct the Midheaven would pull a person into the limelight and toward the future path, while at the same time a planet conjoining the South Node ties them to the past, especially to resolving family issues. A similar complicated scenario would be to have the North Node on the Ascendant while another planet falls in conjunction with the South Node. There would be the need to establish individuality at the same time that there are some residual issues affecting close relationships. In these and other situations in which both nodes are emphasized, it is more necessary than ever to achieve a workable balance between the matters signified by the two opposing houses and signs. Opposing planets must also make peace.

Starting at the North Node, planets that fall between the North Node and the South Node, going in the order of the signs, show qualities and new faculties to be developed. Activity is being built up of the nature of those planets. Planets in the opposite position, between the South Node and the North Node, indicate tendencies and talents previously developed. These inherited elements may be released in a positive way throughout life—or negatively, they may be underutilized or left idle. Take note of whether there are lots of planets in one or the other of these hemispheres, indicating much to learn or much already learned. The pace of life may seem swifter with several planets in the to-be-built-up half of the chart. On the other hand, if there's already a lot of accumulated experience, it might allow one to concentrate more fully on a couple of areas. Many subtle mental and emotional factors can be found from this study.

Note in particular which of those positions the natal Moon falls in. If the Moon falls on the future-oriented side of the North Node, there is a striving to build up power and focus on the fulfillment of personal desires. While services may be provided to others, the individual ego also thrives. When the Moon is in the other position, behind the North Node, an individual acts more as a savior to others. Sacrifices are made on behalf of others.

Swami Vivekananda and his teacher, the great Hindu mystic Ramakrishna both had their Moons behind the North Node, while many politicians have the Moon in front of it. When you combine this bit of detail with the factor of whether the North Node is high or low in the chart, you can make even more determinations. With North Node low, plus Moon in the rear of it, there are ever-greater sacrifices. Consider John F. Kennedy, who had such a chart. With an upper North Node and the Moon in the forward position, the waves of destiny can propel one into a powerful position. JFK's successor, Lyndon B. Johnson, had that kind of chart. Swami Vivekananda had his North Node high, and with opportunities for an education, he founded the Vedanta Movement. His Moon was behind the North Node, however, so he utilized his gifts to be of service to others. Ramakrishna had the South Node up top and this great religious teacher was the son of a poor family with little formal education.

Now, let's focus on the individual planets in aspect to the nodes. With any of the conjunctions, the North Node gives a greater degree of personal volition and control associated with the nature of the planet, whereas a South Node conjunction signifies less personal control over those affairs. There is a degree of karma at work, where the greater cosmic forces have final say in those matters. There are opportunities to grow spiritually with South Node conjunctions; opportunities for gaining worldly influence and outer material abundance with North Node conjunctions. Planets in square to the nodes represent obstacles to achieving the purpose.

NODAL ASPECTS TO THE SUN

With nodal contacts to the Sun, the planet of individuality and awareness of self, the node making the contact determines how much notice a person can achieve and how much freedom of spirit opportunities will provide for.

With the North Node conjunct the Sun there are special privileges or a boost to achievements—it is like being in the right place at the right time, having considerable luck, mingling and interacting with important people, plenty of material abundance, and so forth. Things just seem to click for such a person and they may be drawn into the limelight or onto the stage. They ride the mainstream. The Sun is a beneficial planet, and this soul may have been given this extra help to ensure sufficient development of his or her ego. In the past there was likely a lack of self-esteem and not enough personal recognition even though the person worked for the benefit of others. The house where the conjunction falls will show where the individuality and leadership may best be expressed. If anyone can get by without having to make retributions, even for wrongs done in this

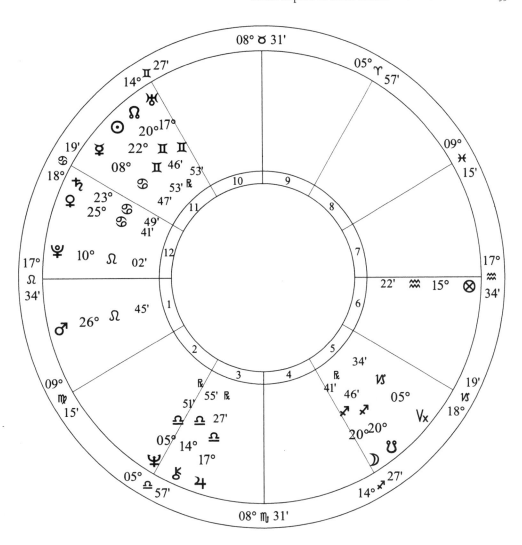

Figure 19: Donald Trump birth chart: June 14, 1946, 9:51 AM, Queens, NY

life, it is the person with North Node conjunct the Sun. He or she is spared for now, as in this lifetime they are slated for personal elevation. Arrogance and egotism may result when these cosmic blessings are misused. Masculine figures, including the father, are ruled by the Sun, therefore with the Sun conjunct the North Node, there are strong ties to a father figure, who is of exceptional benefit. The paternal side of the family may be of special help in finding their direction. There are many of royal blood in this group.

Some famous persons with this aspect are J. P. Morgan, Elisabeth Kübler-Ross, Bo Derek, Abigail Folger, Tim Robbins, and Donald Trump.

With South Node conjunct the Sun, the individual's mission requires making a sacrifice. It may be that the sacrifice is to bring attention to some matter that would be a considerable contribution to the world. These individuals appear to give a lot of themselves to something greater than themselves—they are not so ego-driven. Actually they may not really be allowed full recognition this time around, because spiritual development is needed now to balance out the degree of individuality achieved in the past. Due to previous lives of great ambitions and ego development, one must now slow down and the ego must be submerged to some degree. Though leadership talents are brought over, these can't be used to expand one's own ego. This soul will attract those who will help ensure this. One way or another, circumstances will force this if the person does not do it consciously. These individuals are not allowed to come fully out into the light (of the Sun), similar to those having South Node in Leo. In fact, they may be drawn to the dark, working in a reclusive environment or in the wee hours, or having an interest in "dark" works. There may be some unresolved issues with the father or dealings with an insensitive father figure. A lack of self-esteem and confidence may be noted. However, deep insight and penetrating concentration are talents of the more highly evolved.

A drain of physical vitality, premature death, or a decrease of life longevity is possible, although other chart factors would agree in such cases. There are a number on this list who experienced unusual deaths—sudden or unexpected, or seemingly tragic situations occurred in their lifetimes, which may have been necessary in carrying out their spiritual missions. Some of those with this conjunction include Helen Keller, Chandra Levy, Amelia Earhart, JonBenet Ramsey (wide orb), Roman Polanski, River Phoenix, Gianni Versace, and Sigourney Weaver.

If taking into account the sign of this Sun/Node conjunction, it will be found that the North Node will boost up the sign characteristics and the South Node will play them down. For instance, if the sign is Taurus, which gives the urge to accumulate material possessions, the North Node conjunct the Sun makes for quite an attractor and a spendthrift, while South Node describes a more frugal Taurus, who is, after all, less benefited by possessions. Much of this may also be due to what the universe provides for them to spend. Sun conjunct North Node is more auspicious for material growth, and Sun conjunct South Node is more favorable for spiritual growth.

With other aspects, milder themes similar to the above would be noticed, with more of the essence of the Sun conjunct North Node with a sextile or trine, and more of the Sun conjunct South Node influence if a square. When the Sun squares the nodes, the self-expression is blocked and it may take longer to identify the destined mission and get on board.

NODAL ASPECTS TO THE MOON

The Moon has rule over our emotions and minds; therefore these nodal conjunctions tend toward strong emotions linking to the senses and imagination. There may be exceptional psychic sensitivities, which may be exalted in the ability to predict trends, or distorted and turned to suspicion and paranoia. The disposition and outlook is lighter with North Node conjunct the Moon, while a more serious tone is noted when South Node conjuncts the Moon. Themes surrounding motherhood or a mother figure are virtually always accented.

With North Node conjunct the Moon, the imagination is enhanced and the mind is stable and strong, with accurate psychic sensitivities and reliable impressions. This contributes to creative talents. Wherever this conjunction is found by house, that house and the matters it governs are strengthened. It is often very fortunate if overhead. The Moon is a feminine planet and, with the boost from the North Node, brings out the positive feminine faculties or gives talents in vocations that cater to women. There's a knack for knowing what women want and sensing public tastes. Thus, there are plenty of beauty queens and fashion designers with this aspect, as well as artists and dancers.

Having the support of a mother figure is important, and there is usually assistance from them. These folks are meant to nurture others and sometimes this is done in a big way, where they stroke the multitudes. There is ability to cater to the whims of the public—many political figures fall in this group. The North Node boosts the ability to gain the support of the public. They have a mesmerizing effect on people, a definite asset in public and political life. Other people respond to their enthusiasm, and with an

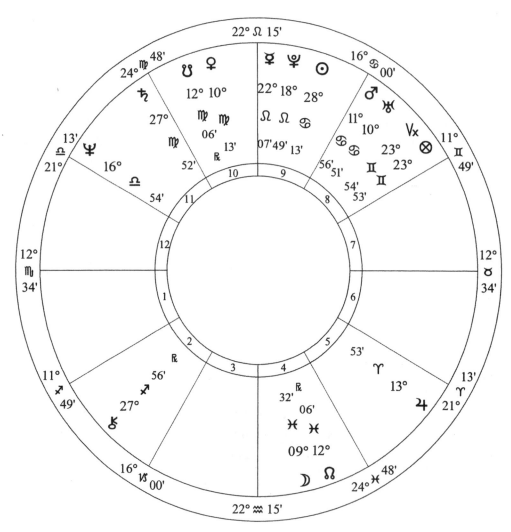

Figure 20: Robin Williams birth chart: July 21, 1951, 1:34 PM, Chicago, IL

abundance of emotional strength they are comfortable dealing with large crowds and audiences. They just click quite naturally with their public. They are provided with the opportunity to increase their popularity, possibly as a reward for past generosity toward others.

Some public figures with this conjunction are Pablo Picasso, James Baker (politician), Jane Curtin, Ron Howard, Rush Limbaugh, and Robin Williams. Two other names that are highly recognizable but show how the blessings can be misused are Jim Jones and Charles Manson. As we would expect to find something spoiling the configuration, in Jones' chart the eccentric Uranus is conjunct the Moon/North Node pair at the bottom of the chart, while Jupiter squares all from the Seventh House. For Manson, the Moon/North Node pair squares the Ascendant/Descendant, while also square Mercury and Jupiter on the cusp of the Seventh House. Due to the misuse of their popular appeal, karmic debts will be owed.

With South Node conjunct the Moon, there are often unavoidable difficult relationships with women, especially the mother, although there is frequently a strong psychic link to her. The emotions undergo difficult spells, especially since those individuals have trouble expressing their sensitive side, causing others to see them as cold or more stand-offish than they really are. Getting the support of others does not come easily, thus they feel alone, forced to rely on themselves. Losing loved ones is extremely hard on them. The mind is of an unusual nature and the thought processes are different. There are anxieties—some verging on paranoia or causing crippling fears. Many of these individuals are not comfortable dealing with crowds. Remembrances of difficult experiences working with the public from previous incarnations may inhibit them. This soul is working on strengthening and balancing the emotions, stabilizing the mind, and handling the impressions coming in. If the impressions get away from them, there can be a fascination with occult practices of an unhealthy sort. In some cases the South Node influence destroys the sensitivity of the Moon, bringing out a cruel and hurtful personality. When working positively, this conjunction provides an elevation of the mind that can bring one in touch with the mysterious workings of the universe. As one of the health-giving luminaries, the Moon contacting the South Node could reflect upon health disturbances, or it may mean decreased longevity.

Some individuals with this conjunction are Bonnie Lee Bakley, Vincent Van Gogh, Jamie Lee Curtis, Natalie Cole, Michael Bolton, and Donald Trump. While detailing this aspect I heard about Anna Nicole Smith's death; it struck me that it fits her, and in following up, I found that she did have the aspect, the width of the orb dependent on what time of day she was born.

For other aspects, a sextile or trine of the Moon to the nodes will be of a milder but similar essence as North Node conjunct the Moon. A square of the Moon to the nodes will partake of a similar influence as South Node conjunct Moon in which the individual is emotionally out of tune with society's trends and may especially have difficulties gaining the favor of women. These are the stumbling blocks they meet with in life when they try to move forward.

NODAL ASPECTS TO MERCURY

A nodal connection to Mercury puts a strong emphasis on intellect, communication faculties, and all of the Mercurial talents.

North Node conjunct Mercury boosts the mental capacity and gives potential in areas calling for the use of the intellect. The higher powers have blessed these people with previously untapped talents to communicate and to promote their bright ideas at just the right time to gain support and popularity. In the past lives there may have been limited opportunities to go through learning processes or the communication might have been blocked. This may be a young soul and they often have a youthful quality about them. They introduce fresh new ideas and establish new or modern ways of doing things. That's their purpose. They display wit and a versatile mind that is quick and adaptable. They are progressive and innovative, frequently showing early potential. A drawback with this conjunction is being a debutante, going along with what is popular at the moment, scattering the mental energies. Some might be mere gossips.

Similar to North Node in the Third House, anything using the pen is favored. As we'd expect, there are many authors, writers, teachers, educators, journalists, critics, and attorneys among this group. They make many contacts, and pass along information. Another theme that stands out is the ability to work with the hands. Some may be ambidextrous. There are tennis players, sportspersons, swimmers, and musicians with these aspects. There are also boxers, sculptors, and race car drivers. The activities of the house in which this combination appears will be quite significant in defining potential talents and a progressive mind.

There are good relationships with siblings, with mutual helpfulness. There are an above-average number of twins in this group. A sibling might be well known. There may

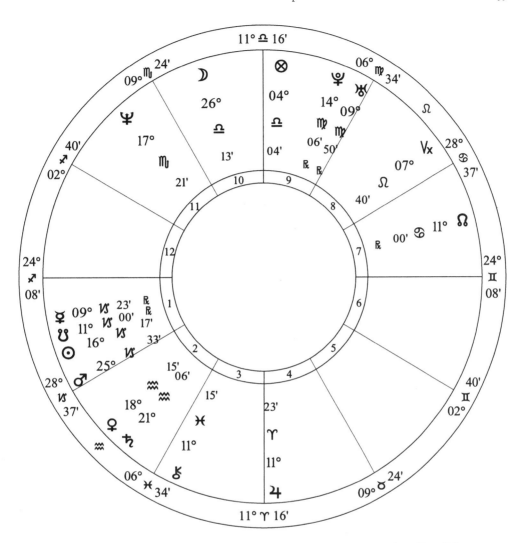

Figure 21: Nicolas Cage birth chart: Jan. 7, 1964, 5:30 AM, Harbor City, CA

be some connection to the youth in society. Something peculiar about the name may stand out—they may have three names, a name change, or the name is in print. Connections with the media are common.

Some of those with North Node conjunct Mercury are the Amazing Kreskin, Peter Hurkos, astrologer Doris Chase Doane, and Edgar Cayce. Mercury is a neutral planet, thus there may be a sort of genderless look or demeanor about these individuals, like Annie Lennox, the brilliant musician, soulful singer, and songwriter.

With Mercury conjunct the South Node, there are similar accents noted as above, except that here, these people have brought over considerable intellectual talents that must be used in a positive way to contribute to the world in the present lifetime. They have asked and been given another chance to develop and bring to fruition the energies they've invested in Mercurian activities. They weren't quite finished working out an idea. The house placement should give clues to the tap they have to past stores of knowledge and it is usually easy for them to redistribute their energy in a way that pays off well. These folks may be more original and independent in their thinking in the long run, but may have some problems with timing. They may be slightly out of sync with the rest of the world when they choose to launch an idea. Unable to gain support from others, they experience frustration and are forced for a time to go it on their own. Other aspects into this one would show the degree of difficulty in bringing out their ideas and gaining support for them. With stressful aspects, there is fear of criticism or ridicule. There could be learning difficulties; what takes others a short time to absorb may take longer for these individuals. Short-term memory may be a problem, or there is a need to go over and over the same material. They may not learn to drive, or they learn late. There are issues with siblings.

Some with this nodal emphasis include Fabio, Hillary Rodham Clinton, Dr. Phil Mc-Graw, Bruce Springsteen, and Jean Piaget, the Swiss psychologist, educator, and author known for his studies of children's learning patterns. Nicolas Cage is one of my favorite actors and I worry a little about his love of race car driving and doing his own stunts with his Mercury conjunct South Node in his First House. But his would certainly be a good example of an attempt to bring out and utilize those previous talents and give of himself in a way that benefits others. He puts himself wholly into each of his roles, researching the character, in order to play an authentic and convincing part.

In either of these groups, there are cases in which the nodal influence to Mercury distorts the mentality, interfering in discretion, enabling a person to become involved in criminal activities. John Hinckley Jr. and Patricia Krenwinkel both had the South Node contact.

The other aspects involving Mercury to the nodes would be of a similar but milder flavor, with nodes in sextile or trine to Mercury like North Node conjunct Mercury and a square more of the nature of South Node conjunct Mercury; ideas are expressed at the wrong time and place, ideas are out of sync with current trends, or problems in expression create misunderstandings.

NODAL ASPECTS TO VENUS

As a Fortune planet, Venus conjunct North Node attracts good things. Creature comforts, a pleasing personality, and social ease are pronounced. The cosmic forces have imbued these folks with excellent potential to establish and further the harmony around them, wherever they go. They have earned karmic credits for past kindness so they also win happiness for themselves through these actions. They find acceptance and attract the finer things in life. They exude beauty, glamour, and grace. They are charming and loving, always with a smile that lifts the spirits of others. They are social creatures, moving in and out of social circles, distributing their personal charisma to increase the joy and happiness of others. Even if they have some melancholy times on the inside, it usually isn't apparent on the surface. Relationships go well, or at least there are plenty of opportunities for them. In its most positive potential, this encourages diplomatic talents and acts of compassion. These are peacemakers. When working exclusively on the material plane, it can cause self-love and narcissistic tendencies to the point that all that matters is me, me, me. They may be terribly self-indulgent, pursuing personal luxuries and material things. Nothing much is accomplished, because they are so caught up in the social whirl, indulging in passing whims and fancies. Still, this is their prerogative.

There is potential for success in Venus ruled pursuits, such as singing, music, entertaining, the arts, and anything that caters to the pleasure of others. Many poets, painters, dancers, and composers fall in this group, and these individuals are quite progressive—interested in moving in new directions in music and art. There is luck in the house where the conjunction falls. Elvis Presley had it in his Tenth House, making it easy to find professional success. Like Paula Abdul, who has this aspect in a wide orb, there are a number of music critics in this group, which really plays up the essence of Venus, fostering the ability to make accurate judgments and spot singing talent. We also note that Paula is the judge on *American Idol* who soothes the feelings of contestants after Simon Cowell gives them the undiluted truth. It is part of her purpose to do this.

Others with North Node conjunct Venus are Cher, Connie Francis, Charles Bronson, Tony Bennett, Jimmy Carter, and Merv Griffin.

With South Node conjunct Venus, exceptional artistic talents are brought over that often show up at an early age. These individuals have been working on developing artistic flair of a particular sort. The house position points to a reservoir of past artistic inspiration or knowledge. There are talents here that can be used to help others and contribute in some way. On the other hand, the love life suffers and the individuals have difficulty understanding their emotions when it comes to love. This is often a sign of someone who has suffered heartbreak. Britney Spears has this aspect, and she demonstrates the assets and liabilities. These people are working through some love karma. They may have been self-indulgent in the past and now a time-out is called, as efforts are required to balance out this area of relationships. Finding happiness in marriage is tough. Even with considerable success in other areas, this is often the weak spot. Relationships with the opposite sex may be difficult to impossible. When it comes to the sexual energies, those energies must be converted into developing higher consciousness. There is potential to evolve spiritually. They have the capacity for deep, meaningful love by relating to those who need affection and friendship. These individuals do better with platonic relationships than intimate ones. Spreading the love out widely to include many others brings better results than trying to give it to an exclusive few. More satisfaction comes from giving love than from receiving it.

In social settings, they also suffer rebukes. Their timing may be off as to when or how they approach others. If the other person isn't receptive at just that moment, they feel misunderstood and may develop an inferiority complex. Thus, they frequently feel lonesome. Some resort to drug indulgence. While the house position shows where struggles take place, there are usually some benefits available with Venus conjunct the South Node. These people enjoy being surrounded by comforts and beautiful objects, but at times they feel that caring for them is a burden, giving away possessions and much of their wealth. They may go through extremes, accumulating and then letting go of worldly goods.

People with this aspect include King Henry VIII (married six times); Cameron Diaz, who started out in modeling, having this conjunction on her Ascendant; Robin Williams, comic and actor; and Dennis Wilson of the Beach Boys. Others are Christian Dior, the

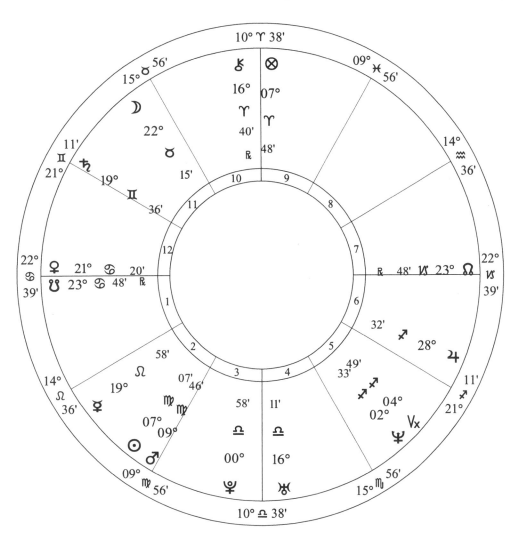

Figure 22: Cameron Diaz birth chart: Aug. 30, 1972, 2:53 AM, San Diego, CA

French fashion designer; Rita Mae Brown, activist (wide aspect); and Robert Reed, who played the father role of Mike Brady on the *Brady Bunch*.

Other aspects of Venus to the nodes will take on similar but milder themes, with the sextile or trine being of the nature of Venus conjunct North Node and the square like Venus/South Node. In the latter, the social expressions are off the mark of acceptability, and they frequently experience difficulties in finances and relationships.

NODAL ASPECTS TO MARS

North Node conjunct Mars is a powerhouse aspect, providing physical strength, endurance, and initiative. These people are driven and intensely involved in life. They've been endowed with the stamina to pursue adventures and get themselves noticed—in the past they were perhaps busy doing for others and not given this chance. Such an individual is not content to wait for opportunities to find him or her. They go out and make their own. No matter what line of work they take up, they will establish their identity and excel in their field. Mars is always first in line and these individuals often make a name for themselves by being the first to accomplish a thing. They set the pace, frequently having a huge influence on those following in the same footsteps or having similar interests. There are many athletes and military people in this group, as there is usually a strong interest in physical activity and building endurance. They are brave, rugged, and tough; willing to venture out first, and not afraid to act decisively and quickly in reaction to situations. They make excellent entrepreneurs because they aren't afraid to pioneer into new territory. They have special potential in fighting causes on behalf of others. They may win championships or become Olympic stars, or be awarded medals for bravery. Lance Armstrong is a shining example of the aspect. Mars rules the action urges and, with the North Node, usually proves the benefit of good timing in gaining the confidence and cooperation of others. In its negative manifestation, this aspect can bring about extreme anger, aggression, or fits of temper. Often, both the admirable and the less appealing qualities are apparent in the same personality.

Some famous individuals with this aspect include Albert Einstein, Queen Victoria of England, actor and politician Clint Eastwood, basketball coach Phil Jackson, gymnastics medal winner Cathy Rigby, and American astronaut Charles "Pete" Conrad, the third man to set foot on the moon.

With South Node conjunct Mars, Mars-ruled talents and instinctual abilities are brought over that must be utilized in a harmonious way. Otherwise, the dynamic and highly combustible Mars energy may turn inward, causing neurosis, obsession, or fighting some demon or adversary within. While there are excellent resources to draw from, the Mars energy is most in need of direction. South Node conjunct Mars presents a delicate situation because people with this aspect must learn to use the energy in a more diluted form than what is really possible. A sort of brake is applied to the degree of aggression they are allowed to express. Some karmic balancing is going on that involves the previous use of the physical powers. These people may have been overly aggressive, accidentally or intentionally hurting others in the wake of practicing the strength of their will and power. Now, the soul is learning to release the controlling energy at a gentler, more subdued or graceful pace. For example, there are a number of ballet dancers with this position. If they can't learn to curb these energies themselves, it will be done for them. Circumstances would tend to restrict them from expressing very temperamental or angry feelings, or of becoming overly aggressive physically.

The health of persons with this aspect may start out as robust, but there is a tendency to put excessive strain on the body, which weakens it, causing eventual weariness or breakdown. The energy level may appear outwardly to be very weak, or the energy level fluctuates, going from one extreme to another. There may be accident-prone tendencies. Occasionally, violence is attracted.

There are fewer people with this aspect involved in athletics requiring a great amount of physical exertion. In addition to dancers, swimmers, and ice skaters, there are many skilled actors, musicians, composers, astrologers, and entrepreneurs in this group, and it appears favorable if these people can draw on their mental energies, uniting those with physical energy reserves in whatever they pursue. They may be skilled in math, science, or engineering.

Sexual relations may prove to be difficult, nonexistent, or tainted in some way, possibly due to some overindulgence in sex in the past. Marriage and relationships with the opposite sex are often difficult. The personality and temperament is highly volatile, unusual, and impulsive. At worst, these people are antagonists.

Ted Bundy murdered women for no apparent reason other than his desire to kill. Bundy, a necrophiliac who told of his fascination with images of violent sex, enjoyed his reign of terror as a serial killer, raping and killing at least thirty women over a four-year span. He died in the electric chair for his crimes in 1989. Next time he would be afforded even less physical power.

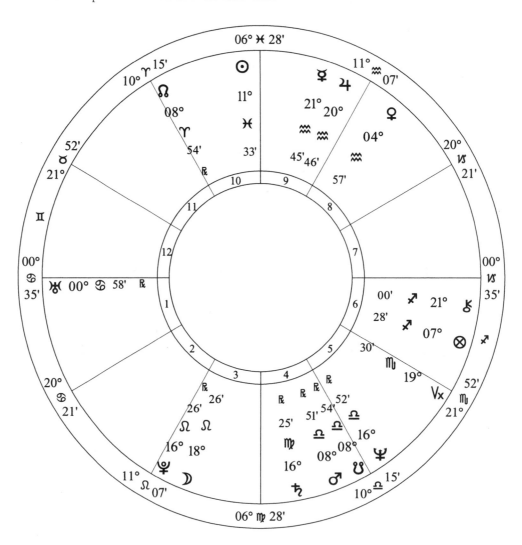

Figure 23: Karen Carpenter birth chart: Mar. 2, 1950, 11:45 AM, New Haven, CT

Karen Carpenter, who died of cardio toxicity due to anorexia, had Mars conjunct South Node. From age seventeen, the famous singer/drummer dieted obsessively, developing anorexia. After seven years, she sought therapy for her disorder and was planning to go public about it upon her recovery, but it was too late. Her death in 1983 finally brought attention to anorexia and bulimia, which was not previously discussed openly. So, we see how the gifts of an aspect may help others even when the individual suffers ill consequences.

Some successful people with Mars conjunct South Node include Willie Nelson, Ann Wilson, Tom Selleck, Mark Spitz, Roger Maris, and Carol Burnett.

The trine or sextile of Mars to North Node has similar, but milder, themes than North Node conjunct Mars. A square indicates milder issues of the South Node type. The actions and impulses of this individual are ill timed or rub against social norms. It is hard for them to harmonize their actions with the needs of others, thus they appear to have bad luck.

In the next chapter we'll examine nodal aspects to the outer planets.

Chapter Eight

NODAL ASPECTS TO OUTER PLANETS
IN THE NATAL CHART

An outer planet in conjunction with one of the lunar nodes is a planet of special sig-nificance. This increases the significance of that outer planet throughout life. Simi-lar to having an inner planet conjunct a node, outlined in the previous chapter, an outer planet conjunct the North Node indicates qualities to be consciously developed in the current lifetime. The individual may feel somewhat compelled to develop the qualities attributed to the planet. There are opportunities and great potential associated with a planet in conjunction with the North Node.

A planet near the South Node indicates qualities developed previously. They are ha-bitual and it usually takes little effort to call them into play. In this scenario, something has been brought over to this lifetime for more perfecting. Talents associated with the planet can be further developed or utilized more fully, more positively, and with more consciousness. Sometimes a planet conjunct the South Node represents working through past failures associated with the planet, or that it is taking more than one lifetime to complete the lessons signified by the planet.

If there are planets on both ends of the nodal axis, there are past lessons to work through but also enticements to make the effort and have a successful mission. This ensures a busy life and suggests a special crossroads in a soul's evolution. There are ample opportunities to advance during the current life, both in a material sense and in a spiritual sense. North Node conjunctions are usually more auspicious for material prosperity and worldly influence while South Node conjunctions favor spiritual advancement.

These conjunctions can be given a pretty wide orb, up to seven degrees or more, although narrower orbs are used for the individuals cited here (three degrees in most cases). The closer the aspect, the stronger the influence will be.

NODAL ASPECTS TO JUPITER

Good deeds in the past bring opportunities for spiritual and/or material wealth when the North Node conjuncts Jupiter. There is a healthy desire to acquire material things, and many advantages may result from developing financial self-sufficiency. Madonna has the aspect in her Second House, which is interesting, as many of us remember her phase as the "Material Girl." The aspect fits her in other ways as well, since it points toward the development of higher philosophies and gaining wisdom. There is a lot of optimism present and in its more negative effects there may be extravagance or over-optimism. The house position of the contact shows where there may be a degree of enthusiasm, over-optimism, or where things are taken for granted. There may be some excessiveness showing up here. This is pretty much fine though, because that house also shows where there is luck. Similar to North Node conjunct the Sun, there are blessings, benefits, protection, and often a life that is free of karmic debts. At its worst, there may be greed, though this is quite a benign aspect as far as any harm that may be caused to others.

Sometimes the aspect offers more in the way of spiritual blessings than material ones, but these people may do a lot of whatever line of work they take up. For example: if in drama, they will appear in many films or roles; if in singing or composing, they will produce a lot of recordings; if in writing, they will publish many books; and so on. Their works are well received and often loved by the public, adding to their material prosperity. There are a wide range of talented people with this aspect. The sign placement provides information as to the talents and whether these will manifest most along social, material, or spiritual lines. Many are simply enjoying the fruits of their past-life good deeds, often

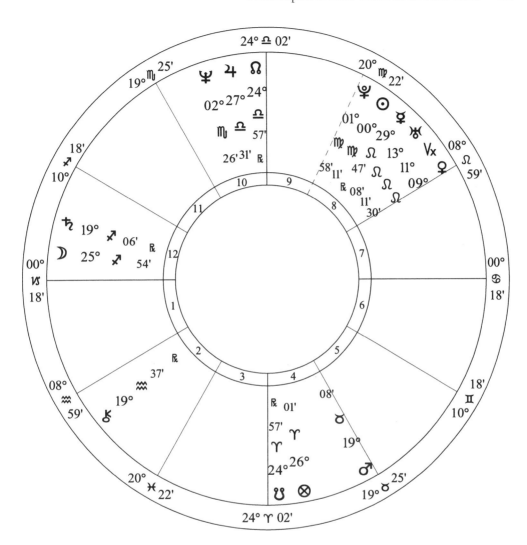

Figure 24: James Van Praagh birth chart: Aug. 23, 1958, 4:18 PM, Queens, NY

in a material way, and are not pressed or challenged to overcome obstacles. The cosmos smiles on them. There is often a youthful quality about them as well.

The conjunction of Jupiter with North Node is expansive in many ways and can also cause weight gain. Judy Garland had this aspect and while she gained the assets, she also became addicted to several drugs after starting out trying to control her weight. Other notables with the aspect are James Van Praagh, Julio Iglesias, Dick Cavett, Andy Gibb, Audrey Hepburn, and Alois Alzheimer, the German psychiatrist, neuropathologist, and professor for whom Alzheimer's disease is named.

South Node conjunct Jupiter is also a philosophical aspect. Jupiter rules philosophy, law, and religious study, so these souls enter this life with experience and knowledge that has contributed to their belief systems. They have some very definite views and now feel a responsibility to pass along what they've learned. They may use their wisdom to contribute to the social morals in a positive way or, negatively, they might be narrow or forceful in their views.

L. Ron Hubbard, founder of Dianetics and the Church of Scientology, had the aspect in a close orb. Not only did his philosophies gain the following of millions of people, but he was also a prolific writer; authoring numerous massive texts on processes meant to rehabilitate and free the "Thetan" (the human spirit) from past encumbrances. Though he is a prime example of the potential in this aspect, with more than a thousand published works, including his science fiction series, and declared by Guinness the most published author ever, there are many prolific writers in this group. Tennessee Williams also had the aspect. While there are actors, sportsperson, politicians, and sundry others among this group, the overwhelming theme involves writing and philosophy. There are many authors, composers, songwriters, teachers, and educators. Their communication skills are notable. These folks spread the word. Spreading beliefs and contributing to moral standards are common patterns. Twin sisters Ann Landers and Abigail Van Buren had the aspect in a wide orb. Each had their own syndicated newspaper column as advisors to people with pressing questions about proper behavior and etiquette. The intuition is usually good and with previous experience and knowledge, individuals with Jupiter conjunct South Node often appear to display talents that were not learned in this lifetime. This aspect also gives wonderful potential for spiritual advancement.

There are usually some benefits, even with the South Node conjunction. Some are born into a prominent or royal family, although material fortune does not always flow as well for these individuals as for the previous group. There are often struggles, but patience serves them well. Problems may relate to higher education, religion, or travels to distant places. Sometimes their social or philosophical views are unacceptable to the majority. Over-expansion is a potential problem and can lead to downfall. At worst, there can be a lack of kindness when the Jupiter quality of benevolence is destroyed by the restrictive influence of South Node.

Others with the aspect are Chastity Bono, Ennis Cosby, Vincent van Gogh, Jennifer Aniston, Lucille Ball, Steffi Graf, Herbie Hancock, Peter Hurkos, and Cheryl Tiegs. Controversial shock rocker Marilyn Manson also has the aspect.

The trine or sextile between Jupiter and North Node acts in a similar, milder fashion to the conjunction. With a square, the individual may hold social or religious philosophies and attitudes that cross with the majority of society. Opportunities may be lacking, and financial struggles may present problems, making it difficult for them to move forward in life.

NODAL ASPECTS TO SATURN

North Node conjunct Saturn often helps lift away some of the usual Saturn restrictions. It increases patience, conservatism, and practicality, and promotes good relationships with elders and authorities who can help in achieving ambitions, especially since there is a good sense of timing as to when to approach these people. There are often connections with older people, frequently those in the family, who are of special assistance in meeting goals. This individual is to develop more self-reliance now, as in the past he was under the guardianship of the family. This may be a soul approaching maturity; learning to take responsibility, and the cosmos has lent them this extra bit of assistance. Self-discipline is one of the strongest, most positive features of this aspect that can be utilized for good works. When working constructively, the aspect has produced champions of all sorts. When organization, patience, methodology, and self-pacing are combined, there's no limit to the potential achievements. There are singers, actors, musicians, writers, astrologers, educators, politicians, athletes, and clothing designers in this group. Bill Blass, Zoe Fontana, and Pierre Cardin all have the aspect. Since Saturn is exalted in Libra, this conjunction works especially well in the air signs: Gemini, Libra, and Aquarius.

Saturn, best known as the taskmaster, brings some challenges. Sometimes this manifests as health problems in youth, although these folks may ultimately enjoy increased

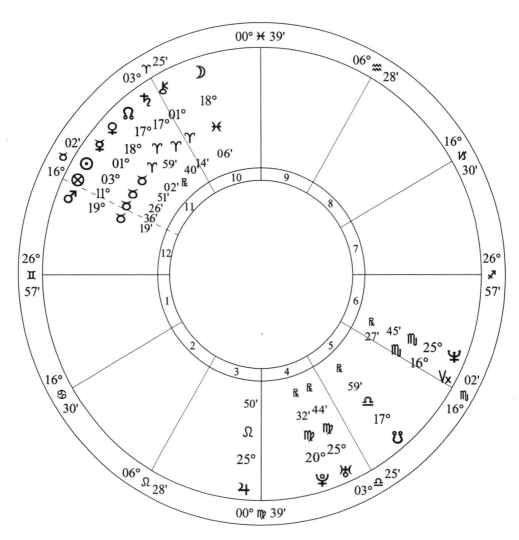

Figure 25: Timothy McVeigh birth chart: Apr. 23, 1968, 8:19 AM, Lockport, NY

longevity. Struggles in life may be seen coming from the house of the aspect. These tests contribute to the development of patience and self-sufficiency.

When the negative traits of Saturn are increased by the influence of the North Node, this can cause the individual to be depressed and melancholic—more of a risk when the conjunction falls in one of the emotional water signs. At extremes, it can cause a person to be pessimistic, insensitive, selfish, greedy, even ruthless, leading to all sorts of problems, both for the person and those around him or her. This latter theme appears to be more in evidence when the conjunction falls in fire signs, most notably Aries, or in cases when Mars is involved in the configuration. This was the situation with Timothy McVeigh, whose chart will be discussed in a coming chapter. A number of individuals with this aspect on my public figures list committed homicide.

Others with this aspect of more positive works are Hank Aaron, Carrie Fisher, John Fogerty, Florence Henderson, Ashley Judd, and George Segal.

With South Node conjunct Saturn, this suggests a person who has come over with a good dose of Saturnine attitudes. While this can come out in a positive way, it is a potentially constricting aspect right from the start, due to the limiting and pessimistic nature of old, worrying Saturn. The rigid habits, outlook, and ambitions may be so far removed from what is the accepted norm by modern society that he or she could create a world of isolation, detached from life, ignoring social duties. This is potentially the hardest past-life influence from which to escape. It is easy for these individuals to become stubborn or stuck in the past. They are bound to the old methods and mindsets, having many connections with elders. The house placement shows where ideas or attitudes of the past keep them a prisoner. There is usually a measure of worries signified by the house placement of the conjunction as well. Sometimes there is tragedy, a series of upsetting events, or generally difficult situations that result in feelings of despair. The outlook may be gloomy or the person may appear as miserly or selfish. Physical vulnerabilities may be noticed in areas ruled by Saturn: weakness in the bones, rheumatism, or dental or skin problems.

When the aspect can be more favorably accessed—drawing on the Saturn discipline, responsibility, organization, and respect for boundaries—it provides the opportunity to do work of such remarkable mastery, precision, and expertise that people with this aspect are in a class by themselves, where the competition simply cannot touch them. They are inimitable. When doing individualized work requiring painstaking methods, they are not influenced by outer elements and are able to see it through to the bitter end. The major influence of this combination is a life of hard work and handling restrictions that are imposed upon them. One of the greatest assets of this combination is that these people have more coping abilities than most. Breakthroughs or rewards often don't materialize until the final hour. When such challenges are met, the individual is greatly rewarded.

There are wide ranges of talents that may stem from this aspect, although the ability to take a philosophical view or a detached and scientific view seems to be a helpful asset. Well-known people with this aspect are Paula Abdul, Tom Brokaw, Greta Garbo, Mario Lopez, Tina Turner, Jack Nicklaus, and Grace Slick. Jim Bakker, the fraudulent evangelist, also had the aspect.

The sextile or trine of the nodes to Saturn indicate that the individual's goals and ambitions are more in harmony with that of society and they can more easily get the support they need. With the square, their ambitions are not so easily attained—they may be fearful, reclusive, conservative in their views, their timing is bad, or they isolate themselves.

NODAL ASPECTS TO URANUS

With Uranus/node combinations, there is frequently a streak of brilliance or genius. These are colorful characters with a unique creative flair. There are similar traits attached to either node conjunct Uranus, the main difference being that North Node is newly developing the Uranus characteristics while South Node comes possessed of them.

With North Node conjunct Uranus, the soul is encouraged to become more daring and innovative; more progressive in their way of thinking. They've come from a life in which conservatism was forced on them—they've been constricted, stuck in a rut, and now the cosmic forces lend help to ensure they learn to see the advantage of change. Perhaps they feared change in the past. They are to become more original, inventive, liberal, and creative in their thinking. Life comes at them in surprising ways—they meet with unusual or sudden situations, thus becoming mentally nimble.

When drawing on the highest potential, these individuals introduce new techniques or unconventional methods that have a wide impact on humankind or at least upon the groups to which they belong. They break new ground. They are avant-garde, on the leading edge, contemporary, expounding new techniques, methods, or styles in whatever line of work they are involved. They may have an attraction to gadgets, computers, science, and new technology. There are many scientific minds in this group: researchers, physicists, psychoanalysts, physiologists, as well as politicians and artists, but few athletes. Some

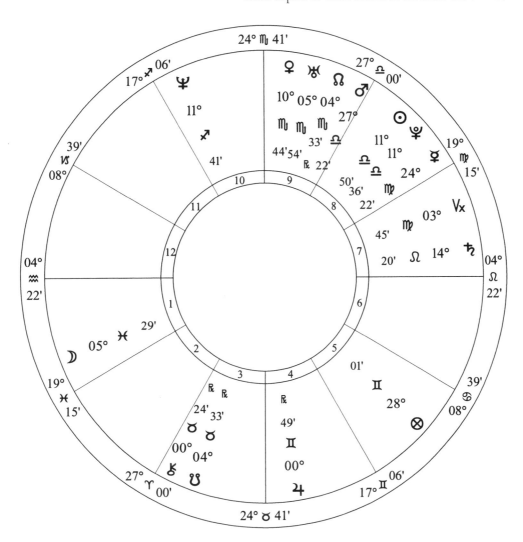

Figure 26: Alicia Silverstone birth chart: Oct. 4, 1976, 3:44 PM, San Francisco, CA

public figures with this aspect are George W. Bush, Bill Clinton, Barack Obama, Cheech Marin, Linda Ronstadt, Alicia Silverstone, Frank Sinatra, Donald Trump, Kenneth Starr, and George White, the astrologer who originally named the line of advantage.

There is some nervousness, often coming out in the house holding the conjunction, which can be utilized and channeled constructively. Some benefit in this house involves embracing the new and novel, being aware of changing tides and taking advantage of this foresight. This is such an extreme energy and electrical influence however, that the chances are for them to get carried away. They may become overly excited, swept up in an idea that has group enthusiasm, and fail to consider the long-term consequences. They are revolutionaries, for good or ill, and can be radical or shocking in their deeds. At worst, this person is bizarre, unconventional, a nonconformist, or a rebel. Hitler's evil genius, Martin Bormann, had the aspect, as did Marshall Applewhite, who led many to suicide. There may be some fascination with euthanasia or with choosing the time of death with either node conjunct Uranus.

With South Node conjunct Uranus, this individual has brought over creative genius of some sort. There may be noticeable talent without benefit of a formal education. Mozart, the classical music genius who began his compositions at age four, had the aspect. This soul may have lived a life in an ancient advanced civilization, like Atlantis, Maya, or Lemuria, and arrives possessing superior insights. Swami Vivekananda had the conjunction in Gemini. Yogananda, the Indian preacher who brought word to the Western world about Kundalini awakening, had the conjunction in his Third House.

These individuals think differently, coming up with unusual ideas and methods. As long as there is a measure of practicality about them, their unique solutions are often workable and they may be balls of energy, meeting with sudden success. There are many artists who produce colorful work—not surprising, since Uranus rules the color spectrum. There is often a love of color, especially combinations of colors—prints, paisleys, or patchworks. Artists such as writers, actors, comedians, and singers are also known for the many and varied shades of work produced.

At some point, however, these people are forced to deal with some sudden or unusual upset relating to the house of the placement, often precipitated by new or changing conditions.

Some famous people with this aspect include Louisa May Alcott, Carol Burnett, Evel Knievel, filmmaker Michael Moore, John Travolta, Willie Nelson, and Jennifer Aniston.

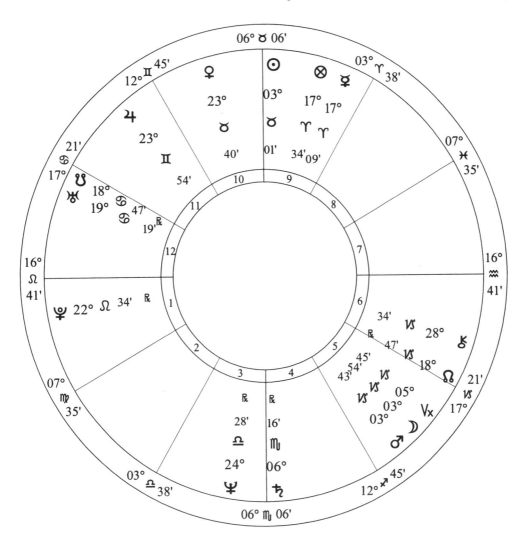

Figure 27: Michael Moore birth chart: Apr. 23, 1954, 12:45 PM, Flint, MI

There are also some notorious people with South Node conjunct Uranus. Some behave in erratic ways or become very eccentric and scattered due to the inherent nervousness of the aspect. Some revolutionary event experienced in the past had a disturbing impact. They may be highly nervous types. Cyrano de Bergerac, who lived a life of reckless bravery and danger, had the aspect. At worst, some of these people can go berserk or freaky as the energy of the aspect works in an internalized way. They may be very weird in how they go about things or outlandish in the methods they use to solve problems. They go to extremes and burn bridges. Some have been called traitors, betrayers, or provocateurs for their actions. Within days of my writing the previous lines, Seung-Hui Cho went on a homicidal rampage at Virginia Tech, killing thirty-two people before committing suicide. He had Uranus conjunct South Node in Sagittarius, linked with Ninth House affairs. His upset occurred in a country far from his birth; his madness came out in a facility of higher education. More on this event is in chapter 9.

With a sextile or trine of the nodal axis to Uranus, this will have a similar but milder flavor as the positive traits mentioned above: the ability to take advantage of new or changing public opinions and introducing new methods. With nodes square Uranus, these individuals are nonconformist and often out of step with current social standards. Their ideas meet with disapproval or resistance, which frustrates them, and may cause them to become insensitive or rebellious.

NODAL ASPECTS TO NEPTUNE

With North Node conjunct Neptune, the imaginative faculties get a boost. These souls are encouraged to become more sensitive and intuitive. They are visionary and can prosper through activities linked to Neptune. They may possess an attraction to film, cinema, the arts, photography, or portrait painting. Design, decorating, and dance are other attractions. Poetry and writing offer favorable paths. These individuals are highly creative and artistic. They are inspiring and can bring positive transformation to whatever fields of work they take up. Occult works may intrigue them, or they are wrapped up in Neptunian realms in one way or another, usually with big dreams to impact the world. They also have a refined sense for what is socially acceptable; therefore they tend to be popular. The house holding the placement indicates where imagination is significant. There may be dreams or visions attached to this house.

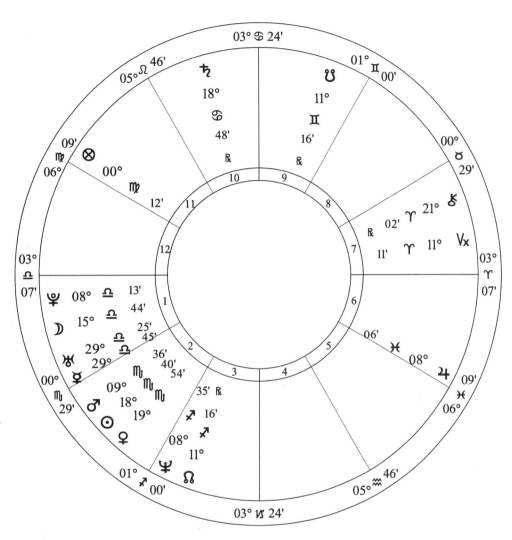

Figure 28: Leonardo DiCaprio birth chart: Nov. 11, 1974, 2:47 AM, Los Angeles, CA

There is an attraction to the sea and to water. Such people may enter the navy or engage in activities that put them near the water. Leonardo DiCaprio, who starred in *Titanic*, has Neptune conjunct North Node. Artists are often particularly drawn to depictions that include water scenes. Individuals with North Node conjunct Neptune also like to take journeys and could make a career of it, as travel benefits them.

One pitfall is an attraction to drugs. Initially these individuals may use drugs as an avenue to enlightenment, but the Neptune aspect is seductive. They can be swept along in its current without realizing it. They are also prone to being misled by their own desires or being deceived by others. Criminals, such as kidnappers, molesters, and sexual predators, appear in this group.

Public figures with this conjunction include Jimmy Carter, Mary Chapin Carpenter, Michelle Pfeiffer, Andy Gibb, Michael Erlewine, Ronald Reagan, and Martha Stewart.

Those with South Node conjunct Neptune have come possessed of visionary gifts. When working through its higher form, these people succeed in similar fields as above. There are cinematographers, filmmakers, painters, artists, sign makers, photographers, dancers, singers, musicians, actors, and designers. Carrie Underwood, fourth season winner of *American Idol*, is a shining example of its highest potential, though it should be mentioned that her pairing has Saturn and Pluto in sextile, strengthening the favorable influences. Her North Node is also strongly placed in Cancer, quite significant for her to become the nation's "country" sweetheart. She should enjoy long-lived fame and adulation.

It is questionable how many will put their unique gifts to superlative use, however. The liabilities are high with South Node conjunct Neptune. They might have led a mystic kind of life and it may be difficult to draw them out, though they could share spiritual insights that contribute to the overall karmic growth on the planet, but many prefer to stay out of the limelight. Their work may require seclusion—however, some are reclusive types or real hermits who prefer the background. Some are so sensitive they want to hide away. This is an emotional aspect, especially when falling in water signs. The South Node influence may distort the emotions, which fuels the mind. Some may not feel like they are part of this world—disconnected, as if they live in an alien world. In fact, Sigourney Weaver, who has this aspect, starred in the 1979 science fiction thriller, *Alien*. Such feelings of alienation and psychic distortions increase the chances they will resort to drugs or other strange methods for handling their crises. Drug dealers and others who prefer to work below the radar are in this group. The house of the aspect shows where the imagination and vision is enhancing those affairs or merely distorting things and showing where there are some secret goings-on.

Some cannot get themselves noticed. There is an interesting case in which a young boy was tagged "mousy" by his classmates in his puberty stage, in order to differentiate him from a more popular boy with the same name. The name stuck, labeling him an inferior. He had Neptune with South Node in the First House, so he was also shorter than his peers, which didn't help. A punishing blow, he remained more or less invisible.

There is often some form of intrigue touching the life. Jessica Lynch has South Node conjunct Neptune in Sagittarius. During her military mission in a foreign country she became a prisoner of war, though finally rescued. The fact that every aspect of her rescue has been questioned or disputed (even by her), and that her POW status is a matter of controversy, only adds to the intrigue. Linda Tripp also has South Node conjunct her Neptune.

Ernest Hemingway is an exemplary illustration of the various influences. With his conjunction in Gemini, he was an imaginative writer. One of his greatest works was a novella called *The Old Man and the Sea*. But his works were fueled and inspired by excessive amounts of alcohol, and he became an alcoholic. He had incredibly bad luck through travel, and was seriously injured in two plane crashes. Later, he underwent shock treatments for depression, his memory failed him more and more frequently, and he ended his life by suicide. Several in his immediate family also committed suicide, leading to speculation of a genetic predisposition for excessive iron in the blood, leading to instability of the cerebrum, depression, and other disorders.

Others with this aspect are Louisa May Alcott, Carol Burnett, Shari Lewis, Willie Nelson, Elizabeth Montgomery (star of *Bewitched*), Jacques Chirac, and Bonnie Raitt (all also had Uranus conjunct South Node, and many were born in 1933).

The sextile or trine of nodes to Neptune has milder themes, similar to North Node conjunct Neptune working at its best. When Neptune squares the nodes, psychic sensitivity is blocked, or the mystical tendencies conflict with current customs, causing the individual to feel alone, shut out, or misunderstood. There may be problems with drugs or danger of poisoning.

NODAL ASPECTS TO PLUTO

North Node conjunct Pluto boosts determination, stamina, and willpower. It provides power, control, and physical strength, which the individual is learning to handle. It may be that this soul was bullied or beaten down in the past life so they couldn't quite attain their goals, and now the higher forces have ensured they don't cave in again. Thus, they will now battle through whatever odds are set against them if they feel passionate about their cause.

These people may succeed in multiple areas. They have the oomph to follow through to their goals. They may even be compelled or obsessed about it. There are successful people in various areas: surgeons, athletes (quite a few), mathematicians, artists, and sundry others. The house of the conjunction reveals where there are opportunities to develop power. Supermodel Lauren Hutton has the aspect in her First House—her power was in her physical assets. Ernest Gallo had the conjunction in his Ninth House and found his power far from his birthplace. Billie Jean King had the aspect in her Seventh House and found her power from taking on competition.

Others with the aspect are George Clooney, John Denver, Wayne Gretzky, Diana Ross, and Mary Wilson (the latter two of the Supremes).

There is potential talent for understanding trends from an intuitive level that can be taken advantage of in very deliberate ways. Those with this aspect are masters of strategy. Working on the highest plane, in highly evolved individuals, this aspect stimulates a deep interest in the meaning of life, a search for truth and illumination. Of course these talents can be used wisely for the advantage of society, or selfishly. Some are tempted to use their powerful insights to manipulate, getting caught up in unrelenting power games and struggles. They might opt for gaining power and control in external ways, through money or politics, exercising power over the people. There are many politicians with this aspect. This nodal influence on Pluto can distort the energies as it magnifies them, causing a person to never feel satisfied with the command they do achieve. It is one aspect that can run away with them, especially since they are very charismatic, usually with no lack of people willing to bend to them. Some create severe problems for themselves. There are aggressive vibes that must go somewhere and can become destructive. Some are the perpetrators of crimes or use their power to bring harm or destruction to others. Serial killer John Allen Muhammad had the aspect. There may be sinister dealings or connections. Sometimes the life is touched by illness, violence, or tragedy. For example,

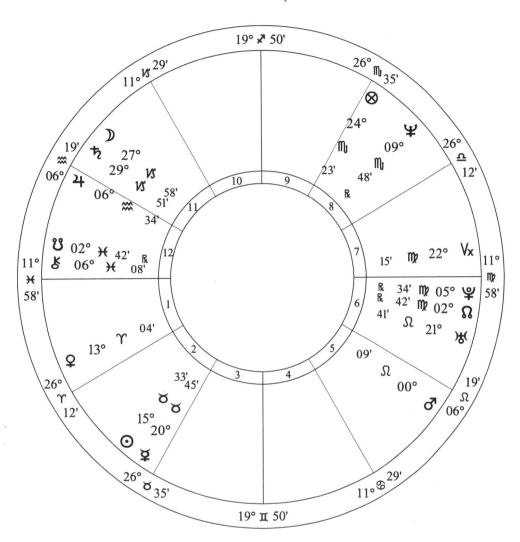

Figure 29: George Clooney birth chart: May 6, 1961, 2:58 AM, Lexington, KY

Frank Sinatra Jr. was kidnapped at gunpoint and held for ransom at age nineteen. Others with the aspect are JFK Jr., Marilyn Monroe, Jim Morrison, Sydney Omarr, John Ramsey, and Michael J. Fox.

With South Node conjunct Pluto, the individual arrives with an incredible amount of power, as a result of having weathered some tough storms in the past. Now this power is to be distributed carefully. There is a pact with the higher forces about how the power is to be used, and this should not be for selfish purposes. The Dalai Lama has the aspect.

These people are not so concerned with what is happening on the surface as with what is going on beneath it. They are questioning, curious, and probing, often aware of the underlying motivations behind people's actions. Erich Fromm, the German-American psychoanalyst and social philosopher, is a good example. A variety of skills are noted, including those of athletes, physicians, political figures, composers, and entrepreneurs. However, there is difficulty getting this energy properly harnessed so that it doesn't work against them. Remembrance of the old crisis can make them suspicious—thus they can become manipulative as a way to stay one-up on others. This could be their greatest undoing. Some have a distracting preoccupation with sex and the sensual side of life. Or, there is an intense fascination with death—with the morbid or strange.

There may be some personal loss connected to the house placement of this conjunction. Christopher Reeve had the conjunction on his Ascendant, signifying the physical body. He used his power to become Superman, a superhero of screen and drama, with this pair in Leo. His conjunction was square Jupiter, the planet ruling large animals, and it was during a horse-riding competition that he sustained debilitating injuries that paralyzed him. His determination and will to overcome his affliction, as well as the unprecedented progress he made, was of great inspiration to other paralysis victims. So, we see how he made his loss our gain. This is the nodes working at their best—a soul who remembers their allegiance.

Others may be the victim of bad health, physical limitations, sexual abuse, or may somehow be connected to violence, catastrophe, trauma, suffering, or sinister dealings. Elvis Presley had it in the Fourth House of endings, suffering a tragic end to his own life.

A sextile or trine of nodes to Pluto will work out in a more positive way, similar to North Node conjunct Pluto, but minus the heavier liabilities. With the square, the person is blocked in the expression of his or her ideas and suppressed in their actions by society at large. They are very ambitious and want to do something big, but there's no audience or stage. There are disruptive and destructive tendencies that may be demonstrated by these people, causing others to regard them as a threat.

NODAL ASPECTS TO CHIRON

Chiron's placement reveals how, where, and with whom some wounding exists, and how healing can be brought to others. Individuals with Chiron conjunct either node live out themes traced to Chiron. They play the role of the wounded victim, the wounded healer/teacher/initiator, or the one who wounds. There is often some personal wounding that must be embraced, expanding personal consciousness, and then using the understanding to help others.

People with North Node conjunct Chiron are particularly encouraged along these lines. Some event motivates them toward work in a healing capacity. An experience in youth may be significant, from which they get a sense of this calling. They undergo a personal emotional or physical crisis, or they have a close personal relationship with someone ill or handicapped. They often work in a capacity strongly linked to healing fields, advocating progressive therapies or promoting processes as a route to recover from painful wounding and move on. Other times, they have connections with those who act in a healing or teaching capacity, sometimes following the principles of a personal guru.

When working constructively, these individuals don't waste much time feeling sorry for themselves when they do experience hurt. They get over it and move on, and feel that others would be better off doing the same thing. Many of them exhibit a tough-love attitude. They rarely get sick, as they simply have no time for it. They take a firm, no-nonsense approach when dealing with a painful crisis, though some can be excessively severe and harsh. Besides teachers and healers, there are many activists and politicians in this group, who have influence over the masses and often play a positive role in bringing attention to larger situations in need of remedy. There is often a charismatic quality about people with Chiron conjunct either node. This gains them a following, which they may take advantage of in either a constructive or destructive way.

Some celebrities with North Node conjunct Chiron are Jennifer Aniston, Chastity Bono, Dick Clark, Larry Flynt, Jimi Hendrix, Janis Joplin, Judith Sheindlin ("Judge Judy"), John Travolta, Barbara Walters, and Oprah Winfrey.

It is easy to see from this list that most have experienced personal wounding. How constructively this is dealt with is shown through the aspects to the lunar nodal axis.

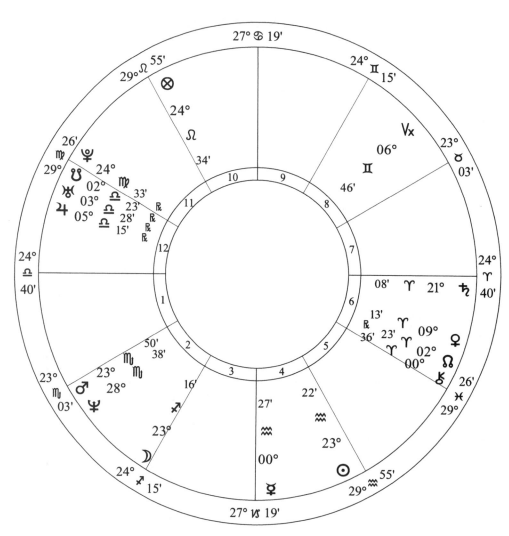

Figure 30: Jennifer Aniston birth chart: Feb. 11, 1969, 10:22 PM, Los Angeles, CA

Sometimes the personal wounding experience has a distorted effect in which the hurt and suffering they ultimately bring to others far outweighs any good they do. Hitler had the aspect (wide orb), though he also had South Node conjunct Moon, which sometimes causes a heartless quality.

With South Node conjunct Chiron, a soul arrives having first-hand experience as a healer, or with recall of wounding experiences. There may be painful remembrances, including early wounding in this life. They may be very private people with such vivid recall of the past that they are prone to get stuck in it. Some use their personal wound to control others. Others become activists but may champion causes that have less popular appeal. It is advantageous if there is a planet on the North Node end of the axis to provide balance and help move them forward.

Some with this aspect are Warren Beatty, Helen Gurley Brown (editor of *Cosmopolitan* magazine), Billy Carter, George Clooney, Ted Danson, King Edward VII, Michael J. Fox, Kenny Loggins, Dick Martin, and Jack Nicholson.

There's a sort of quietness about them, as though they have been initiated and could assist, should one face a painful crisis. Jack Nicholson, who has played some touchy characters, has his strong, quiet side, as if he has access to esoteric wisdom that not everyone has. Certainly he has experienced wounding. His acting career was a long time in taking off and not until he was in his thirties did he learn, after both were dead, that his mother was his grandmother and his sister was his mother. Unsure of his father's identity, he chose not to pursue the matter.

Micheal J. Fox, who suffers from Parkinson's disease, uses his understanding and popularity to bring awareness to how stem cell research could potentially remedy many physical diseases.

There are also some notorious people with this aspect, like Saddam Hussein and Edward Gein, the homicidal maniac that Hitchcock's thriller *Psycho* was based on. The real guy was more frightening than the movie character. He made suits and leggings from the skins taken from his women victims after killing them or digging up their bodies from graves. He was prevented from going in the direction of his North Node by his mother, who forbade him to have anything to do with women and kept him secluded so that others could not influence him. A religious fanatic, she once scalded him when she found him masturbating. His South Node/Chiron was in the Ninth House. His nodes were square his Vertex and there were numerous oppositions in his chart. However, with nodes in fortunate aspect to Part of Fortune, he avoided death by execution and eventually died in a mental institution, with a history so bizarre that his case was studied in depth to understand how his mind worked.

The trine or sextile of Chiron to the nodes gives similar themes to the positive descriptions above. They find ways to help others, based on their understanding of painful wounding. With squares of the nodes to Chiron, the painful issues, wounds, and limitations noted by Chiron's house position indicate continued and recurring troubles that pose stumbling blocks, causing difficulties in getting on board the North Node end of the axis.

In the coming chapter, we'll talk about how to identify major life themes based on time periods when the nodes come in contact with other planets or angles by progression.

Chapter Nine

PROGRESSIONS AND NODES

Secondary Progressions is a predictive technique based on simple symbolism. It assumes that a single day of planetary transits equals a year in the life. Simply put, if you wanted to find the progressed planetary positions of someone aged twenty, you'd look up the position of the planets on the twentieth day after birth. The Sun, which moves one degree each day would therefore progress about one degree for each year of life. As it does so, it forms aspects to the natal planets. When the aspect is within a one-degree orb, it reflects on major themes in the life during that period. For example, when the Sun reaches the Ascendant or Midheaven, it usually brings some attention, important life happenings, sometimes marriage for a woman, and so forth. The inner planets move along at a steady pace too, and each aspect formed to a natal planet or to another progressed planet reflects on current life themes. The Secondary Progressions are most reliable for predicting trends and events based upon the combination of aspects within orb during the same period.

The outer planets in their transits move at a much slower pace and therefore will not progress very much over an entire lifetime. In fact, if you review the ephemeris for the ninety days following birth, you can pick out important years in the life based on the number of days to exact that an aspect will form from one of the transiting planets to a natal planet. The lunar nodes progress backward but not very much. By age ninety they would have regressed maybe five degrees. Like the Sun, the Midheaven progresses forward approximately one degree per year.

PREDICTING TRENDS

When the natal North Node is overhead and left of the Midheaven, at some point in time the progressed Midheaven will reach the node. At this point in time, there are noticeable effects for good in the life, as some advancement will usually come about. If the node by progression has regressed a degree or two by the time of this meeting, the blessed trend will continue beyond the one-year time frame to include the progressed Midheaven conjunction—first with the progressed, and then with the natal North Node. Karmic rewards and favors are forthcoming as far as elevation of outer status and moving forward on the destined path.

To illustrate a couple of points, let's take a look at Ron Howard's chart. His North Node is only a little more than six degrees into the Tenth House. Ron started acting at a very young age, propelled by his parents into show business, and this is signified partly by the North Node conjunct his Moon. He would be fairly thrust into the spotlight with the prominent and assisted North Node overhead. He appeared in bit roles starting at just sixteen months old. Although there wasn't a lot of notice in his earliest childhood, it was only a matter of time before he'd get noticed. It's promised in his chart. In 1960 *The Andy Griffith Show* debuted, with Ron playing Opie Taylor, the role that won him an early claim to fame at age six and a half. This was just as his progressed Midheaven came to natal and progressed North Node (using the mean lunar node). It wasn't until one or two years later that true node met progressed Midheaven. This is still significant as he was riding high at the time, but as far as timing his lucky break, the mean node proved most precise.

This entire trend is reversed when it is the South Node overhead in the Tenth or Eleventh House. Then—when that angular contact of progressed Midheaven meeting progressed and natal South Node comes about—difficulties, trials, and strains appear.

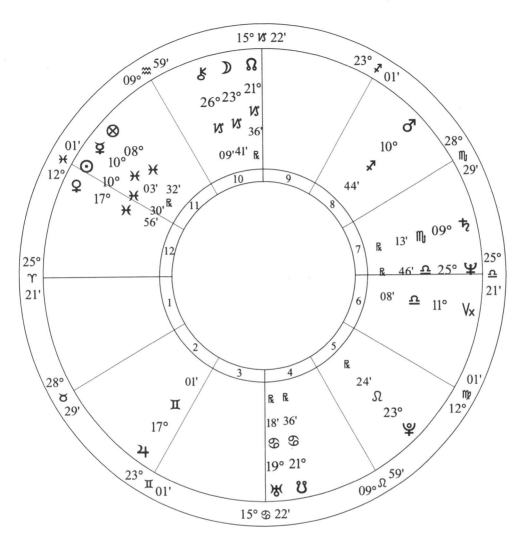

Figure 31: Ron Howard birth chart: Mar. 1, 1954, 9:03 AM, Duncan, OK

Things may take a downward spiral, or a sort of dive in extreme cases. Progress is slow as various barriers crop up. Unfortunately this trend may last a few years, depending on the age and how far apart the progressed and natal nodes are. There may be a series of challenges, coping with more than one problem at once. One thing to know in advance is that many of these problems are a direct result of previous actions. The lifestyle may invite them. Health problems may arise. At the very least, it's a struggle to maintain the previous momentum. As much of a testing time as this is, with lessons learned, it is also cleansing in many ways. Some old ways are shed, old baggage or habits are let go, and one can move into a new era and new conditions.

During this period progress can be made and it can be a breakthrough point in retrospect, but it does require extra efforts. For example, Sonny Bono struggled for years to become known. He dropped out of school to concentrate on his songwriting, taking odd jobs to support himself. For him, this contact occurred between the ages of twenty-two and twenty-four, during which time he became a father and peddled his songs to record labels. He tried various ways to break into the music industry, but couldn't make a go of it. When he landed a job as assistant to record producer Phil Spector, he honed his skills, and soon after this contact ended in the early 1960s, Sonny became a star.

Judy Garland had the contact occur at age twenty. This was a very challenging period for her too, as she tried to move from acting in child roles to adult roles, especially to break away from the image of "the girl next door" after her starring role in *The Wizard of Oz*.

I was discussing all this with a friend when I realized that one of the most challenging periods in my own life had indeed occurred during this contact phase. It reminded her of a critical period in her early adult years when she experienced major setbacks: credit and finance problems, and relationship problems. She left her husband, got fired, was involved in a nasty car wreck, had a hysterectomy, and on and on. I thought how very interesting, and just knew there was something going on with her nodes at that time—likely a contact to an angle in the progressions.

The Secondary Progressions can also be used in what is called *converse* fashion. Instead of looking at the days following birth, one notes the transits on the days prior to birth. Counting backward from the birth date, when you come to the day that equates to your present age, those planetary positions will be very relevant to the current themes in your life. (The better astrology programs do this for you.) Knowing that the converse progressions are just as valid as the more usual forward motion progressions, when I didn't see

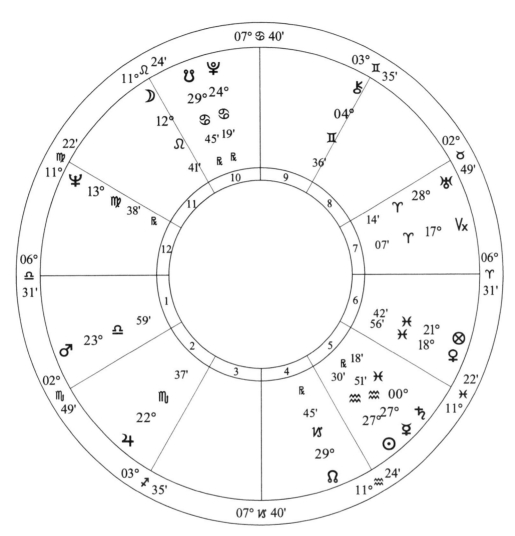

Figure 32: Sonny Bono birth chart: Feb.16, 1935, 9:21 PM, Detroit, MI

an angular contact in my friend's regular progressions involving her nodes, I decided to check her converse progressions for the year she'd indicated was such a disastrous time. Sure enough, with her natal South Node in the Twelfth House, it had been a period when her converse Ascendant met up with her South Node. This is another angular configuration that tends to be climactic and was especially difficult for her. In Libra, it explains volumes. In the usual set of forward motion charts, she did have the long lasting influence of transiting Pluto conjunct her natal South Node, which also summed up the difficult experiences.

While transits will be discussed fully in a coming chapter, they are mentioned briefly here to show that there is usually a combination of factors at work in the progressions and transits when important events occur. The progressions set the stage and then the transits set things off, or hold things off.

It is more auspicious to have the progressing Ascendant meet up with natal North Node, which happens when the natal North Node is in the First House. There are predictable benefits from such a natal placement. On the other hand there are predictable difficulties when the natal South Node appears there.

By converse direction the progressing Ascendant will meet a natal Twelfth House node at some point in time and the node that meets up with the Ascendant describes the general trend for a year or so, and by converse direction, the Midheaven will meet a Ninth House natal node. Count the degrees between these two, and that is the age they will meet by converse direction. This explains why a Ninth House North Node is also auspicious.

When the angles progress to meet one of the nodes, it will be a very significant time in the life and how wonderful or how difficult the period might be can be judged not only by the node involved but also by the natal potential combined with the overall influences of progressions and transits at the time. These angular contacts in the progressions are similar to the natal aspects discussed in chapter 2, except these reflect on more temporary conditions.

Aspects formed between a planet and a node by progression are also important, showing predictable trends, especially the conjunctions. These are quite karmic in nature, realigning individuals with their destiny, and often the free will factor appears negligible. With less desirable contacts, events may occur before one realizes or understands what is happening, and therefore are hard to counteract.

When there is a conjunction of a planet to one of the nodes in the natal chart, it should be judged whether the aspect is applying or separating. Remember that the lunar nodes are always retrograde and they only regress a few degrees over the entire lifetime. If a planet is within a two- or three-degree range *clockwise* of the node, they will meet at some point as the node progresses backward over the natal planet. If this happens, it will be a long-lasting influence, as the progressed node will not change degrees any time soon. If the planet is just ahead of the node by zodiac degree, the aspect is separating. Therefore, the most potent effects of the aspect will not come about unless that planet is retrograde at birth and continues retrograde long enough to reach the node, or unless it is an inner planet, like Mercury, Venus, or Mars, and goes retrograde after birth. Check the ephemeris for the ninety days following birth to see if it will go retrograde, and at what age it will meet the natal node, using the day-for-a-year method. A good friend having such a condition experienced a serious health fright when his progressed Sixth House ruler, Venus, eventually moved through the degree of his South Node.

If a fast-moving planet like the Sun or one of the inner planets is just clockwise from the node in the natal chart, by a few to several degrees, by progression it will move forward over the natal node during youth, describing a set of conditions and circumstances lasting from one to three years, usually. But, gradually, the planet moves along and conditions described by the contact come to an end. This is again assuming it is not an inner planet (Venus, Mercury, or Mars), and the planet happens to make a retrograde station while conjunct the node. The Sun never goes retrograde, nor does the Moon. The Moon progresses forward through the zodiac very quickly, about one degree per month, so when it goes over a node it describes temporary influences in effect for only a couple of months, while within the one-degree orb.

PROGRESSED NODAL ASPECTS

Following are brief descriptions of the influence of an inner planet meeting a node by progression. These can be applied also in the case of a progressed node meeting the planet, but in that case the influence is longer lasting:

Progressed Moon conjunct North Node: A period when one prefers to stay out of the limelight and take an emotional reprieve from the usual efforts. Some alone time is needed and taken by choice. The influence of women is significant; bonding occurs. Domestic harmony.

Progressed Moon conjunct South Node: A low period emotionally, due to circumstances that block one's efforts and prevent success. There are feelings of inadequacy. Problems with women are significant. Concern over the health of someone close is very likely.

Progressed Moon square Nodes: Similar to previous. Efforts needed to overcome blockages that are having a considerably negative impact on the emotions and expression.

Progressed Moon trine North Node: A happy state of affairs results in a natural flow of expressions, with feelings of security and emotional comfort. The sextile is less noticeable.

Progressed Sun conjunct North Node: An uplift of the individuality and career follows a temporary squeeze. Inner stress is experienced initially. An illness or death in the close family is possible. May be a testing time for the male figures in one's life. Male associations are significant.

Progressed Sun conjunct South Node: Similar to the above, but a much more difficult testing period that may cause depression or an inferiority complex. A male figure is under focus; association with one of low moral fiber. A separation or death may occur in the close family.

Progressed Sun square Nodes: Quite similar to the previous aspect. Circumstances block opportunities. Problems or difficulties arise through father or strong male figure. Health is taxed.

Progressed Sun trine North Node: Things are going well, with luck, opportunities, and assistance that boosts recognition and shows off talents. Things go well for important masculine figures, and beneficial circumstances surround male children. The sextile is similar.

Progressed Mercury conjunct North Node: Increased mental activity and focus on the communication skills and business affairs. Some change in the vocation or job, usually constructive in nature. Affairs surrounding siblings, young people, and short trips are significant.

Progressed Mercury conjunct South Node: Mental stamina and abilities are taxed. Communication and comprehension skills are tested. Difficulties in coming to agreements cause relationship and business problems. Nerves are overwrought and one may be accident-prone. Trouble may involve siblings.

Progressed Mercury square Nodes: Similar to the previous aspect, though less difficult. Extra efforts are required when it comes to logic, comprehension, and communicative responses.

Progressed Mercury trine North Node: The mental skills are operating at maximum levels, absorbing ideas, originating ideas, and presenting them easily. The ability to communicate effectively is increased. Excellent period to make plans. The sextile is similar, but less spectacular.

Progressed Venus conjunct North Node: Brings about circumstances meant to restore a healthy balance in Venus activities, protecting one from painful experiences. Love relationships are tested. Financial management skills are tested. Frustrations are experienced initially, but things work out okay. There are new acquaintances; gifts or gains may come through females.

Progressed Venus conjunct South Node: Frustrations in Venus-ruled activities, often caused by outer circumstances or other people. There's a lack of harmony, especially with females. The love/romance area is difficult. The finances take hits and undergo depletions. General dis-ease.

Progressed Venus square Nodes: Similar to above. There's a possible break-up, divorce, or separation.

Progressed Venus trine North Node: General ease and harmony. Social life increases, new acquaintances made, with gains possible through a female. Love life goes well; possible engagement. Financial increases, with gifts coming in. Self-indulgence must be watched.

Progressed Mars conjunct North Node: Brings a big boost of energy and a desire to do purposeful things. This energy needs a good outlet or it can internalize and cause physical difficulties. The masculine figures in the life may likewise be overly excitable and passionate.

Progressed Mars conjunct South Node: Lack of energy. The physical energy must be monitored and paced so that one doesn't overdo. It is time to be low-key and less aggressive in pursuits. Health needs guarding, as it is vulnerable. Accident-prone tendencies. Problems arise with men. General conflicts. There are difficulties or trouble in sexual relationships.

Progressed Mars square Nodes: Similar to previous.

Progressed Mars trine North Node: Circumstances make it easy to put big plans into action. Increased stamina and constant energy flows. New enterprises are entered into, often in concert with a masculine figure. Sexual relationships go well. May bring a marriage or a birth.

For the outer planets contacting one of the nodes by progression, the influence is often very similar to the aspect in the natal chart, given in chapter 8, so descriptions for these combinations will be brief:

Progressed Jupiter conjunct or trine North Node: A good-luck phase, with help coming from associations. Much activity surrounds the family, with happy increases through marriages and births. Self-indulgent tendencies must be watched. Overexpansion and weight gain are possible.

Progressed Jupiter conjunct or square South Node: Reverse of the above; a bad-luck phase and washing karmic debts. Business associations prove unhelpful to disastrous. Legal involvements, business losses, trouble with in-laws.

Progressed Saturn conjunct or trine North Node: Older, wiser, or influential people tend to be of benefit. Brings a possible romance with someone older. Relationship with a parent deepens.

Progressed Saturn conjunct or square South Node: Relationships bring responsibilities and problems. It is hard to get cooperation. There may be a death or separation from a family member.

Progressed Uranus conjunct or trine North Node: New, exciting friends and acquaintances are made. Through them come unexpected events and new experiences are enjoyed. Gains come through groups. New-age interests develop.

Progressed Uranus conjunct or square South Node: Problems or separations involving a friend. Problems arise through the groups to which one belongs. Unexpected developments tend to be upsetting; separations, accidents, conflicts, or catastrophes.

Progressed Neptune conjunct or trine North Node: Psychic activity. May be a blissful era; relationships formed involving unusual people. Secret alliances or gains from hidden sources.

Progressed Neptune conjunct or square South Node: Trouble comes from deceptive people who may wish to exploit you. Involvements with low-life individuals: the drug addicted, the criminal minded, or people with severe mental or emotional problems. Associations are unreliable.

Progressed Pluto conjunct or trine North Node: A major transformation in life occurs due to a new and powerful association. There are new interests in healing or contacts with healers.

Progressed Pluto conjunct or square South Node: Power struggle ensues or heavy burdens are placed on one through an association. A death occurs in close circles or there is a separation from someone close.

Progressed Chiron conjunct or trine North Node: Positive connections formed with healers, teachers, or counselors who can assist in healing of painful wounds. Assisting others who are experiencing pain. The sextile is similar.

Progressed Chiron conjunct or square South Node: Facing a painful crisis and working through it. There's a possible connection with someone who is experiencing wounding.

To glean the meaning of progressed aspects of the nodes to points like the Part of Fortune or Vertex, chapter 3 can be referred to, except that here it is a temporary influence.

The North Node conjunct a planet is generally more favorable than South Node conjunct a planet—as in the former case there is more free will and, due to cosmic assistance, some good to come of it. Still, the North Node is quite an excitable influence upon a planet—there can be some distortion and unusual effects noticed in the affairs ruled by the planet and in the matters of the house ruled by the planet, even if in retrospect it is judged to have been a constructive period. Some unexpected event may precede a new, more favorable era. When it is the South Node, there are difficulties, losses, depletion, sacrifices, and a downshift surrounding the associated affairs ruled by the planet and in the matters of the house ruled by the planet. The individual is undergoing some karmic testing, paying debts, and washing karmic liabilities.

To get the most information from your interpretations, it is important to judge the house occupied and ruled by a planet that gets the stimulation of a node due to progression. If it is the natal planet joined with the node, look to the natal houses that planet occupies and rules. If it is the progressed planet involved in the aspect, look to the progressed houses that planet occupies and rules. With a contact of a node to a planet, the affairs that are impacted are three-fold: first according to the activities and people the planet is naturally associated with, secondly according to the house it occupies, and thirdly according to the matters of the house it rules.

Taking some illustrations, Al Pacino rose to popularity after his portrayal of Michael Corleone in *The Godfather* in 1972. The release of the film occurred as his progressing Moon formed a trine to his natal North Node, gaining him publicity. His progressed North Node was also transited by Uranus, which gained him sudden notice. The houses benefited included his Second of earnings, his Sixth of work, and his Eleventh of hopes and wishes, as North Node was in the progressed Second, and Moon was in the progressed Sixth while co-ruling the Eleventh.

Timothy McVeigh, who was executed for the 1995 Oklahoma City bombings, had an upper North Node in his natal chart, closely conjunct Venus. This accounts for his near-perfect childhood, a happy one, with many opportunities. He was a popular student, in the honor society, among other activities. While Venus was just slightly ahead of his North Node, and separating, Saturn was slightly behind it. So by progression, Saturn was moving forward to conjunct his natal node while his progressing node was moving backward to conjunct Saturn, creating a double aspect. It was after these contacts took hold and after a stint in the army that McVeigh's life took a dramatic turn. In April of 1994, he claimed that he'd been implanted with a computer chip while in the army and declared himself a nonresident alien. This was just as transiting North Node crossed his natal-afflicted Neptune, coinciding with these apparent self-delusions. He met up with Terry Nichols and then used the patience and resolution of that nodal conjunction to Saturn to carry out the bombings a year later. When he died by lethal injection on June 11, 2001, his progressed Part of Fortune was square his natal nodes.

Judy Garland's life ended under similar chart signatures, after her natal North Node, which was situated between Saturn and Jupiter, progressed backward and met up with progressed Saturn coming toward it. She died of an overdose when transiting South Node was conjunct her progressed Part of Fortune. All this occurred in the natal Fourth House of endings.

When John F. Kennedy was assassinated in November of 1963, his progressed Part of Fortune was square his natal nodes. This was in addition to having transiting North Node conjunct his South Node and transiting South Node conjunct his North Node, a major life turning point.

Althea Flynt's death occurred as the natal square between her nodes and her Vertex came closer by progression, with additional stress from progressed Neptune square her

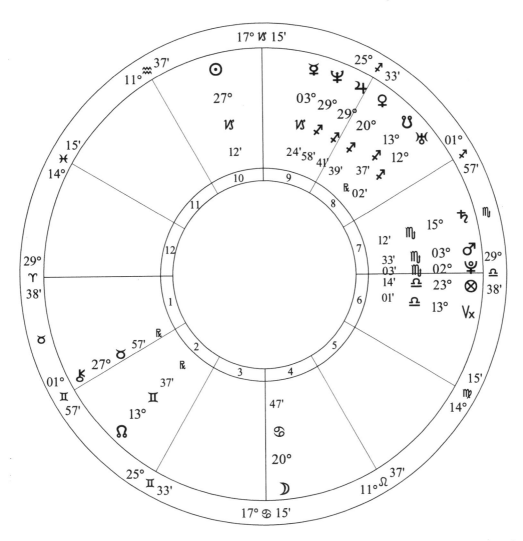

Figure 33: Seung-Hui Cho birth chart: Jan. 18, 1984, 12:00 PM, Seoul, South Korea

progressed nodes. Progressed and transiting Mars also joined to put pressure on that square.

Though I do not have the time of birth for Seung-Hui Cho, who carried out the massacre at Virginia Tech in 2007, his chart still affords an excellent illustration of how a natal nodal aspect becomes stimulated, excitable, and prone to act out. The chart shown is set for noon to see the approximate location of his Moon, but no matter what time of day he was born, his South Node was closely conjunct his Uranus with Uranus slightly behind the node. By the time of his rampage, by progression the two had come to share the same degree—as progressing South Node was moving backward and progressing Uranus was moving forward. Thus the nervousness of his natal South Node/Uranus conjunction was reaching a high pitch and poised to explode.

The transiting nodes were at 13 degrees of Pisces and Virgo, square his natal conjunction of Uranus/South Node in Sagittarius. At the time, transiting Uranus was also within five degrees of transiting North Node so that this pairing, similar to his own natal pairing, were both involved in the square, a very potent aspect to produce sudden unexpected results. In this scenario, the actions are usually quite unpredictable. The action or event has quite an impact, raises awareness, and then afterward, in retrospect, the cause can be traced. This appears to be exactly what is happening. It is unfortunate that such drastic and radical measures that caused so much suffering were necessary to bring light to the weaknesses in the mental health system when it comes to treating those in need. This is where some good can come as everyone sees the ignored warning signals along the way. As you can see, Cho also had a wide conjunction of Venus/South Node, making it difficult to feel accepted and enjoy a social life. If you notice also in his chart, Cho was born near a Full Moon. Unlike people born nearest the New Moon, Full Moon people usually want to get noticed and will go to greater lengths to achieve it.

In the next chapter we will talk more about the transiting nodes and their specific influences as they travel through a house or make contacts to natal or progressed planets.

Chapter Ten

THE TRANSITING NODES

We are evolving at a fast pace in the matters signified by the houses transited by the nodes. We are having experiences that add to our wisdom in those areas. We are going through changes, with a little help from cosmic nudging.

The transiting nodes represent guideposts or checkpoints to help ensure that we accomplish our soulful and spiritual tasks. They show our connections to time, space, and people—where we play a role or perform a function in this larger universal system. We aren't here solely for our own pleasure, but to make a contribution from our accumulated experiences that will enrich the greater humanity. We do many services for each other and these interactions can be observed through nodal contacts. Contracts are started or ended, things we've taken for granted may cease, or new opportunities fall from the sky. We are part of a grand design—a grand orchestration, led by a higher force. We're a spark of it, here to do great work. We've made agreements and appointments we can't get out of. We may not fully remember them now, but there were sacrifices we were willing to make for the opportunity to come and serve a purpose, learn a lesson, and gather experience for the greater whole—for the greater good.

We have tons of free will 99 percent of the time, but when the transiting nodes are involved, it means there are some things happening over which we have little control. Some things are meant to be. This is all part of a plan that may be bigger than our limited perspective while we're here. The nodes operate on many levels, physical, emotional, and spiritual—but a lot is happening automatically as a very natural process.

It is not at all necessary to try to control every little thing in your life when you have a nodal transit or aspect. It would likely do little good anyway. Just live your life as wisely and ethically as you can and trust in the universal system. Enjoy life's processes and envision your bright future. Beyond that, it can be helpful to understand the processes at work and do what you can to assist.

We take in at the head and we eliminate at the tail.

With the nodal transits comes a degree of awareness about the affairs of the house or planet. The North Node *thinks* about exciting possibilities and the South Node *knows* there is a responsibility or an obligation.

In a general way, you can track the transiting North Node through your chart to note areas of opportunity where rewards, good fortune, and happiness can be found. The North Node provides those. The house transited by the North Node gets the most attention. Similarly, you can track the South Node to find potential areas of vulnerability, loss, or sacrifice, where you are working through issues. South Node offers chances for spiritual growth. Look for contributions to make in that area for the good of others, aligned with your spiritual task and staying on your path. The house transited by the South Node requires the greatest caution.

NODAL TRANSITS THROUGH THE HOUSES

The First House governs your personality, temperament, appearance, and physical health. Attributes of the First House show the color lens through which you view the world and the experiences you attract, based upon the first impression you make on others. The key phrase is "I am," and this house naturally corresponds to Mars. Your attitude is changing, and you are apt to take everything more seriously when a node transits this house. You may become more health conscious, and make changes in your appearance.

The Second House governs your income-earning power, portable possessions and property, and general finances and resources. It indicates how you earn and spend your money. It also reveals your value system and how you set your priorities. The key phrase is "I have," and this house corresponds to Venus. You may make or spend big money with a nodal transit through this house.

The Third House governs your mentality, communications, short trips, vehicles, immediate environment, neighbors, and siblings. It's the house of basic concepts, ideas, and written and spoken agreements. The key phrase is "I think," and this house naturally corresponds to Mercury. Life is busy with errands, contracts, and paperwork with a node transiting here. Communication and transportation are key issues.

The Fourth House governs your home, family, parents, heritage, and real estate. It reveals the way you feel about yourself on the inside, based upon the degree of security and foundation provided to you from your heritage and background. The key phrase is "I feel," and this house corresponds to the Moon. Home, domestic, and family matters are all important with a nodal transit here.

The Fifth House governs children, romance, artistic expression, entertainment, sports, and speculation. This house corresponds to the urge to create something that will live on as an extension of the ego. This may be a child of the body or the mind, or some other individual contribution. The key phrase is "I will," and this house corresponds naturally to the Sun. Children, the pursuit of pleasure, friendships, and hobbies are highlighted with a nodal transit through this house.

The Sixth House governs routine responsibilities, schedules, duties, service, occupation, co-workers, employees, health maintenance, and pets. The key phrase is "I analyze," and this house corresponds to Mercury. Jobs, schedules, pets, or new diet and exercise regimens are some of the things that often come into focus with a nodal transit here.

The Seventh House governs "others" who attract your attention. This house rules marriage partners, business partners, adversaries, open enemies, counselors, and advisors. The key phrase is "I balance," and this house corresponds naturally to Venus. This is an important relationship house, and multiple relationships are apt to be transformed with a nodal transit here.

The Eighth House governs taxes, insurance, inheritance, shared property, and resources—as opposed to the personal resources and earnings of the Second House. It rules regenerative processes, sex, and death. It also governs transformational processes like divorce or surgery. The key phrase is "I desire," and this house corresponds to Pluto. You may take out a loan or have concerns about debts when a node transits this house.

The Ninth House governs higher learning and the abstract mind, long-range vision, philosophy, professors, religion, publishing, propaganda, and long journeys. It also rules in-laws and travelers. The key phrase is "I see," and this house corresponds to Jupiter. Education or travel may come into focus with a nodal transit here.

The Tenth House governs your public reputation and status, profession, career and authority figures. Whereas the Fourth House was the most private area, the Tenth House is the most public area, and where you gain notice. The key phrase is "I use," and this house corresponds to Saturn. You'll certainly get noticed with a nodal transit through this house, so be prepared.

The Eleventh House governs friends, social groups, long-term hopes, wishes, and ideals. It is an outer extension of the Fifth; here creative goals are shared in common with a whole group. The key phrase is "I know," and this house corresponds to Uranus. Changes in friendships, clubs, and group affiliations are likely with a nodal transit through this house.

The Twelfth House stores past deeds. It governs the subconscious mind, secrets, behind-the-scenes activities, recovery, confinement, or retreat. The key phrase is "I believe," and this house corresponds to Neptune. Introspection, a need to regroup, or the desire for solitude may coincide with a nodal transit through this house.

THE NODAL TRANSIT TIMES THE RESULT OF PRIOR CHOICES

Where the South Node transits, we may have a sense of knowing that there is something there that we could lose; something we might desire to keep very much. Anything that is neglected, ignored, or insecurely attached may be lost. Some sacrifices may have to be made. These sad matters often make us look to the advantages of the house of the transiting North Node, where we think about the exciting possibilities. There is a sense of anticipation there. You can often lighten the load of the South Node transit by pushing toward the North.

Say a middle-aged lady is having South Node transiting her First House; she may feel her looks are fading as she sees imperfections starting to appear. She may go through a period of trying to save her beauty. The effects of these kinds of changes would affect different people differently, of course—it would be much worse for the woman with

Libra or Venus rising, who has a healthy share of vanity. Of course, she has a year or so to come to terms with what is happening and, if aging gracefully, she finally comes to the realization that looks really aren't the most important thing anyway. She evolves above the need to be dependent on her looks. She reevaluates her priorities and looks to her relationships with others as more important.

Now, this South Node transit through the First House could have a more serious impact for someone who has been lax about taking care of his or her physical body. At this point a health crisis could occur, especially if a natal planet falls there too. It is the universe's way of saying, "Hey there, wake up—your job's not finished!" It may seem like the free will is operating at a minimum when some full-blown crisis erupts, but it is really the legacy we left (our past habits and actions) that is having an impact on us *now*. Past crimes done to the body may be atoned for now. Those attracted by North Node in the Seventh might be the experts consulted who can offer hope and treatment to restore physical health.

The houses show the general significances, a planet being transited shows more specifics, and the house ruled by a planet being transited gives even more specifics, so there may be multiple manifestations of a nodal transit through a house or over a planet. Gains come in the area (house) ruled by a planet getting the North Node transit and sacrifices, or debts come due in the house ruled by a planet getting the South Node transit. The North Node brings an increase while the South Node brings a slowdown or complications.

Old karma relating to the affairs governed naturally under that house or associated with the planet transited is burnt off with the South Node transit. Remember the suitcase you brought with you into this life that held all your past-life debts? Well, what if a good portion of the old karma was automatically distributed to the appropriate house and the rest to the appropriate planet?

For instance, if you brought with you into this lifetime, or created in this lifetime, karmic debts in the area of sexual relations, the transit of the South Node through the Eighth House could be when learning experiences relating back to those debts occur. You might feel the pangs of hurt or loss in that department. The fear of loss of potency or sexual desirability may lead to acting out in a desperate fashion to prove otherwise. As the South Node acts as a drain now, in the Eighth House, there may also be losses through investments.

There are usually some growing pains where the South Node transits. In the Second House, there could be financial losses or frozen assets, similar to transiting South Node going over Venus. In the Third House, there could be problems surrounding siblings or communication difficulties, problems with contracts and so forth, similar to South Node going over Mercury. The South Node cleans house. The energy of this node is like an evacuation tube, where we work through things and come clean, easing the load. The South Node acts as a drain, relieving you of the old burdens and residue that are casting a shadow over your soul. Find ways to fill the empty cup in the area under focus. Once the South Node has transited a planet or a house, you have a new clean slate in those matters. It is quite normal for you to experience some losses,.

However, it is possible to create so much good karma at such a swift rate that you can help offset your debt or earn a reprieve. Think of the health situation. What if you saw this transit coming and did all kinds of good things for your body—gave up the bad habits and consulted an expert nutritionist or weight trainer, for instance? You are still giving something up, but in a way that you have some control and show good intentions. Depending on how soon you start the new regimen, very likely there are immediate benefits. It may not save you completely, but could offset or reduce negative effects. There is always some karmic balancing going on with the South Node transit, and the best way to handle it is to make willing sacrifices and remain low-key.

If in any situation there is a debt still owed, based on the Prarabdha karma, which are debts that *must* be paid in this lifetime, the universe will hook you up with the right circumstances, experiences, or people to ensure you get the chance to wash away the old karmic residue. Temptations are all around us; virtually none of us get past them all without committing a spiritual crime here and there that will have its eventual effect. Even if the crime done to you is not exactly the same as the one you committed, it will somehow match the form.

We all have some good karma stored up in each department or house. The more good that is stored there, the more the North Node transit will open those flows and time the rewards. Gains or losses experienced are in direct proportion to what one has earned, and the major effects of a nodal transit to a planet become most apparent right after the contact. The nodal transit times the effects of past actions, decisions, and choices.

As we move on to discuss the transits of the nodes over each planet, the orbs of the transiting nodes are very narrow. Usually, you will experience the effects of a nodal transit over a natal planet within two weeks of the exact aspect. That gives about a one-month span, six weeks at best. The strongest impact of the transit is felt when the node is within one degree of the exact aspect. Often it is less than this, just half a degree, or very nearly exact. Other transits and progressions help to more precisely identify the main effects, but the nodal transits to a planet or an angle are a very good timing device for determining when an event will occur. By checking any progressed lunar aspects falling in the same time frame (based on an accurate time of birth) you can get an idea of how the nodal contact may be mitigated or strengthened.

Sometimes a planet appears to go out of control with a nodal contact. Or we might say that the psychological urges associated with the planet go out of control. Andrea Yates had transiting North Node going over her progressed Mars when she drowned her five children. Even when the effects of such a transit are more positive, there is often some compulsive action with these nodal contacts to Mars that brings an almost uncontrollable urge to take action and attempt large things.

With South Node transits, trouble and sacrifices sometimes occur because it's easy to make errors in judgment regarding the matters ruled by the planet while it is getting the South Node stimulation. Thus one brings about his or her own self-undoing. With the North Node contact, it is more likely to become overly stimulated and exuberant regarding the matters ruled by the planet.

If by lucky chance transiting Jupiter happens to be near the transiting South Node when it moves over one of your planets, Jupiter will act as a buffer, protecting against the worst of the impact. Venus also acts as a cushion. On the other hand, should transiting Uranus happen to join a node when it makes a pass to a natal or progressed planet, the effects of the nodal transit will have some unpredictable elements. Always check to see if the transiting node has the accompaniment of another transiting planet when making a contact, and judge your interpretation accordingly.

NODAL TRANSITS TO THE PLANETS

North Node to Sun: Changes in recognition of a positive sort follow some initial inner stress and tension. There are usually increased opportunities, elevation, successes of a personal nature, and confidence gained. Significant matters are tied to the father or fatherly figures, with assistance from them as well as gain for them. Important beneficial acquaintances are made, opening new doors. Stronger expression of one's individuality and more freedoms are noticed after the contact—much like the natal aspect, except this is a temporary influence. The house reveals where success or freedom is experienced and the house ruled by the Sun will also be affected for good according to the rewards due one. Transiting North Node over the progressed Sun is also favorable. Help and assistance from masculine figures, personal elevation, increased recognition, and opportunities open up for the important masculine figures in your life.

South Node to Sun: Changes in recognition, often with unexpected problems cropping up. The ego and identity is somewhat suppressed or forced into a downshift and it is difficult to maintain status and position. You feel off your game and must assume a low-key position. There may be low self-esteem, feelings of despair, an inferiority complex, or an identity crisis. Health or vitality is often below par. Changes occurring for those who have been helpful figures impact the life, having a negative effect. Important figures may experience setbacks, losses, or are unable to help, much like the natal aspect, but having a temporary influence. The houses occupied and ruled by the Sun also undergo trials. Similar themes are noticed with transiting South Node over the progressed Sun, with setbacks experienced in the progressed house ruled by the Sun.

North Node to Moon: Changes in mood and temperament with increased sensitivity. There are new domestic conditions and changes involving family members—often an increase through births. The nesting instinct becomes stronger. Women play a significant role in the life, often with some benefit from them. Affairs of the mother or a mother figure come into focus. There may be increased support from others, favor, and popularity. Benefits and joy of a personal nature that are forthcoming are more in evidence after the contact. The matters of the house ruled by the Moon prosper, and opportunities open up. Similar themes are noticed with transiting North Node over progressed Moon, with positive developments in the progressed house ruled by the Moon.

South Node to Moon: Changes in mood and temperament. The emotions go through a melancholic period or they are blocked. The creative faculties feel suppressed. The imagination works overtime, causing excessive fears or paranoia. Personal, domestic, or family changes bring some upset. The health and affairs revolving around a mother figure are significant. There may be trouble through a woman who is overly domineering, and a separation could occur. The health is vulnerable, especially in functions and body parts ruled by the Moon. This is much like the natal aspect, but for a temporary time. The matters of the house ruled by the Moon experience setbacks, frustrations, or a slowdown. Similar themes are noticed when South Node transits over the progressed Moon, with a downshift noted in the affairs of the progressed house ruled by the Moon.

North Node to Mercury: A busy time. There are changes in job, environment, or communications that are usually of a positive nature. The mind becomes activated and nervous energy needs a good outlet. Important discussions and decisions take place. Travel is highlighted and plans are made. One may get a new car and become interested in exploring the vicinity and interacting with neighbors. Activities or conditions surrounding siblings take an up-turn. Young people play a significant role in the life. Note the house occupied and ruled by Mercury also, as these undergo a positive increase of activity. Similar increases in related activities are noticed when North Node transits progressed Mercury, with happy results affecting the progressed house affairs ruled by Mercury.

South Node to Mercury: Job and other changes of a dismal or depressing nature. Areas of contracts, communication, and travel are likely to become complicated and unsatisfactory. Ideas may be challenged, although this is often an appropriate time to work through an idea. Communications become blocked or misunderstandings occur. One must meet the demands of others, and it is likely they do not have his or her best interests at heart. Nerves and anxiety, feeling unable to cope with changes is evident. The houses occupied and ruled by Mercury become difficult. Similar themes are noticed as transiting South Node moves over progressed Mercury, when the progressed house affairs ruled by Mercury undergo difficult changes.

North Node to Venus: There is the need for a reassessment of the finances and/or affections. Romantically there may be an initial cooling-off stage as one reflects upon the relationship and doesn't want to feel suffocated or possessed while doing so. There may be a karmic attraction, attachment, or romance that begins under this transit. Financially, this is usually a positive aspect with increases, assuming one deserves such a boost. The North Node magnifies and sometimes distorts the energy attributed to the planet it touches, so one may experience increased self-indulgent tendencies. This is something to watch that may need to be controlled. There is often an increase in the social life, with celebrations and happy occasions. Young women and their interests come into focus, playing a significant part in the life.

South Node to Venus: One must watch for misdirected priorities when it comes to love and money. This is usually a low point when it comes to the affections, romance, and feelings. One feels misunderstood or on a different wavelength with the partner or the romantic attachment, and much effort is needed to keep things alive. It is time to reassess things, as one may be involved in the wrong relationship. Karmic attachments, especially of a romantic nature, may come to an end at this time—not necessarily a separation, but the karmic element is removed and one is released from the obligation. The finances undergo a sudden squeeze, with a freeze of the assets or an inability to draw on them. Sudden and unusual troubles or losses revolve around finances. It is time to take precautions and reassess things. The social life is discouraging.

North Node to Mars: Taking on large projects and a tendency to push the physical limits is a major theme with this aspect. The urge may come on suddenly to do big things that one would normally not consider. It feels largely uncontrollable, as if one is a puppet. As a result, the blood pressure may go up or the person feels irritable or overworked. He or she may even become accident-prone, so it is a good time to watch physical movements, and the amount of stress and pressure placed on the body. Significant experiences may revolve around a strong male figure. New acquaintances are made and new enterprises begun. This is an exuberant but somewhat reckless vibe, and caution should be applied in any actions. Take into account the various dangers of Mars from cuts, burns, fire, and so on. Check the house ruled by Mars for increased activity.

South Node to Mars: Easy to make mistakes in undertakings, especially new enterprises. One needs to be very aware of all the factors and persons involved when launching new projects. Circumstances or people may tend to block progress, and confrontations or conflicts are common. Frustration occurs. Disappointments or difficulties come through masculine figures. Sorrows, problems, or setbacks connected to them may be inescapable, especially if this is a female chart. Sometimes they face danger. Accident-prone tendencies are significant with this aspect, and the physical health is quite vulnerable. Energy levels may be low and one might experience feelings of weakness. There may be mechanical problems with automobiles. This transit is one in which people need to be very aware and cautious overall. Check the house ruled by Mars to find affairs that will likely be negatively impacted and complicated.

North Node to Jupiter: Jupiter is the Greater Fortune, while Venus is the Lesser Fortune, therefore there are similarities to transiting North Node conjunct Venus regarding the material and financial matters. While this aspect gives a lot of control over these activities, one is learning about spending habits and there may be a reappraisal of the financial affairs and often some initial frustrations before one works with the circumstances to find the proper solution. Extra money coming in may only cover an increased amount going out. Large expenditures may bring gains of a spiritual or philosophical sort. There is increased interest in philosophy or religion. There is often a helpful person in the life who acts as a catalyst to financial or spiritual growth. Publishing ventures go well or there are opportunities here. Long-distance travel usually turns out favorably. North Node is an expansive vibration, thus one can easily gain weight.

South Node to Jupiter: Just the reverse of the previous position. Sudden unexpected expenditures come up that were not taken into consideration, thus shortages and depletions of a financial sort are common. One may take large risks that prove to be their undoing, seeing opportunities where there are actually many drawbacks. One may take on too much, making promises that cannot be honored, which has a negative impact on the reputation. Over-expansion is a problem, or thinking that one has more time than he or she really does. One's philosophies and belief systems are tested. Publishing ventures do not go well and long-distance travel is unsatisfactory. Weight loss may occur.

North Node to Saturn: This is quite a powerhouse aspect for good if one has invested much time and effort in doing the right thing, laying strong foundations for success, and playing by the rules of society. One gets all the rewards due for such sustained efforts and hard work. Lessons and learning experiences take place now, but of a sort that is ultimately quite constructive, allowing for more stability. One learns to appreciate patience, and comes to know oneself and one's capabilities better, resulting in an improved self image once the contact is over. There is usually an older person who can be of much guidance, or who plays a significant role in the life at this time. One is willing to take on more responsibility and make commitments. Relationships begun now or circumstances entered into have a good chance for long-term survival, especially if of a professional nature.

South Node to Saturn: This places considerable restrictions on the life efforts. This may be as a result of weak health, or a low point in the emotional demeanor and outlook, or from obstacles and heavy responsibilities placed upon one. One sees life and limitations in a more negative light than at other times, and may feel as if a black cloud is overhead. Authority figures, such as a boss, a business associate, a judge, or someone else of advanced rank and knowledge, present problems or there are issues with them. Saturn-related problems are common and normal, such as dental, bone, or skin problems, increased colds, etc. There may be disturbances, upsets, or losses that connect to older folks. An illness or death may occur. Look to the house ruled by Saturn in addition to the house occupied by Saturn to learn more of where the discouraging trend is operating and affecting your life, where circumstances are undergoing a shift.

North Node to Uranus: This is often a very potent aspect capable of producing sudden unexpected events. Anything can happen, although it may have a Uranian twist to it relative to the house position. Chance meetings may occur. Brief encounters or temporary relationships are formed that tend to be quite significant in the life, often acting as a catalyst to open up new vistas. One may gain sudden notice. Interests may increase in new age topics or in other fields ruled by Uranus such as astrology, computers, gadgetry, and technology. This is usually a constructive transit in which unexpected developments tend to have a positive outcome. Look also to the house ruled by Uranus for out-of-the-ordinary developments.

South Node to Uranus: Surprising or unplanned-for developments take place. It is difficult to plan and one must be flexible and learn to go with the flow. This is a disruptive and destructive vibration. Stability is lacking. Unexpected developments tend to come out of the blue and have a negative outcome. It is a time to protect the reputation and avoid unwise risks, as there is increased vulnerability for scandals or black marks against one. The house ruled by Uranus may also undergo unusual circumstances or developments causing difficulties.

North Node to Neptune: The imagination is stimulated, thus this is often a very creative trend. Previously untapped artistic talents may reveal themselves. One may feel highly inspired, loving, and sympathetic toward others. The spiritual side of the nature expands. It is a lofty kind of vibe; in love with life and everyone around, with feelings of appreciation and happy contentment. An interest in meditation and dream work may increase. The intuition is stronger and more reliable, and spiritual or psychic experiences may occur. Visualization exercises are likely to bring swift results due to the happy frame of mind, combined with the ability to *see* and feel the desired outcomes. Hypnosis is an avenue for self-improvement. Successful journeys are made.

South Node to Neptune: There may be involvement with intrigue, with alcohol or drugs. The imagination is misleading, excessive, and one tends toward self-delusion. There may be connections to sinister persons or those who will deceive you, and caution should be used in letting someone new into your life at this time. It is a time to question your own judgment, and you need someone trustworthy whose advice you can depend on. Some likelihood of fraud is apparent, depending upon how prominent Neptune is in the natal chart. There is a degree of confusion or unsettled matters, one's direction is foggy, and there may be fearful feelings that something is about to go wrong. Travel or journeys turn out less satisfactorily than anticipated.

North Node to Pluto: A change in consciousness, with some significant and permanent change in the life. One is ready to confront obstacles, and there is increased power and inner strength to make changes that were previously put off. This is often a time of reckoning with deep psychological issues. Decisions are made that impact the most personal areas of life: the domestic life, financial situation, or personal habits. One becomes compelled to carry out some activity. Large undertakings. Transformations and reorganization take place and it is a constructive period when one has the power to greatly improve circumstances. It is a good time to kick a bad habit. There may be contacts with healers, or a new association marks a turning point in life. Activities that are highlighted include joint resources, taxes, and insurance matters.

South Node to Pluto: Intense and complicated relationships, often with power struggles or confrontations. Something breaks down. Some profound or forceful event that takes place may act as a catalyst to a new experience and a change of consciousness. Circumstances may force a change in plans and you are suddenly forced to adapt to new conditions. There may be closure of some significant issue that has been the source of conflict in the past. Sometimes a death occurs in your immediate circle, or there is an estrangement or separation. There is some danger of personal attack, or violence entering the life. One must be careful and alert to the surroundings. Contacts of Pluto with the nodes have been connected to all sorts of unsavory things like kidnappings, miscarriages, abortions, suicides, and other dramatic incidents.

North Node to Chiron: The natal house placement of Chiron shows an area of wounding, but also where one is gifted and can be of assistance in bringing healing to others. The North Node transit may bring a peak in activities relating to the house of Chiron and the associated wounding, while also timing important connections with others, with opportunities for inner healing to take place and bringing it to others.

South Node to Chiron: Some sad development that relates back to the initial wounding symbolized by the house position of natal Chiron or aspects to Chiron. Some loss, setback, or painful event occurs. Contact with someone who is ill or experiencing wounding. May have multiple effects, but often in regard to the matters ruled by the natal house holding natal Chiron. There are growing pains and experiences that force one to confront the issues. Transiting nodes square Chiron are similar.

In addition to the natal house occupied and ruled by a natal planet receiving a nodal transit, the foregoing descriptions may also be applied to a progressed planet receiving the transit of a node. In that case, check also the progressed house position of the planet and the progressed house it rules to find the areas where benefits or losses will come about. The following descriptions may also be applied to progressed angles receiving a nodal transit.

NODAL TRANSITS TO THE NODES & ANGLES

North Node to North Node: This marks a major crossroad, as it is a period of karmic transitions. An important year follows. It is a time of wrapping up an old phase of growth and experience, and moving into new areas of growth with different projects underway, and new lessons to learn. The higher forces seem to be guiding things. An individual has had the past eighteen and a half years to fulfill the karmic lessons of the previous stage—the new era he or she is entering into depends on the evolutionary level of growth achieved up to this point. Whatever stability, maturity, and spiritual insight gained up to this point will only contribute to the positive possibilities ahead. Some initial confusion or frustration may be noticed as one is still working with the old circumstances, but experiencing new urges. One may become aware that the focus is beginning to shift just prior to this contact. Others may want to hold you to the same old groove. May take a year to see the transition.

South Node to North Node: This also often marks a crossroad in life, as it is a highly developmental stage. There is new awareness, made possible chiefly through interactions with other people. One must meld what has been learned about the self with an appreciation for other people and varying viewpoints. There are many exchanges with others, many new connections.

North Node to Ascendant: This is a dynamic period for personal changes and events. Major transitions often occur and connections of a karmic type are formed with others. You are in a coming-out phase and more noticed by others. You have good self-control and a positive outlook. Personal efforts tend to get more support. It is easy to draw other people into your life. There is a need to balance the personal goals and needs with those of a partner or other people, who may tend to feel like a burden. This is generally a busy time. There is likelihood of weight gain.

South Node to Ascendant: You may just want to be invisible for the time being. You are going through inner changes. Others may see you as quite successful and having the perfect life, but you may not feel this way at all. Your tendency is to do for others and to make concessions and sacrifices for others. Others seem to have the upper hand, or are calling the shots, and your choices seem severely limited. Relationships are going through changes. Weight loss is possible.

North Node to Midheaven: This is usually a very positive transit for career recognition, an increase of status, and renewed ambitions of a worldly sort. Neil Armstrong had transiting North Node approaching his progressed Midheaven when he first set foot on the Moon. There are good relations with superiors. Difficulty balancing the activities of home and career may mean some sacrifices in the home life. Or, the home and family life may be unsatisfactory or draining, causing one to put more energy into the outer life. Sometimes a move occurs and many experiences revolve around the parents and the home base. Home repairs may be needed.

South Node to Midheaven: The home and family life is very activated, so that attention is turned there, and there may be less involvement in the professional life for the time being. It's taking an effort to balance the activities of home and career and the career may suffer as a result. Some sacrifice is made in the career area. The status may go down, or superiors or beneficiaries may be dissatisfied with the job performance. The ego nature and the outer ambitions take a back seat as inner growth is occurring. There may be changes in goals or changes in the home base. Experiences and events surrounding family members are significant. Parents may be enjoying happy circumstances and may be of some help.

North Node to Part of Fortune: Conditions are favorable and frequently there is a meeting with someone who can be of special benefit. A change in trends may come about through this fortunate connection. It is also a time when hunches pay off—timing and choices may be right on target for bringing about improved conditions. Check the house to find the areas that will most benefit from this aspect.

South Node to Part of Fortune: Support is lacking for one's efforts and this is a less fortunate phase overall. The choices seem limited, and you may be pushed into a corner or confront someone who has counter intentions and goals. You can easily err through making inappropriate choices and unwise decisions. The house of the aspect reveals the kinds of troubles one runs up against and the area in which to proceed with caution.

North Node to Vertex: This is a very fateful contact. You seem to have little control as you meet with destined encounters and experiences. You are quite vulnerable to being taken advantage of or hurt by others. You may feel suppressed, lonely, or isolated. It is time to closely scrutinize those with whom you are intimately involved and beware of giving over your power. Important decisions have long-term effects. Even when things are stable and going well, it seems you cannot make your own decisions, depending on what others tell you will be best. Work with the circumstances. Nodal squares to the Vertex are likewise difficult.

South Node to Vertex: This is the same as the above as far as there seems to be a momentum for events that was set in motion by forces outside of your control, forcing you into new experiences, limiting you in your options, but here the final results are often fortunate. The cosmic forces are working more in your favor. Others are more agreeable to your needs and desires and may be quite beneficial to your cause, although there is still some dependency on them. Important decisions have long-term implications. There may be a major shift in close affiliations. Karmic connections of the past may come to an end, while new ones begin.

The trine and sextile aspects of the nodes to the planets or angles are of the nature of the North Node transit. A square of the transiting nodes to a planet or point is more of the South Node influence. The affairs of the house ruled by a planet are affected accordingly.

In the next chapter, we will consider the various effects of the contacts of transiting planets to the natal nodes.

Chapter Eleven

TRANSITING PLANETS IN ASPECT
TO THE NODES

The transits of the planets over the natal nodes bring forth similar themes as do the nodes over the planets, outlined in the preceding chapter. Here, however, the transiting planet over a node reflects upon passing circumstances that may seem to be largely out of one's hands, for better or worse. As a result of these often-fleeting circumstances, which are always related to the quality and nature of the particular planet making the contact, the individual is generally encouraged (North Node) or forced (South Node) to take some action, utilizing the free will. These are opportune times to make modifications or needed changes that will ensure one's continuation on the intended soul journey. Actions or modifications are with an eye to the future when it is the North Node being transited, while actions are taken with an eye on the past when the South Node is being transited. For the latter, this is often due to prior commitments, or based on what one has learned from previous actions. Previously neglected problems are dealt with.

The house ruled by the transiting planet is significant in the interpretation. Look to that natal house for the affairs that circumstances are affecting during the time frame of the contact, and according to the nature of the contact, whether uplifted by the planet's contact to the North Node, or undergoing a downshift by the planetary contact to the South Node. Here, unfulfilled expectations may result. To avoid the worst, be sure your responsibilities have been met in these house affairs prior to the transit. Watch especially for transits involving the chart ruler. When it contacts one of the nodes, the effects will be more personal in scope.

Since the progressing nodes move backward slightly from their natal position, a transiting planet crosses the progressed node first and then the natal node. You may be aware of the appropriate energy and manifestations slightly before the contact to the natal planet. The orb recommended is plus/minus five degrees in which to expect the manifestations of the transit, but with the most noticeable effects when the planet is within three degrees of the node.

The influence of the North Node expands, opens, increases, and magnifies the qualities of the planet coming into contact. The influence of the South Node contracts, closes, depletes, and shrinks the qualities of the planet making the contact. The transit of a planet to the North Node usually times some personal increase or favorable conditions coming from others, while the transit of a planet to the South Node usually coincides with times that we are doing for others, or conceding to others, making these times more strenuous. Opportunities come one's way when the North Node is transited, and concessions are in order when the South Node is transited. It is often someone described by the planet that offers something to you or seeks something from you.

PLANETARY CONTACTS TO THE NODES

Transits of the inner bodies—the Moon, Sun, Mercury, and Venus—crossing the nodes are very temporal contacts, showing fleeting circumstances. Unless multiple inner bodies happen to transit a node at the same time, the effects may be only slightly noticeable. They are, however, significant enough that they can counter other aspects to a strong degree. You might not enjoy all the fruits of some other nice transit that coincides with a planet transiting your South Node, nor should you expect the most difficult themes reflected by a nasty transit that occurred during the same time frame that a planet transits your North Node.

We will begin with the fastest moving body and move outward.

Moon conjunct North Node: Sensitivity is increased. Women play a significant part in the events occurring, often with some favor for you. There are mothering, nurturing themes, usually with someone taking on this role toward you. There's an increased interest or focus on domestic life. Health matters may be significant. Developments may be noticeably connected to the affairs of the house ruled by the Moon, and in a favorable way.

Moon conjunct South Node: Increased sensitivity or change in temperament. A woman plays a significant role, and domestic matters are under increased focus. Here, it is more likely that you play the part of the mother or the nurturer for someone else. You are in the giving role. Female interests and health issues are highlighted. Events may be noticeably connected to the affairs of the house ruled by the Moon. Efforts are required there.

Mercury conjunct North Node: News, information, and communications of an uplifting sort and having a futuristic tone to them. Very busy with Mercury-related activities, such as correspondence, paperwork, planning, or travel. Contacts with agents, advisors, and messengers go well. Young people may play a more active role in events. The matters of the house ruled by Mercury are improved and enhanced as a result of this transit. If Mercury goes retrograde around this time, it may make multiple passes within a short period.

Mercury conjunct South Node: Wrapping up on business matters, with logistics to handle. News, information, or communications tend to present challenges. The past is somehow significant. There's a need to resolve or update something from the past. Data coming in and the present circumstances may allow you to unload or purge an old idea. Nerves become frazzled by errors in schedules, travel-related upsets, dealing with agents, etc. Young people play a significant role. Frustrations felt in the matters of the house ruled by Mercury. If Mercury turns retrograde around this time, it may make multiple passes within a short period.

Sun conjunct North Node: Occurs on the same date each year. Usually some praise, admiration, or honors. Those who can be of benefit encourage your efforts and offer you gifts or opportunities. Masculine or beneficial figures often play a significant role in affairs. This aspect usually brings a boost in energy and brightens the outlook. Improvements arrive in the house ruled by the Sun.

Sun conjunct South Node: Things take a discouraging turn and there are compromises to make. Others question your credentials, may be unappreciative of your efforts, and the ego is injured. Those who can be of benefit require something from you. It is hard to push through barriers and there are frustrations dealing with others. Men often play a significant role. This is the time to make adjustments in your methods, using the present circumstances as a guide to modifications needed. Efforts may feel like an energy drain.

Venus conjunct North Node: Think all things Venus! There is usually extra money coming in and these flows are open. At the same time, you feel quite indulgent, buying new things to beautify your surroundings or yourself. There are connections with young women, hair stylists, decorators, financial advisors, and so on. Social life is on the increase, with parties, showers, etc. Gifts and flowers may arrive from a lover. The matters of the house ruled by Venus are benefited. If Venus turns retrograde around this time, it may make multiple passes within a short period.

Venus conjunct South Node: There are financial or relationship problems. Extra money is going out that was not budgeted for, and you need to review your financial situation. If your own relationship is going okay, which is questionable, you may hear from others who are having problems, and possibly need your advice. Others require something from you, a young lady perhaps. There is some general disharmony. The matters of the house ruled by Venus experience a downshift or suffer restrictive elements as a result of this transit. If Venus goes retrograde around this time, it may make a prolonged contact or multiple passes within a short period.

Mars conjunct North Node: Someone is willing to take positive action on your behalf. Men often play a significant role. The energy level is high and one experiences increased initiative, ready to take on a challenge or conquer the world. Beginning some demanding project to be completed in the future. The matters of the house ruled by Mars benefit from this transit. If Mars turns retrograde around this time, it may make multiple passes within a short period.

Mars conjunct South Node: Things are not going your way. There may be confrontations or differences of opinion and someone is asking you to make compromises that annoy you. Great effort is required to control impatience, aggression, and anger. Encounters tend to be difficult and sap your energy. Others need you to take action on their behalf and you can spread yourself thin. You may be dealing with unsatisfactory results of past actions and decisions. Health issues may surface. The matters of the house ruled by Mars experience a downshift or suffer upsetting elements. If Mars goes retrograde around this time, it may make multiple passes within a short period of time.

Jupiter conjunct North Node: There may be opportunities to travel, or for higher study—getting a diploma or certification. Involvement with publications or publishing tends to go well. There may be someone of a philosophical mind who can be of some special help and assistance. It is a feel-good contact, often tempting you to take on too much and make big promises. Weight gain is possible. The house area ruled by Jupiter gets a significant boost, with happy increases. If Jupiter goes retrograde around this time, it may make multiple passes within a few months.

Jupiter conjunct South Node: Travel plans or journeys may have unexpected and troubling outcomes. Legal entanglements could arise. Problems relating to religion, philosophy, or individuals or groups one belongs to with these interests. One re-evaluates the life beliefs and philosophies, letting some pass away. Publishing ventures require extra efforts; agents expect more from you. Weight loss is likely. The affairs of the house ruled by Jupiter require attention; it is ill-advised to take risks as the South Node neutralizes Jupiter's luck qualities and expanse potential. If Jupiter goes retrograde, it may make multiple passes within a few months.

Saturn conjunct North Node: There is often a superior or someone in an authority capacity who can be of assistance, offering opportunities to utilize the inborn capabilities. One enjoys increased status or recognition. Material expansion. There is an eye to the practical and a mature outlook. The matters of the house ruled by Saturn benefit, with increased stability and an improved future outlook. One feels more satisfied, self-assured, and secure in those affairs. If Saturn goes retrograde, it may make multiple passes within a condensed time frame.

Saturn conjunct South Node: It is hard to find supporters and there are difficulties or differences of opinion with superiors, authorities, or older people. They are demanding. Restrictions and limiting circumstances crop up. It is taking time to re-establish status and recognition as it enters a nebulous or undefined period. There are material decreases. Physical weakness or health issues of a Saturn nature arise. Much effort is required in dealing with old issues or problems that were put off in the past. This is a time when a most important contribution may be made, even though considerable sacrifices might have been required. The matters of the house ruled by Saturn undergo obstacles and problems. If Saturn goes retrograde around this time, it may make multiple passes within a condensed time frame.

Chiron conjunct North Node: Some painful experience that one is forced to deal with results in substantial healing in the area occupied by Chiron. As a result, doors are opened and one is more capable of sharing the gift with others in a way that uplifts their lives. This is similar in influence to transiting North Node conjunct Chiron. If Chiron goes retrograde, it may make multiple contacts to the North Node over the course of a year or so.

Chiron conjunct South Node: An emotionally low point. This may be a painful learning period in which the self-undoing may result from improper management of the skills symbolized by the house holding Chiron. One thus realizes the power one has to hurt others by such misuse and does better in the future. This is similar in influence to transiting South Node conjunct Chiron. If Chiron goes retrograde, it may make multiple contacts to the South Node over a period of a year or so.

Uranus conjunct North Node: Unexpected situations that arise are usually of some personal advantage. Chance meetings and circumstances develop. Unusual ideas or unconventional methods are entered into. Involvement in activities ruled by Uranus goes well. This is similar in influence to transiting North Node over Uranus. The matters of the house ruled by Uranus tend to take on an expansion factor or elevation from this transit. If Uranus goes retrograde around this time, it may make multiple passes within a year or so.

Uranus conjunct South Node: Very uncertain and surprising incidents. Unexpected situations arise that tend to be of some personal disadvantage. Thrown into forced changes when least expecting it, one reflects upon the cause and the past mistakes afterwards. This is similar in influence to transiting South Node over Uranus. The house affairs ruled by Uranus come into focus; the individuality in that area is suppressed or unusual circumstances produce restrictions. If Uranus goes retrograde, it may make multiple passes within a year or so.

Neptune conjunct North Node: Quite a creative and often a spiritually enlightening period. Very much like the transit of North Node over Neptune, bringing about increased and reliable impressions and instincts, dream states, and psychic awareness. There may be unusual experiences along these lines. You may often feel very blessed, empathetic, and giving to others, trying to do good in the larger scheme of things. The matters of the house ruled by Neptune undergo a progressive trend. If Neptune goes retrograde around this time, it may make multiple passes within a couple of years.

Neptune conjunct South Node: An individual may get some glimpses of the larger scheme of things and the individual role, but may opt not to act on them, especially if the past mistakes must be confronted. He or she may prefer to pretend that all is well and continue the same path, likely using some method to escape reality, such as alcohol, drugs, or even sleep. There are similarities to transiting South Node over Neptune. The matters of the house ruled by Neptune undergo a period of confusion or uncertainty, or things are simply hard to define and understand. If Neptune goes retrograde around this time, it may make multiple passes within a couple of years.

Pluto conjunct North Node: Constructively regenerating. A person is able to work with the situation, conditions, circumstances, and resources to build up and improve various life areas. It is a time for making corrections in strategies based on experience, and for putting forth great self-initiative and the strength to carry through to desired results. This is similar to the transit of North Node over Pluto. However, due to the slow movement of Pluto, this contact is in orb for an extended period. Thus, the total effects of this successful period are not realized until the transit completes. The house ruled by Pluto may be in focus for some of the most improved circumstances.

Pluto conjunct South Node: A transforming, regenerating influence. Circumstances beyond one's control occur suddenly, tending to be disruptive, and forcing one through changes. There is a need to adapt to new conditions and circumstances. Frustrations may bring an unsettling end to a power struggle. This is similar to the transit of South Node over Pluto—however, due to the slow movement of Pluto, this contact is in orb for an extended period. Thus, the total effects of the transit, with changed conditions, may seem slow to materialize. The matters governed by the house ruled by Pluto may be most in focus for transformation.

KARMA AT WORK

With contact of a planet to either node, the individual is not totally in control of events and circumstances. The cosmic powers have control. There is more control for the individual when it is the North Node that is transited, but not always complete control. Here, it depends on how much reward is due one. Any time that more rewards are due than one actually receives, the excess goes toward the future good karma savings fund. With contacts to the South Node, the personal control is even less. This brings in opportunities to repay debts, finish up old business, be of service, or make sacrifices. Much of this we are aware of, as needed actions may be linked to obligations created in this life-time—often not that long ago. Extreme frustrations or unexplainable incidents and developments may be as a result of interactions in the far past that were karmic controlled, and about which we may have no conscious recall. The unresolved difficulties and residue are explained by the nature of the planet making the contact; the debts owed are to someone described by the planet. So, if things go unexplainably wrong with authority figures or a benefactor when the South Node is transited by the Sun, this is likely a result of some wrongdoing in the distant past to someone who acted as a benefactor. Each planet can be judged this way and you may find that you have more issues with certain planets than with others. There might be more imbalances in certain types of relationships than in others. If there is not much old karmic residue or outstanding problems tied to a planet and the people or things it represents, then not much distress will come from a transit of that planet over the South Node.

Transits of your nodal rulers may be especially significant and personal.

One final word: Be aware of any other strong aspect a transiting planet makes to another natal or progressed planet at the same time it makes a nodal contact, for this will have a bearing on the overall results. For instance, if the natal Sun and the natal nodes are in square to one another, every time a transiting planet goes over the natal North Node, it is also squaring the natal Sun, therefore reducing the amount of good received due to other obstacles encountered at the same time. You must modify your interpretations accordingly.

In the next chapter we'll talk about Solar Returns, and how we can use the nodes independently of any other chart factors to discover many things about the year to come.

Chapter Twelve

NODES IN THE SOLAR RETURNS

The Solar Return chart is a chart cast for the precise moment that the Sun returns each year to the zodiac position it held when one was born. This usually occurs within a day of the birthday. Such a chart—when calculated accurately, based upon the known birth time, and set for the current residence—reflects conditions, circumstances, and events for the coming year. The Solar Return chart is like an auxiliary birth chart, a personal map just for this one-year period.

Now, it won't be necessary to give you a lot of special instructions to interpret the nodes in your Solar Return because this chart is read very much like a natal chart. Everything we've talked about up to this point can be applied to interpret the nodal influences appearing in your Solar Return. You can find the general themes for the year based on the node that has prominence, discussed in chapter 2, for instance. The only difference is that the themes in the Solar Return are for one year.

In my studies of the Solar Returns, begun in the early 1990s before much was written about them, I started my research by running all of my own previous returns, comparing them to my journals and to my excellent memory of dates and events. In virtually every chart, unless there was a planet conjoined with one of the nodes, it seemed that the easiest and happiest years, when there was more free will available and things were going quite well personally, were the years that the North Node fell in the uppermost portion of the chart, or near the Ascendant. These were the years of increased opportunities and opening doors, where the judgment was good and when helpful people arrived to be of assistance, often resulting in an expansion or improvement of the status.

I noticed just the opposite when it was the South Node holding that upper position in the Solar Return. It showed more trials, when it was hard to achieve goals. It was more difficult to get support for projects and interests, and troublesome connections were sometimes formed. I came to the conclusion that here, it seemed that I was moving into a season of bad choices, when status, reputation, and employment might be adversely impacted as a result. Complications arose in any plan, losses and setbacks occurred, and there seemed to be much less control over the outcomes. Burdens were heavy and life was a struggle.

I continued to study these factors in the returns of others, noting similar conclusions. Again, there are these karmic implications, with the nodes showing whether one is reaping some good karma or paying off some debts. The cosmic forces are quite active, working in your behalf and granting personal favors, if the North Node is most prominent, while they are being particularly severe and restricting if the South Node is prominent. With the latter, there is the chance that you are working against your own best interests and the universe imposes blocks as a reminder. At other times, circumstances created from previous actions deny the opportunity to make much forward progress until the past is resolved. Again, this is similar to what the natal nodal positions indicate, according to which node is above the line of advantage, except that in the Solar Return, the indications are just for this one-year period.

You may be asking what happens when the natal chart shows one node overhead while the current Solar Return has the positions reversed. I asked myself the same question. But, it is not so difficult to understand. The natal map shows the dominant life-long influential node and the Solar Return shows the dominant node for just this one year. If you have North Node most prominent in the natal and then South Node overhead in the Solar Return, this year you will be making a contribution, making some concessions. It is a critical time for decision making, as every choice will have its result right away and possibly have some long-term implications. If South Node is prominent in the natal and

North Node dominant in the Solar Return, you will have a year of incoming energy, opportunities, and new foodstuff to assimilate that replenishes your reserves. Things will go easier and smoother, and it is safe to trust your judgment as you move into and welcome new conditions. Progress can be made for the future.

Of course there are exceptions to how much good or how much stress will be experienced, according to which node is prominent in the Solar Return by being above the line of advantage. Other features in the chart will tell you this. If there are strong squares to the Midheaven, this will present some challenges even if the North Node is uppermost. This would be more severe if the square comes from a planet like Mars, Saturn, or Pluto. Conditions would be more treacherous if the same conditions were present, but with the South Node uppermost.

If the Solar Return North Node is conjunct the Ascendant, this reflects on some cosmically controlled conditions, as discussed in chapter 2. While there may be many advantages, there may be some events occurring that one is only able to respond to. There are learning experiences. Fortunately, a person is in an excellent position to take things in stride and profit or benefit as a result. Taking the reverse position of the nodes, with Solar Return South Node rising on the Ascendant, this again reflects on very karmic conditions and here one is more in a position of having to sacrifice for someone else, making concessions on someone else's behalf. If, however, there's a beneficial planet in conjunction with the North Node in the Seventh House, there should also be some personal benefit or favor.

Frequently, there is significant activity during the year in which a node falls on the Ascendant or Midheaven. There is usually some effort required to get the personal areas to flow harmoniously and come into balance. Relationships require attention or adjustments are needed to bring the domestic life and the professional life into better alignment. The closer this conjunction, the more dramatic the effects for changes, with moves, job changes, relationship changes, or a change of outlook. If there are supportive aspects to the Ascendant or its ruler, however, the changes are welcome and one is indulged. So, take into account any major aspect to the Ascendant, its ruler, the Midheaven, and especially to the nodes themselves.

Having a planet conjunct one of the nodes will always result in more complicated or colorful themes. Since these are temporary influences, you can refer to the descriptions given in chapter 10 to interpret the meaning of a Solar Return node in conjunction with one of the Solar Return planets or points. You can give these Solar Return aspects a fairly wide orb—up to ten degrees in some cases, although the closer they are, the stronger the themes will be. Applying aspects are experienced more intensely than separating aspects.

If there are multiple planets on one end of the nodal axis, or planets on both ends of the nodal axis, judge which aspect is the nearest by degree to find the strongest influence. Each contact will have its effect, but the nearest one should result in the most noticeable effects. If two aspects are close to the same strength, give prominence to the node nearest the Midheaven.

Once the Solar Return chart is cast, it is essential to compare it to the natal horoscope. Use a bi-wheel with the natal chart outside the Solar Return chart or write in the natal planet symbols, near the center of the Solar Return wheel. Check to see if there are connections made from a natal planet to one of the Solar Return nodes, or a connection from a natal node to one of the Solar Return planets. In such cases, the information in chapter 11 will come in handy for interpretation. Say you have the Solar Return Moon in conjunction with your natal South Node. From the last chapter you'd find that you'll experience increased sensitivity, that there will be increased focus on domestic matters and some health concerns, possibly primarily for your mom. Or, if the Solar Return North Node is conjunct your natal Neptune, from chapter 10, you'd know there's a chance of travel, that you're feeling creative and happy about life, etc. For any one of the possible contacts, including aspects besides conjunctions, you could check descriptions in any of the three previous chapters for the fullest coverage. Since the Solar Return is a chart of the transits for a particular moment in time, these are temporary contacts, most like the influences described in the progressions and transits. However, the themes shown in the Solar Return chart will continue for the whole year.

The more nodal contacts there are, the more eventful your year is going to be.

Let's take a look at Paula Abdul's Solar Return just prior to her becoming a judge on *American Idol* and her successful run on the series. The Solar Return North Node is above the line of advantage, giving it prominence and indicating that there is potential for worldly influence and material gain. It is conjunct Solar Return Saturn. In chapter 10 we find that:

> This is quite a powerhouse aspect for good if one has invested much time and effort in doing the right thing, laying strong foundations for success, and playing by the rules of society. One gets all the rewards due for such sustained efforts and hard work.

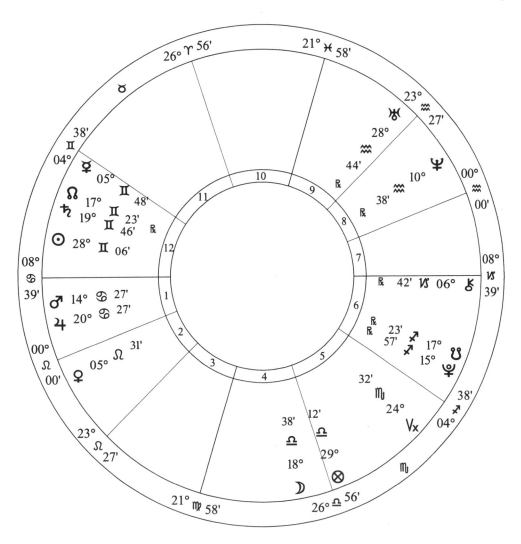

Figure 34: Paula Abdul's Solar Return: June 19, 2002, 6:33:13 AM, Los Angeles, CA

Lessons and learning experiences take place now, but of a sort that is ultimately quite constructive, allowing for more stability. One learns to appreciate patience, and comes to know oneself and one's capabilities better, resulting in an improved self image once the contact is over. There is usually an older person who can be of much guidance, or who plays a significant role in the life at this time. One is willing to take on more responsibility and make commitments. Relationships begun now or circumstances entered into have a good chance for long-term survival, especially if of a professional nature.

All seems true for Paula that year. The trine of the Solar Return Moon to Solar Return North Node and Saturn improves the possibilities. We also observe that Paula's Solar Return Venus is approaching a conjunction to her natal North Node, which falls at 11 degrees Leo. In chapter 11, we learn that:

> "…There is usually extra money coming in and these flows are open. At the same time, you feel quite indulgent, buying new things to beautify your surroundings or yourself. There are connections with young women, hair stylists, decorators, financial advisors, etc. Social life is on the increase, with parties, showers, and so on."

Those things can be easily observed in her life that year. She also had two other nodal conjunctions: Solar Return South Node with Pluto and Solar Return Neptune conjunct her natal South Node, so there were also some personal matters that the public was less aware of. So you see how many things you can find based only on the nodes.

Now, let's examine Patricia Krenwinkel's Solar Return prior to her committing murders for Charles Manson in August of 1969. Her Solar Return South Node falls in the Tenth House, giving it prominence and indicating problematic conditions. South Node aligns closely with Uranus. In chapter 10, we find that:

> "Surprising or unplanned-for developments take place. It is difficult to plan and one must be flexible and learn to go with the flow. This is a disruptive and destructive vibration. Stability is lacking. Unexpected developments tend to come out of the blue and have a negative outcome. It is a time to protect the reputation and avoid unwise risks, as there is increased vulnerability for scandals or black marks against one…"

This would be especially damaging with that conjunction falling so close to the Midheaven.

We also note that Krenwinkel has double nodal aspects attaching Neptune to South Node. Solar Return Neptune is near her natal South Node and Solar Return South Node is near her natal Neptune. Again, in chapter 10, we find that:

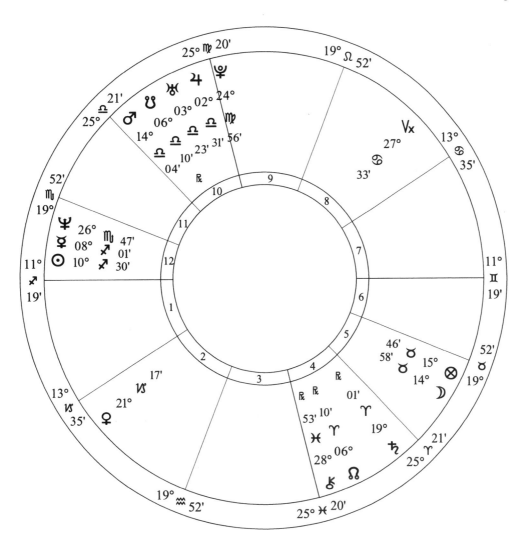

Figure 35: Patricia Krenwinkel's Solar Return: Dec. 2, 1968, 7:49:48 AM, Los Angeles, CA

"There may be involvement with intrigue, with alcohol or drugs. The imagination is misleading, excessive, and one tends toward self-delusion. There may be connections to sinister persons or those who will deceive you and caution should be used in letting someone new into your life at this time. It is a time to question your own judgment, and you need someone trustworthy whose advice you can depend on.... There is a degree of confusion or unsettled matters, one's direction is foggy, and there may be fearful feelings that something is about to go wrong. Travel or journeys turn out less satisfactorily than anticipated."

Solar Return South Node is not that far from Solar Return Mars, an indication of difficulties coming through masculine figures, when significant problems, setbacks and sorrows connected to them may be inescapable. Her North Node control planet is Mars; by joining the South Node and Uranus energy, it became more destructive and uncontrollable and brought her undoing. She basically gave her power to someone else.

So, again, it is impressive how many clues to the year ahead may be found only by an examination of each nodal feature appearing in the Solar Return.

I had an inquiry from an author friend about her Solar Return nodes soon after starting this book. I wondered just how much I could find about her year ahead based only on the nodes. They occupied the Third and Ninth Houses, with North Node in the lower part of the chart. They fell in the opening degrees of Aries and Libra, potent degrees for something potentially very big. Putting two and two together, knowing she's an author of many novels, I knew this had to do with a book project. On the one hand, it could be an uphill year for her, harder to get her projects to fly, but looking on the bright side, it seemed she could make a contribution of special significance.

An idea struck me that I asked her about. I thought that she might be contemplating doing a totally different type of book than her usual novels and that it would be in association with a Libra and that it was something she would do more as a service to humanity than for personal gain. We were both blown away when it turned out that she had been thinking of writing a nonfiction book about how to cope with a parent with Alzheimer's disease, which her mom died of. She hadn't done it yet because it would infringe on her time and the current novel she was working on. But she felt a sense of responsibility or some calling to do it recently as she'd been coming across notes on Alzheimer's, left by her recently deceased father—a Libra!

Now, the thing is, this is not what happened. She continued to work on her time travel novel, which was taking a lot of time and effort, and which was hard to get support for. The chart also reflected the actual developments. The time travel novel was also different for her. It was an adventure, going in new directions with her writing, requiring much energy, all symbolized by Aries North Node in the Third House. The opportunity to do the other book did not present itself. It would have been an ideal time for it, but Mercury squared her Solar Return nodes and they squared the Solar Return Ascendant, showing how present circumstances, based on previous commitments, can interfere with one's higher purpose and forward progress.

So, the house and sign positions are important. The house position of the North Node usually indicates where benefits arrive, while the house containing the South Node shows where drains are possible or opportunities are lacking. Frustrations attach to that house.

Let's say you have Venus in the First House conjunct the South Node. This will have a personal effect; you may be just generally out of sorts and experiencing a lack of harmony in your life. Sacrifices are made for your partner. The sign tells more. If that same aspect fell in the Fourth House, there might be dis-ease or disharmony for a family member; in Scorpio a female family member may require surgery. If it were Mars with the North Node in the First House, you might be very selfish in pursuing your own goals, possibly having little regard for the ideas of others but being very self-accomplished, especially if this conjunction falls in a fire sign.

Each of the points discussed earlier can be examined in the Solar Return. Let's say your Solar Return shows the North Node with the Part of Fortune in the Tenth House. This should be very good for your career and recognition, unless there is something preventing it at the south end of the nodal axis. On the other hand, having the North Node on the Midheaven could hardly bring all of the potential good if the Solar Return South Node aligns with your natal Part of Fortune or with personal natal planets.

Contacts of the nodes to the Sun or Mercury are always significant, since they have to do with the ego/identity and business/job affairs. One of these contacts would influence indications given from which node is prominent by being above the line of advantage. It will not do as much good to have the North Node uppermost if the South Node aligns with one of these bodies.

Struggles might be particularly intense should the South Node fall on the Midheaven with another body; with Pluto there may be power struggles affecting the vocation and the domestic sphere; with Neptune, one may feel especially confused about the direction in life; with Uranus, unexpected developments impact both the professional and the domestic spheres, etc.

If a node falls right on a house cusp, it is especially significant for those affairs.

The Solar Return Moon progresses one degree per month, advancing forward twelve degrees over the course of a year. It may form aspects to the return nodes as it progresses. An aspect formed by the progressing Moon to a node is descriptive of influences during the month of the contact.

If you are married, you can also judge how your partner is doing, going by your own Solar Return. Your Solar Return Seventh House is your partner's First House. So you can start from there to read his or her other houses. Flip the chart upside-down. For instance, your Eleventh House is your partner's Fifth House. If you married later in life and each of you have children, that house most closely reflects your partner's children, your step-children. If a node fell with a planet in that house, you can read that this will not only be of some effect involving your friendships or the groups to which you belong, but perhaps also have something to do with your stepchildren. If you were more interested in how things are going for your child, you'd begin at the Fifth House, which is your child's First House. Turn the chart to bring the Fifth House into the Ascendant position and proceed to read. You'd find that your Solar Return Sixth House is your child's money house, your Solar Return Ninth House is your child's house of children and your Solar Return Eleventh House represents your child's partner, being seven houses from your child's First House. So, you can do multiple interpretations from this one Solar Return chart.

The actual house position of a planet is most significant, more so than the house ruled.

Use the Solar Return like a natal chart and apply transits to it for the year to time events.

Feel free to use the material in any of the previous chapters to interpret your Solar Return nodes. For some remarkable insights, apply these techniques to your last nodal return. The nodal return marks an important crossroad in life when a new phase of karmic growth begins. The planetary patterns in the nodal return provide a map for the coming eighteen and a half years, especially as it relates to your mission, the work you must do, and the help you will have. If you need general interpretation help with your returns, my previous books are listed in the bibliography.

In the coming chapter we will explore the nodes in relationships.

Chapter Thirteen

NODES IN SYNASTRY

Since the nodal axis indicates lessons to be learned in this lifetime, showing the compelling forces of destiny, when there are nodal connections between two people, they may be drawn to one another as if by a magnet. One or both individuals usually want some interaction, and oftentimes one or both get a sense of the importance of the other in their life. The planet person may play a valuable role in the life of the nodes individual, an instrument with which the nodes person can work through some of the issues suggested by their nodal axis. They are not compelled or forced into a relationship and may simply pass and leave the interaction for some future time. However, for a deep and meaningful relationship to come about—intense and karmic oriented, if you will, whether of the most pleasant or the most unpleasant type—a nodal connection virtually always exists.

North Node connections usually mean that this is a new relationship and that the two of you are building good will for a future meeting. Both parties want the exchange but circumstances are such that one or the other will be unable to fulfill or complete it in this lifetime. This relationship is future oriented and to be continued. In this relationship, the two individuals are often on equal footing and there are no prior obligations, just a feeling that they have an opportunity to experience new growth and create something exciting together in the future. The nature of the planet involved describes the relationship they feel bound for.

In this North Node connection, the planet person is bringing new growth opportunities to the North Node person. The nature of the learning experience or qualities the planet person can share is all wrapped up in the nature of the planet involved in the connection. The planet person represents, expresses, or owns qualities that the North Node individual needs to develop in order to grow spiritually, experiencing fulfillment as a result. However, if the North Node person is not ready for the experience, the planet person makes her or him feel nervous or anxious. The North Node person who considers the planet person to be a distraction is in a comfort zone and not yet ready for the new learning experience.

Yet, often there is a breezy, uplifting feel to the association. Both can benefit from the interaction. The planet person is inspired and encouraged by the North Node person to continue to build on the qualities associated with the planet involved in the connection. There's often something in it for the North Node person and some effort needed on the planet person's part. Depending upon the planet involved, these North Node connections are more or less positive in nature. For example, a Saturn connection would entail much more effort for both people than a Sun or Jupiter connection, which would tend to be effortless. With Mercury or Mars involved, the planet person might push North Node too hard with his or her endorsements and recommendations.

South Node connections have a familiar feel to them, as if you've met before and spent considerable time together. It is initially an easy, comfortable association. The planet person represents or offers a comfort zone in the areas associated with the planet, putting the South Node person at ease.

With this contact there is a previous obligation or set of circumstances that the planet person wants to balance out; some debt owed to South Node. The South Node person has contributed something or done favors (described by the planet involved). Now, the energy flow goes mostly toward the South Node person. The planet person may feel an unconscious need to do things for the South Node person in the areas represented by the planet, sometimes using skills or attributes associated with the planet that will somehow help South Node. South Node could drain the energy of the planet person eventually. The South Node person collects on debts, which is why these relationships sometimes appear to involve losses or making sacrifices.

These relationships sometimes become more difficult or impossible to maintain as working out some prior karma is involved in the association. There may be some past life residue that puts pressure on the current relationship. The past may have to be repeated in some way to remind them of their obligation. At worst, they fall into the same old groove. The South Node person may act as a restraining influence toward the planet person, cautiously advising against getting caught up in the latest trend or whim (identified by the planet). South Node freely gives the planet person advice in the areas ruled by the planet. Sometimes this works out well, but other times the planet person may eventually feel suppressed by the negativity. At some point, the South Node person may feel as if the planet person offers no new growth and sees no future in the association, thus the South Node person outgrows the relationship and wants out, or simply drifts away. South Node connections are more appreciated as one grows older and becomes more interested in spiritual growth and development. Though these South Node associations are frequently more difficult, this is not always the case. It all depends on how the past relationship went and whether there was an imbalance when they parted.

Current lifetime North Node connections often become South Node connections next time. So, take a look at how you're handling yourself in your North Node relationships. If there is an imbalance in the give and take in the relationship, the karmic scales will need to be balanced in the future.

When there are both North and South Node connections between two people, there are both future and past associations. They may be part of the karmic growth possibilities for one another for several lifetimes. Sometimes there are multiple contacts of a South Node type or North Node type, or both. Each contact should be analyzed, with priority given the closest.

There are various ways to consider nodal aspects between two people. We'll begin with aspects involving the two natal charts, where one person's planet or point conjuncts the other person's node. You can give these connections a five-degree orb. Nodal connections involving the angles are strongest and most compelling due to the double intensity and magnetism of the axis alignments. Inner planet connections to the other person's nodal axis are more significant and personal than outer planet conjunctions. With the outer planets, whole groups of people—born at certain periods, would have their outer planet conjunct your node or their node conjunct your outer planet. Nevertheless, if two of you should come together, it may be an intense contact.

NODAL CONNECTIONS IN CHART COMPARISONS

Sun—North Node: A new connection that is future oriented. This is a mutually beneficial contact in which each person can be a boost in furthering the career of the other. The North Node person is like a ray of sunshine, promoting optimism for the future, and can help the Sun person to gain more recognition for any creative efforts, while the Sun person provides a boost of energy that helps the other in their social ambitions and getting a better sense of their unique identity. This is a harmonious, free-flowing, encouraging contact. Each person is willing to invest in the relationship even if it is deficient in some departments, because they anticipate a future (lifetime) connection. The luck or fortune for each will be found mainly in the respective houses occupied by the North Node, and occupied and ruled by the Sun. This tie is improved if one of the individuals is a male. There is often a fatherly role taken by one of the individuals.

Sun—South Node: A past life connection in which the South Node person has done much to further the interests and wishes of the Sun person. Now, the South Node person holds the empty cup, happy to accept repayment or whatever the Sun person offers. The Sun person instinctively feels an obligation to the South Node person, usually feeling some attachment and familiarity. The Sun person may take on a fatherly role or just be there to give South Node a boost of support when needed, helping South Node overcome fears. South Node may attempt to restrain the Sun person in the ways that Sun goes about seeking recognition and individuality. Problems may crop up due to unresolved ego or authority issues between them. Sometimes, the South Node person begins to feel that the Sun person is a burden or a block to personal progress, and outgrows the association. This tie is more binding if this is a male/female relationship.

Moon—North Node: An intense emotional tie and instant attraction. While this relationship immediately feels meant to be, the Moon individual often initiates this association and offers nurturing to the North Node individual, feeling that North Node is lacking in that department. Moon tries to be a good role model, demonstrating a commitment to protecting the safety and security of North Node. The North Node person does much to encourage these nurturing/mothering qualities in the Moon person. These become the dominant themes in the relationship, creating an almost unbreakable bond. Sometimes the two become so wrapped up in these roles of providing mutual emotional security and sympathy that they lose touch with the outer world. The Moon person often gives the most, though content with this role. The North Node person usually feels the most nervousness in the exchange. This tie is stronger if one person is female. This relationship may have continuations for many lifetimes.

Moon—South Node: An instant attraction and strong feelings of comfort and familiarity, with mutual sympathy and security as its basis. One of them may have been mother to the other in a previous lifetime. The Moon individual feels an obligation to provide for, shelter, and nurture the South Node person. The South Node individual feels emotionally indebted to the Moon person. The bond is strong but may turn problematic as they fall back into old ruts and habits, trying to keep one another within certain emotional boundaries. They may come to amplify one another's mood swings and emotional fears, rarely coming out to see what is happening in the world around them. The Moon person may eventually feel emotionally suppressed by the negativity of South Node and South Node feels held back, with little chance for new growth.

Mercury—North Node: Mutual intellectual compatibility and an excellent communication connection, with new growth potential. Both people feel the stimulation to exchange ideas and they have much to discuss. The North Node individual gives a boost to the Mercury person in properly expressing himself and getting his ideas accepted—thus Mercury has much to gain. The Mercury person instinctively feels that this is an advantageous association for the future and wants to establish a bond. The Mercury person also encourages the North Node individual to consider new ideas and analyze the possibilities in regard to current trends, in order to capitalize on the latest fads. North Node may feel it is too much effort, however, or it may be going down a different path than he or she sees for themselves for now. Thus, North Node could begin to feel Mercury is too pushy. This is usually an enjoyable interchange—good for business, among friends, and often having a sense of brotherly love.

Mercury—South Node: This gives a comfortable mental link and intellectual exchange. There is a brotherly feeling to the association and they may have been siblings previously. South Node may have assisted Mercury on some intellectual level or business capacity in the past, offering ideas or solutions that benefited Mercury. Now, Mercury feels obliged to repay the service, giving information and sharing ideas freely with South Node. If overdone, Mercury may eventually feel drained in South Node's presence. South Node may exert a somewhat restraining influence on Mercury's ideas though, feeling that Mercury is perhaps too scattered or a dilettante. In business, South Node may feel they know what's best for Mercury. Mercury can end up feeling that South Node is preachy or too conservative in their views, and unreceptive or negative toward Mercury's ideas. But, this is often a mutually beneficial aspect for the exchange of wisdom or logic and along the lines of mentoring, teaching, and advising capacities.

Venus—North Node: Instant attraction. They want to impress one another, having the feeling they will meet again and willing to invest in the relationship. If this is a male/female association, sometimes they wonder what it would be like to be lovers, although realizing it won't happen in this lifetime as circumstances are not convenient for it. This is just the casual meeting stage. They are content to bide their time and enjoy one another's company in the meantime. North Node is impressed with the charm and easygoing way of Venus. Venus likes the way North Node makes them feel, stimulating their awareness of their own attractiveness or creativity. This is a friendly, cooperative relationship, excellent in social and public relations and business associations, especially if this is along Venus lines, relating to art and beautification. They share common interests and a high degree of compatibility.

Venus—South Node: A comfortable association, often social. This contact suggests a past life connection in which the South Node did something nice for Venus. Now, the Venus person wants to make South Node person happy. Venus gives compliments, appreciation, love, money, favors, and gifts of art or beautiful things, anything to indulge and make South Node happy. South Node could eventually drain Venus. South Node gives Venus advice about how Venus handles love and money, usually with cautious or conservative tones. Venus may feel that South Node is a gloomy damper. However, there is a beauty, love, and harmony transference that may be mutually satisfying. At some point South Node may feel there is no further growth and drift away unless the relationship is durable enough on other levels to continue once past imbalances have been neutralized. If this tie is between male and female, this may be a past romance that couldn't get off the ground. Now they feel compelled to get together but circumstances may again deny it fully developing. They may settle for stolen moments or get together in some capacity other than lovers, just to be together. This explains otherwise unexplainable attractions between two who are of different generations or backgrounds.

Mars—North Node: A dynamic and stimulating interaction. This is an animated, spirited, lively exchange where both people are forthright and open with one another. Mars acts as a motivator to the North Node person, often taking the lead role in the association. Mars is ambitious and sees ways that North Node could take some action that would bring improvement to his or her situation; often either financially or career wise. It is obvious to Mars that North Node is in a position to gain by exploiting the current trends, fads, or popular beliefs, and Mars is willing to lend energy to help. Mars does tend to be a little presumptuous and North Node may or may not be ready to take the advice. Sometimes the Mars ego gets in the way of what is meant to be an equal exchange. North Node offers direction and a boost of energy that enables Mars to be more effective in activities. The houses occupied and ruled by Mars and the house of the North Node indicate the activities they are most excited to explore together. If between two females, the Mars individual may introduce North Node to an exciting man.

Mars—South Node: Though it starts out fine, with both enjoying the energy of the other, this is a difficult relationship and seldom lasts. In the past, this may have been an association of love or marriage, between athletic competitors, siblings, or soldiers, in which South Node has put forth energy in behalf of Mars. Some conflict likely occurred and Mars may have mistreated South Node or acted in anger toward him or her. Now the debt comes due South Node, which Mars readily feels is owed. As a result South Node can easily drain the energy of Mars. South Node acts as a restraining influence on Mars, considering Mars to be overly impulsive. Mars considers South Node an imposition and feels stifled. Then Mars feels inner resentment and hostilities building and may eventually erupt in rash actions. If Mars is a woman and the aspect is close, she may give herself sexually to a South Node man. If vice versa, the woman drains the energy of her partner. If between two of the same gender, Mars may try to accommodate South Node's demands, but in this situation the building tension may not be noticed until it is too late. This relationship has a better chance of working if there is some distance between them.

Jupiter—North Node: A mutually supportive and optimistic association between equals. They are building good will and would tend to always be there to fend for or provide for one another. They share similar values, philosophies, and beliefs. They bring out the best in one another. Often North Node provides the philosophical stimulation and Jupiter offers material support. This is excellent for all types of relationships, although the contact often shows up in teacher/student relationships.

Jupiter—South Node: Jupiter can flow luck or fortune to South Node. This association results from a past interaction, often of a legally binding nature, in which some injustice or unethical behavior occurred, usually done to the South Node person by the Jupiter person and along the lines of religion, education, or finances. Now, Jupiter wants to atone for the character flaw and improve the situation and is willing to sacrifice to South Node. Often this comes across as material and financial support. South Node is happy to receive and could over-drain Jupiter although South Node will offer financial or philosophical advice. South Node may even be preachy but Jupiter will put up with it. This aspect is not all bad. It may feel very spiritual and both can benefit. They are often involved in large dissemination projects together. It may take multiple lifetime associations to set things right. Jupiter may be limited to making contributions coming out of the house with Sagittarius on the cusp. Larry and Althea Flynt had the aspect: his Jupiter conjuncts her South Node. With Sagittarius on the cusp of his Seventh House, he offered her marriage and a legal partnership.

Saturn—North Node: This is a serious association in which both parties assume responsibilities. This relationship is slow in forming and some circumstance must exist that forces them together—they would not simply be attracted through any sort of magnetism. The Saturn person gives tangible material help to North Node and North Node helps ease the burden that Saturn carries. Even though this is a future-oriented association with mutual opportunity and mutual interests, it is among the most difficult relationships to maintain due to the seriousness and responsibility it entails. Once it gets going and stabilizes, it may enjoy longevity, though it is usually too stifling for marriage and works better between two who live apart.

Saturn—South Node: A heavy, serious association that may be too much of a damper for either. They tend to discipline one another, creating a double Saturnine situation. South Node advises Saturn on how to better organize and run their business and Saturn feels it his or her debt to serve some concrete, constructive purpose in South Node's life, often in a teaching capacity. Thus, both tend to set boundaries and present limitations, verging on pessimism as each brings out the seriousness in the other. It could become misery loves company, or just plain misery as they can't get past a chilly association. South Node may take what Saturn has to offer and move on. In mature cases where discipline serves mutual purposes, their like-mindedness with regard to custom and tradition could (maybe) turn into a long-lasting, binding association.

Uranus—North Node: Very futuristic. They share unusual interests in movements that are new, popular, or the latest. There may be mutual involvement in computers, astrology, gadgetry, inventions, or a revolutionary idea. Uranus contributes input that is very new age and tries to show North Node that it is a plus to think for him- or herself in these matters, rather than go with the prevailing notions and beliefs. Uranus sometimes makes North Node nervous. North Node guides Uranus to recognize how the outer world will respond to their unique ideas or abilities.

Uranus—South Node: An interesting or unusual association that begins and ends suddenly. Uranus likes to show off their inimitability to South Node, and South Node is fascinated and stimulated by some element of the association. This is a continuation from a previous encounter that was unexpected, often with Uranus having had a revolutionary impact that was either jolting or liberating to South Node. There are explosive dynamics.

Neptune—North Node: This is a passing, casual affair and association, sharing mutual interests, and may require other nodal contacts to hold them together. There are often similar tastes in music, art, movies, and other entertainment. They encourage one another generally, sharing similar interests and may pursue metaphysical topics or enlightenment concepts together. It is excellent for working together in fields like photography, film, etc. They may encourage one another to a fault when it comes to following the crowd.

Neptune—South Node: Neptune feels obliged to shine a ray of spiritual light in the life of South Node. Neptune may have acted as a mystic or spiritual advisor to South Node previously. Neptune may use visionary methods to express esoteric theories and ideas that he or she thinks South Node will benefit from or be uplifted by. South Node may indeed feel uplifted, want more, and could drain Neptune, but Neptune sometimes displays odd or bizarre behaviors. If extreme, South Node may consider Neptune to be deluded, confused, or immature. Neptune may consider South Node as too conservative or negative. There are sometimes different tastes in music, art, movies, and entertainment, although Neptune will usually indulge South Node. At worst,

Neptune has misled South Node in the past and is now insincere, only pretending to try to equalize an unpaid debt, and continues to commit misdeeds.

Pluto—North Node: They want to know more about each other but may not find enough common ground to get past surface superficialities. They admire a quality of resourcefulness and strength they see in one another. Both are interested in improving conditions. Works well if both are involved in fields relating to Pluto: the occult, or having mutual interests in healing. They enjoy sharing strategies, presenting structured ideas, and flowing stamina to one another.

Pluto—South Node: Due to a previous obligation, Pluto feels he or she must yield to South Node. South Node has used his or her power on behalf of Pluto or Pluto has abused South Node with theirs. Pluto is rebellious and iron-willed but wants to balance the score between them now. Unfulfilled karma is connected to the houses occupied and ruled by Pluto, and by the South Node house. Pluto offers South Node energy and assistance. South Node will advise Pluto in ways to increase their power, whether of a monetary sort or some other, but expects something out of it. South Node restrains and makes demands on Pluto and can drain Pluto of power, energy, money, or sex. It can be an explosive combination like fatal attraction, with each person vying for control. Pluto feels obliged to South Node and a theme of domination may turn to mutual destructive jealousy. South Node may eventually feel Pluto is holding him or her back and break away. This contact is most intense and stimulating when one of the individuals is a woman.

Chiron—North Node: There are often mutual interests along the lines of healing the split between body and spirit. They may experiment with healing through crystals, or explore other forms of healing therapies. The Chiron person offers insights to North Node. North Node supports and encourages Chiron. Occasionally, Chiron person goes over the top, making North Node nervous with progressive or extreme ideas or practices they are not ready for.

Chiron—South Node: There is a real feeling of familiarity. They have come together previously, and the theme between them involves wounding and healing. Each shares or understands the pain of the other and there is mutual compassion. Chiron person may feel an obligation to flow healing energy or therapy to South Node, sensing some pain or wounding that needs to be alleviated. The houses occupied by Chiron and South Node reveal the current interaction and suggest unfulfilled karma between them. South Node offers advice to Chiron on how to bring about their own healing, but could exhaust Chiron of their healing energy.

North Node—North Node: Those of the same age or born apart at intervals of eighteen to nineteen years have the same nodal axis. This is often a good connection for friendship, but is not enough on its own to signify anything spectacular. The individuals are on similar life paths, use similar methods, and often understand one another's underlying motives. The house positions of their individual nodes reveal how complementarily they affect one another, or if the association is tense.

South Node—North Node: An attracting combination. The two have known each other before and will likely meet again. There is often mutual sympathy, appreciation, participation, and response to the other in their basic efforts toward advancement and meeting goals.

Ascendant—North Node: Among the most compelling relationships, as both individuals feel drawn to create something new together in the future. Ascendant usually approaches North Node initially. North Node may feel somewhat nervous due to the fated feeling of their meeting. This has slight similarities to the lunar aspect as far as having a familiar, family, or female element. Ascendant persons must be careful that North Node doesn't consume them and close them off from others. They are certain to meet again in the future, perhaps for many lifetimes.

Ascendant—South Node: Instant attraction and compatibility. Ascendant person wants to give and give to the South Node person, even though South Node puts restraints and limitations on Ascendant. Ascendant person owes much to South Node and feels urged to make this repayment right away in order to be free. There are slight similarities to Moon conjunct South Node.

Midheaven—North Node: With this axis alignment, the North Node person has a strong impact on the Midheaven person's home life and domestic sphere, with some disruption or rearrangement involved. Midheaven owes nurturing or has a parenting responsibility to the North Node person. There is often a family tie, frequently with one taking the parenting role.

Midheaven—South Node: Here, Midheaven person wants to help South Node realize more success in the career and vocational areas and to establish more self-respect.

South Node may drain Midheaven, although this relationship works well in certain roles where one takes on the fatherly or mentoring role.

Part of Fortune—North Node: A futuristic luck and fortune association. The pair bring joy to one another. Together they have excellent chances to experience strokes of luck, joy, and prosperity. The North Node person promotes optimism and encourages Part of Fortune to be more creative in seeking their joy and fortune. The Fortuna individual may make North Node nervous with the way he or she spends, but can help North Node adopt freer attitudes about money flows.

Part of Fortune—South Node: South Node person benefits greatly from this association, and Part of Fortune person is happy to share their wealth and good luck with South Node. Since South Node is usually well aware of how willingly Part of Fortune gives up their fortune to make South Node happy, South Node could drain Fortuna, who could eventually experience losses.

Vertex—North Node: A compelling, binding association with unusual karmic implications. Each person is necessary for the other to fulfill the personal destiny and make the journey. Both gain something from their interaction. Both are necessary to carry out an ideal important to both. The association may feel semi-involuntary, driven by circumstances, but one in which they can support each other in attaining their higher aims. The house holding the Vertex gives clues to their previous association and current mutual interests. This is a complementary association.

Vertex—South Node: Quite a destined association and karmic interaction in which each person needs the other in order to fulfill the destiny. Each acts as a complement to the other, providing an element needed for the other to attain the individuality or accomplish a feat. The houses holding the Vertex and the South Node signify the energy flow of the association. The Vertex/node associations have a long history and a long future, as there are many continuations.

If you know lots of people and have collected their birth data, you can use the above pairings to define many relationships and realize why you have felt or feel the undercurrents in your associations. You may find that much is owed to you or vice versa. You might even find that you have lots of previous associations of a particular type. You might have been a teacher to many, an advisor, authority figure, or a benefactor.

HOUSE AND SIGN ASSOCIATIONS

There is general luck in the matters of the house in your chart where your partner's North Node falls. For example, if your friend's North Node falls in your Seventh House, they might introduce you to new people and open up your social flows. If an association is formed with someone whose North Node falls in your Fourth House, they would tend to somehow improve your sense of emotional security or your domestic sphere. There is a boost or facilitation and free-flowing energy brought to the house through your association. Where their South Node falls is an area that undergoes some disturbance, frustration, or sacrifice. There are issues attaching to this house that require compromise or adjustments in order for the association to flow smoothly. If the compromise is too much, the relationship may not last.

In planet/node interactions, the areas of life that are most impacted by the association or the areas shared most in the relationship are shown by the houses occupied and ruled by the planet in the planet person's chart and by the location of the node in the node person's chart.

If one person's North Node is in the sign or house opposite the sign or house of the North Node of the other person, it is a naturally harmonious and workable relationship. For example, if her North Node is in Aries and his North Node is in the Seventh House, this relationship will allow both people to grow together and transcend their nodes. In this case, she is learning to be more independent and he is learning to be more giving, appreciative, and supportive of his partner. It is a naturally complementary relationship that facilitates new growth for both. House reversals work, sign reversals work, or a mix of the two, as in the example.

The sign of the North Node will often match the Sun sign of an individual who will play quite an important role in the life. The Sun person is there to help North Node work through the issues reflected in their nodal axis, and cultivate the traits associated with the North Node sign.

PROGRESSED NODAL CONNECTIONS IN CHART COMPARISONS

There may be timely interchanges with others when nodal connections are formed by progression. If shown in the natal charts that a karmic interaction is in the stars at some point, the actual meeting may occur when a nodal progression brings them together. These orbs must be kept very tight, within a one-degree orb.

A pair of friends, Mary and Jane, had a natal node connection. Mary's Venus was on Jane's South Node. They came together in this life at precisely the time that Jane's progressed Midheaven met with Mary's South Node. Thirty years later both are still enjoying the friendship.

A male and female, Bob and Sue, had a natal nodal connection involving his Part of Fortune and her North Node. They met when her progressed North Node got within half a degree of his natal Part of Fortune. They have found a lot of joy together, and since this is a long-lasting progressed aspect, their run of happy times should continue for the rest of their lives.

Nancy and Diane, with a wide Neptune/South Node conjunction, met in this lifetime when Neptune and South Node came together, within one degree, by progression.

My friend Steve, who helped me with this book project by running lists and designing a couple of the diagrams, became a friend after he read my book about eclipses. We had a natal nodal connection of North Node to Sun. At the time we met, my progressed Ascendant was approaching his natal North Node.

With a close strong nodal connection between two people who are in the same vicinity, they may meet multiple times, or they may have a strong feeling of recognition for no apparent reason. Ken, a realtor, first met Paul, with whom he shared a South Node/Jupiter connection, when Paul moved to the area. At the time, Paul's progressed Jupiter was exactly conjunct Ken's progressed South Node. They parted after Ken found Paul a home. Eleven years later, they met again when Paul's new wife phoned a realtor from an advertisement in the mail. Lo and behold, it was Ken. Ken and Paul recognized one another immediately. This time, Paul's progressed Uranus and Sun was conjunct Ken's North Node, and the two struck up a long-term friendship.

It is possible that unless a progression brings them together, two people with a natal nodal conjunction might never actually meet or come together in the current lifetime. I can't say for sure, as this could require endless research, but it sure seems that some nodal contact is always showing up in the progressions when these meetings occur. Either the angles or the planet involved in the original aspect are often involved.

It is interesting to note that a temporary aspect by progression works in a similar way to the natal descriptions given previously. Okay, let's say you are a woman, and you meet a guy who you notice has his progressing Venus going over your South Node. He may not know what is going on, but will feel he wants to give you the moon. He feels a compulsion to be of help to you, and it may be just the kind of help you could use. You charm him without trying. He may also feel romantically attracted to you and want to fill your cup. He can't help himself. You could take advantage of this and drain him of all the favors, gifts, goodwill, and love he has. However, this is a passing phase and he may not feel the same later, definitely not to this degree. This aspect generally lasts only a year or two, unless by chance his progressing Venus is nearing a retrograde station. You are in the controller's position here; you will have to be the restraining influence, lest harm be done with you burdening yourself with bad karma. It is even an ethical responsibility, especially now that you know the node's secrets. Check the natal charts to see what shows there. Is there a natal nodal connection and if so, what does it say? Is this a sustainable association and in what capacity will it work best? You are being brought together for some cosmic purpose. Once in a while this is a situation in which he has some general karmic atonement to make to women, and you have some general favors owed you by men. By coming together, you may be facilitating the larger workings of the universe that eventually leads to the enlightenment of all.

Chapter Fourteen

EXTRA TIPS AND TRICKS

Here are a few extra tips for judging the significance of the lunar nodes and their aspects in the natal chart, and for spotting important nodal transits to the natal chart that would otherwise be overlooked. These tips and tricks will be most appreciated by the serious student and by intermediate and advanced astrologers. A couple of the techniques can be applied to any type of chart and will bring special insights to nodal features in progressed and return charts.

A SHORT STORY ABOUT PAST-LIFE THERAPY

I want to point out here that it is rarely a good idea to get too caught up in treading into the past lives if there's an inner planet conjunct the South Node, unless there is also a planet on the other end. Even then, it is chancy. One can get pulled too much into the past, preventing progress now. Bonnie, a newer client, has Venus conjunct South Node on her Ninth House cusp, with North Node/Moon on her Third House cusp. Well, we learned many things. She had the stumbling blocks in her relationships and in social situations, although she was very successful as a purchasing planner for a metaphysical re-tailer, predicting future trends and advising on new product lines. Her nodes were perfect for this. You see, she had that open pipeline to creative inspiration and past knowledge, but it was coming from a very lofty place. It was like a link to a past guru, dwelling on art and beautiful things. It was very tempting to live back there in that place instead of coming out, mingling with others, and getting first-hand experience, as her North Node encouraged. As a child she'd even had an imaginary guru. Now, she spent her time read-ing books, isolated, at lunchtime. She lived alone and meditated at home before making beautiful amulets and prototype products. She fell asleep asking for assistance from her guides to bring her certain information. She'd gotten caught up in researching past lives, and had vivid dreams, some of which made her physically ill. It seemed she was starting to live more of her life in trance states than in the here and now. While meditation in moderation was favored, especially as it contributed to her work, it was not so favorable when overly indulged in. Even with planets on both ends of her nodes to help maintain an even balance, she was overly tempted to fall back on her South Node. She also had a very intriguing fear that demonstrates how we do sense the messages from the cosmos that are available through the nodal axis. Either node conjunct the Moon suggests some phobia—when I asked about this, Bonnie said she indeed had some; her greatest fear was that she might one day lose touch with the third dimension altogether. This was the cos-mos' way of urging her to stay closely involved and connected with other people, which is the area intended for her growth. She has much wisdom to share now with each per-son contacted, as she contributes to peace and harmony in society.

So, listen to those inner guides. They may only be a whisper, but those inner feelings may tell you much about your place in the larger scheme of things and what the right thing is for you to do. However, if the voices begin screaming at you, or coaxing you to do things that are going to hurt you or someone else, that is neither your guide nor your inner voice. It is a demon entity that you're somehow allowing to take control of your mind. It leads nowhere pretty. Also, if your inner voice assures you that it's okay to continue living on your South Node, that is pretty normal and natural—but it is mostly wishful thinking.

HOW NEPTUNE CLOUDS THE ISSUE

It seems that even in these studies, the illusive Neptune lives up to its reputation for throwing confusion into the data. Many of the individuals who made the public figures listings with South Node conjunct Neptune also had Uranus conjunct South Node—thus it seems this particular combination is especially gifted artistically. A large percentage of this group was born in 1932–1933, or in 1949, when both aspects were in place. It was largely the unique combination that contributed to the great works that brought them notice. We may have to wait quite a while before this occurs again. The next time Uranus conjuncts South Node is in early 2015 and the next time Neptune conjuncts South Node will be in late 2016. The two aspects do not form at the same time during the coming century. There are, however, a group of individuals with North Node conjunct both Uranus and Neptune, born in late 1991, who are coming to maturity. We could expect to see a high number of creative individuals from this group make progressive contributions that better the world.

SOLSTICE POINTS

Just in case you don't have enough things to watch in your chart, I'll give you one more and you will find this most fascinating in terms of nodal transits.

Also known as the *Anticisions*, the solstice point of a planet is its *reflex* position on the opposite side of the Cancer/Capricorn axis. It is the planet's distance from 0 degree Cancer or 0 degree Capricorn, whichever it is closer to, taken the same distance over to the opposite side of that axis, using the remaining numbers of degrees of the sign it's in to determine the solstice point. Here are the sign pairings to determine the solstice points.

Capricorn—Sagittarius
Aquarius—Scorpio
Pisces—Libra
Aries—Virgo
Taurus—Leo
Gemini—Cancer

A natal planet in Capricorn has its solstice point in Sagittarius and vice versa. A planet in Aquarius has its solstice point in Scorpio and vice versa, and the same with the other pairings noted above. If natal Mercury were at 7 Taurus 21, its solstice point would be 22 Leo 39, which is the remaining number of degrees of the sign it is in, but carried over to the other side. By subtracting the natal planet's degrees and minutes from 29:60, you arrive at the correct degree and minute of the solstice point in the other sign.

A natal planet becomes *activated* when a transiting or progressed planet meets with its solstice point. The solstice points are like *invisible attractors* in the chart, attracting attention to the affairs of the planet they belong to. It is through the solstice point that a planet attracts attention to its own importance. The nature of the natal planet, its sign, house position, and aspects help determine the type of events to expect as there is always a link back to it. Events that are unexplainable otherwise are frequently explained by the impact of a transiting planet to a solstice point.

So keep an eye on nodal transits to your solstice points to stay ahead of the game. Refer to the description in chapter 10 matching the node and the planet involved in the contact. You can also find your nodal solstice points and watch planetary transits to those.

IN THE DEGREE OF THE NODES

"In the degree of the nodes" refers to any planet or significant point that falls in the same degree of the nodes, no matter what sign, and no matter if a major aspect exists between them. The planet must be in the very same degree as the nodes, regardless of the number of minutes. This shows a fated appointment or fateful event. The planet is imbued with both the excitability of the North Node and the troublesome influence of the South Node. The planet involved often tends to go a little wacko. The things in life represented by the planet are unusual, erratic, excitable, and prone to act out.

Astrologer and author Ivy Jacobson, who did research in this area, suggested that a planet or angle in the same degree as the nodes points to a catastrophe, casualty, fatality, or tragedy in a natal chart, and that the effects are potentially more far-reaching when a malefic planet (like Mars, Saturn, or Pluto) is involved.

There are ample examples in history in which an individual with a natal planet in the degree of the natal nodes acts out in unusual ways or undergoes severe trials and problematic episodes. John Wilkes Booth had Uranus in the degree of his nodes. Examples of a few others with natal planets or points in the degree of the nodes include: Martha Stewart (Part of Fortune), George W. Bush (Uranus), Bonnie Lee Blakely (Venus).

A planet in the degree of the nodes will be prone to take on some of the more negative connotations of having the planet in conjunction with one of the nodes; in particular it takes on the liabilities of a South Node conjunction.

These same rules can be applied to the solar return chart. Any planet in the degree of the nodes should sound an alarm bell when doing the interpretation. The planet and its house position, along with the sign it occupies, is quite significant in showing where, with whom, and in what way a crisis might erupt. There is some trouble brewing here. Mars would suggest a masculine figure, some friction or danger. If in the Eleventh House, this may involve a friend. Uranus would signify something totally unexpected; in the Seventh, it affects the partner. Jupiter says it's a legal or financial issue, the Moon an unhappy move or other domestic changes. The sign is less important than the planet's significance and its house. The angles in the degree of the nodes are also symbolic, and when the Vertex is involved it may be a particularly fateful year.

This tip will best be applied in the natal or Solar Return chart, although you may experiment in other charts. There are always numerous indicators for any one event, and application of this rule should be judged alongside the rest of the factors in any kind of chart.

ELECTION CHARTS

It should not surprise you that the material on the nodes found throughout this book can be applied to election charts for any kind of enterprise or undertaking. For instance, if you can combine the nodal factor of having the North Node near the Moon in the upper portion of an election chart that is otherwise suitable for the particular occasion you are planning, it would only enhance the long-term result. There are specific guidelines and books for choosing appropriate planetary pictures for an event, so this is something to approach with care, but let's take a brief example:

Say you are planning your wedding, having found appropriate aspects in your progressions to enter a happy union. This might be Sun or Mars on an angle, ruler of the Seventh House on an angle, Venus on the MC, with progressing Moon through Libra in nice aspect to several natal planets. Your partner's chart concurs with major Moon aspects and a mix of aspects involving inner planets with the angles. Especially judge the condition of the progressed Seventh House ruler for appropriate aspects for marriage. However, you've done all this, and now you're looking for the best day for the ceremony. For an event of such magnitude the transiting planets will also be forming major aspects to both charts, so you can use those to narrow your search. Multiple transiting planets should form favorable aspects to both charts. You've found a day when there are favorable aspects between transiting Sun and transiting Moon and they are making significant connections to both charts. Transiting Venus and Mars are also harmonious to one another and to your Sun and your partner's Moon. In fact you see that Venus is approaching someone's MC, and trine the other's Moon, Venus, or Mars. Now, unless you can find a more suitable day before or after, go in to find the best time. Try to get a Fortune Planet on an angle and make sure it is well supported by other planets. Finally, consider the nodal placements and aspects in your election chart. You might nudge by a few minutes to get an auspicious aspect of the nodes to the MC, the Vertex, or Part of Fortune to secure extra benefits and joy. What do these nodes say?

DETERMINING THE STRENGTH
OF PLANETARY ASPECTS TO THE NODES

You will notice that the sextile, square, and trine aspects between the nodes and the planets are not always of much influence. The fact that they are sometimes ineffective has thrown the nodal influences into some obscurity among astrologers. I noticed that only the conjunction was consistently reliable, although the other aspects worked sometimes. Then I came across a short passage in George White's little book that helped explained why. Since it is sometimes the astronomical elements of astrology that give the most difficulty, I will try to explain this with the help of an illustration.

Normally we are concerned with where the planets are in the zodiac band, and in what degree of a sign, based on their longitude position. However, they can also be measured according to how far north or south they are of the equator and by how far north or south of the ecliptic.

The equator is an imaginary line that runs around the center of the earth, equidistant from the two poles upon which the earth appears to rotate. Projected out into space, it is called the celestial equator. The planets in their orbits spend half their orbital period above the equator and half their time below the equator. Declination is the measurement

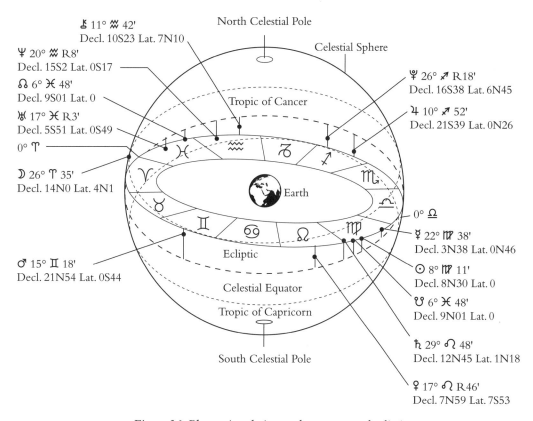

♇ 11° ♒ 42'
Decl. 10S23 Lat. 7N10

North Celestial Pole

Celestial Sphere

♀ 26° ♐ R18'
Decl. 16S38 Lat. 6N45

Ψ 20° ♒ R8'
Decl. 15S2 Lat. 0S17

☊ 6° ♓ 48'
Decl. 9S01 Lat. 0

♅ 17° ♓ R3'
Decl. 5S51 Lat. 0S49

0° ♈

Tropic of Cancer

♃ 10° ♐ 52'
Decl. 21S39 Lat. 0N26

☽ 26° ♈ 35'
Decl. 14N0 Lat. 4N1

Earth

0° ♎

♂ 15° ♊ 18'
Decl. 21N54 Lat. 0S44

Ecliptic

☿ 22° ♍ 38'
Decl. 3N38 Lat. 0N46

⊙ 8° ♍ 11'
Decl. 8N30 Lat. 0

Celestial Equator

☋ 6° ♓ 48'
Decl. 9N01 Lat. 0

Tropic of Capricorn

South Celestial Pole

♄ 29° ♌ 48'
Decl. 12N45 Lat. 1N18

♀ 17° ♌ R46'
Decl. 7N59 Lat. 7S53

Figure 36: Planets in relation to the equator and ecliptic

in degrees and minutes north or south of the celestial equator that a body occupies at any point in time.

The ecliptic is the path that the Sun appears to travel upon during its yearly journey around the Earth. The rest of the planets travel near this same band, but are usually slightly above or below the ecliptic. Latitude is their measurement north or south of the ecliptic.

The ecliptic is at an angle 23 degrees 27 minutes with respect to the Earth's equator. When the Sun reaches zero Cancer, it is at 23 degrees 27 minutes north of the celestial equator and when it is at zero Capricorn, it is at 23 degrees 27 minutes south of the celestial equator. These Sun positions coincide with the longest and shortest days of the year, respectively; the first day of summer and the first day of winter. The point where the celestial equator and ecliptic meet is along the axis described by zero Aries (first day of spring) and zero Libra (first day of fall).

The nodes are always points upon the ecliptic. They maintain zero degrees of latitude. The Midheaven, the Ascendant, Part of Fortune, and Vertex are likewise points upon the ecliptic (thus they possess no latitude), so that any aspects of the nodes to these points always work.

The aspects of the nodes to the luminaries are likewise effective. The Moon's relationship to its own node is always noteworthy, as explained in chapter 7. While the Sun maintains a zero degree latitude, it can have as much as 23½ degrees of declination. Its aspects to the nodes *always* work, and any aspect is strengthened if the declination of the Sun is within one degree of the declination of the node. In that case, the *parallel* is formed, a strong aspect similar to a conjunction.

When it comes to aspects of the nodes to the planets, besides the conjunction, the other aspects may or may not be influential, depending upon the planet's declination and latitude. When the declination of the nodes matches the declination of a planet, within one degree, this is a parallel. In this case, even if no aspect exists between the node and the planet, the parallel relationship will send vitalizing strength and energy to the planet and the planet will be affected according to the condition of the node and the promise it holds. If the planet and the node are forming an aspect and have matching declinations, this is an extra-effective aspect, with the parallel adding strength to the nature of the actual aspect.

When a planet is within half a degree of matching the nodal latitude of +0 and there is a sextile, square, or trine aspect between the two, it is also an effective aspect. The more latitude of the planet, north or south of the ecliptic, the less effective one of these aspects becomes.

Taking a look at the diagram, Uranus and Neptune have little latitude, so an aspect they form to the nodes would be strong and noticeable. (Uranus never has much latitude, so its aspects to the nodes are always effective.) But there is no aspect to the nodes here.

Jupiter, at 10 degrees of Sagittarius, is in square aspect to the lunar nodes at 6 degrees Pisces/Virgo. Jupiter's declination is not within one degree of the declination of either node, so there is no parallel, but Jupiter is barely above the ecliptic at 0N26 latitude. This makes its aspect to the lunar nodes an effective square. The actual aspect is only within a five-degree orb however, so still not as strong as it would be if the aspect was nearer to an exact square.

An ephemeris and the better astrology programs provide information about declinations and latitudes of the planets for any point in time. Use this tip to judge the strength of natal nodal aspects, or nodal aspects in other types of charts.

North Node Ephemeris 1935 to 2054

Use the tables on the following pages to locate the sign and degree of the North Node for any date in question. Find the block corresponding to your year and month of birth. Inside that block, the number on the left is the day of the month and the number on the right is the degree of the North Node. Locate the date nearest your date of birth. Then, unless a sign symbol appears right next to that date, scan your eye upward to identify the last sign symbol entry. This gives you the sign and degree of the North Node for any date in question. The South Node is always exactly opposite the North Node, in the same degree, six signs away.

If you need help identifying the sign symbol:

♈	Aries	♎	Libra
♉	Taurus	♏	Scorpio
♊	Gemini	♐	Sagittarius
♋	Cancer	♑	Capricorn
♌	Leo	♒	Aquarius
♍	Virgo	♓	Pisces

	1935	1936	1937	1938	1939	1940	1941	1942	1943	1944
Jan.	01 ♒ 02 / 16 01	15 ♑ 12 / 30 11	09 ♐ 23 / 24 22	04 ♐ 04 / 19 03	14 ♏ 14 / 29 13	09 ♎ 25 / 24 24	03 ♎ 06 / 18 05	13 ♍ 16 / 28 15	08 ♌ 27 / 23 26	03 ♌ 08 / 18 07
Feb.	01 01 / 16 00	14 11 / 29 10	08 22 / 23 21	03 02 / 18 02	13 13 / 28 12	08 24 / 23 23	02 04 / 17 04	12 15 / 27 14	07 26 / 22 25	02 06 / 17 06
Mar.	01 ♑ 29 / 16 28 / 31 27	15 09 / 30 08	09 20 / 25 19	04 01 / 20 00	14 11 / 30 10	10 22 / 24 21	05 03 / 19 02	15 13 / 29 12	08 24 / 24 23	03 05 / 18 04
Apr.	16 26 / 30 26	14 07 / 29 06	06 18 / 24 18	04 ♏ 29 / 19 28	17 09 / 29 09	08 20 / 23 20	03 01 / 18 01	13 11 / 28 11	07 22 / 23 22	02 03 / 17 03
May	14 25 / 31 24	14 06 / 29 05	09 17 / 24 16	04 28 / 19 27	14 08 / 29 07	08 19 / 23 18	04 00 / 18 ♍ 29	15 10 / 28 09	08 21 / 23 20	02 02 / 17 01
June	16 23 / 30 23	13 04 / 28 03	09 15 / 23 14	03 26 / 18 25	13 06 / 28 05	09 17 / 22 16	02 28 / 17 27	11 08 / 27 07	07 19 / 22 18	01 00 / 16 ♋ 30
July	14 22 / 31 21	13 02 / 28 02	08 14 / 23 13	03 24 / 18 24	13 05 / 28 04	10 16 / 22 15	02 27 / 17 26	12 07 / 27 06	07 18 / 22 17	01 29 / 17 28 / 31 27
Aug.	14 20 / 30 19	12 01 / 27 00	07 12 / 22 11	02 23 / 17 22	12 03 / 27 02	05 14 / 21 13	01 25 / 15 24 / 31 23	10 05 / 26 04	06 16 / 21 15	16 26 / 30 25
Sept.	13 19 / 30 18	11 ♐ 29 / 26 28	06 10 / 21 10	01 21 / 16 21	11 01 / 26 01	07 12 / 20 12	17 23 / 30 22	11 03 / 25 03	04 14 / 20 14	14 25 / 29 24
Oct.	01 18 / 16 17	11 28 / 26 27	06 09 / 21 08	01 20 / 16 19 / 31 18	12 00 / 26 ♎ 29	05 11 / 20 10	15 21 / 30 20	12 02 / 25 01	06 13 / 20 12	13 23 / 29 22
Nov.	01 ♑ 16 / 16 15	10 26 / 25 25	05 07 / 20 06	15 17 / 30 17	09 28 / 25 27	07 09 / 19 08	16 19 / 29 19	10 00 / 24 ♌ 30	03 11 / 19 10	14 21 / 28 21
Dec.	01 14 / 16 13 / 31 13	10 24 / 25 24	05 06 / 20 05	15 16 / 30 15	13 27 / 25 26	04 08 / 19 07	14 18 / 29 17	08 29 / 24 28	05 10 / 19 09	15 20 / 28 19

	1945	1946	1947	1948	1949	1950	1951	1952	1953	1954
Jan.	12 ♋ 18 / 27 17	07 ♊ 29 / 22 28	02 ♊ 10 / 17 09	12 ♉ 20 / 29 19	06 ♉ 01 / 22 00	01 ♈ 12 / 16 11 / 31 11	11 ♓ 22 / 26 21	06 ♓ 03 / 21 02	15 ♒ 13 / 30 13	10 ♑ 24 / 25 23
Feb.	11 17 / 26 16	06 28 / 21 27	01 08 / 16 08	02 19 / 28 18	05 ♈ 30 / 20 29	15 10	09 21 / 25 20	04 02 / 20 01	15 12	10 23 / 24 22
Mar.	11 15 / 28 14	07 26 / 23 25	03 07 / 18 06	11 17 / 27 16	08 28 / 22 27	02 09 / 17 08	12 19 / 27 18	05 00 / 21 ♒ 29	01 11 / 16 10 / 31 09	11 21 / 26 20
Apr.	11 13 / 27 13	09 24 / 22 24	04 05 / 17 05	13 15 / 26 15	05 26 / 21 26	01 07 / 16 07	10 17 / 26 17	06 28 / 20 28	14 09 / 30 08	11 20 / 25 19
May	13 12 / 27 11	06 23 / 22 22	03 04 / 17 03	11 14 / 26 13	07 25 / 21 24	01 06 / 17 05 / 31 04	11 16 / 26 15	04 27 / 20 26	14 07 / 30 06	09 18 / 25 17
June	11 10 / 26 09	08 21 / 21 20	01 02 / 16 01	12 12 / 25 11	07 23 / 20 22	15 03 / 30 03	09 14 / 25 14	05 25 / 19 24	15 05 / 29 05	10 16 / 24 16
July	11 09 / 26 08	06 20 / 21 19	01 00 / 16 ♉ 30 / 31 29	13 11 / 25 10	06 22 / 20 21	15 02 / 30 01	11 13 / 25 12	03 24 / 19 23	14 04 / 29 03	08 15 / 24 14
Aug.	12 07 / 25 06	07 18 / 20 17	16 28 / 30 27	13 09 / 24 08	06 20 / 19 19	16 00 / 29 ♓ 30	08 11 / 24 10	04 22 / 18 21	14 02 / 28 01	09 13 / 23 12
Sept.	15 06 / 24 05	08 16 / 19 15	17 27 / 29 26	07 08 / 23 07	07 18 / 18 18	16 29 / 28 28	08 10 / 23 09	02 20 / 17 20	12 29 / 27 ♑ 30	08 12 / 22 11
Oct.	10 04 / 24 03	05 15 / 19 14	18 25 / 29 24	11 06 / 23 05	06 17 / 18 16	17 27 / 28 26	09 08 / 23 07	03 19 / 17 18	12 29 / 27 28	07 10 / 22 09
Nov.	13 02 / 23 02	08 13 / 18 12	12 23 / 28 23	10 04 / 22 04	04 15 / 17 14	13 25 / 27 25	09 06 / 22 06	01 17 / 16 17	11 27 / 26 27	05 08 / 21 08
Dec.	07 01 / 23 00	09 12 / 18 11	14 22 / 28 21	08 03 / 22 02	06 14 / 17 13	14 24 / 27 23	10 05 / 22 04	01 16 / 16 15 / 31 14	11 26 / 26 25	07 07 / 21 06

	1955		1956		1957		1958		1959		1960		1961		1962		1963		1964	
Jan.	05 ♑ 05	20 04	15 ♐ 15	30 04	09 ♏ 26	24 25	04 ♏ 07	19 06	14 ♎ 17	29 17	09 ♍ 28	24 27	03 ♍ 09	18 08	13 ♌ 19	28 19	08 ♌ 00	23 ♋ 30	03 ♋ 11	18 10
Feb.	03 04	19 03	15 14	29 13	08 25	23 24	04 06	18 05	12 16	28 15	08 27	23 26	02 08	17 07	13 18	27 17	08 29	22 28	03 10	17 09
Mar.	05 02	21 01	16 12	30 11	09 23	25 22	06 04	20 03	15 14	30 13	10 25	24 24	04 06	19 05	14 16	29 15	09 27	24 26	02 08	18 07
Apr.	07 00	20 ♐ 30	16 11	29 10	11 22	24 21	05 02	19 02	15 13	29 12	08 24	23 23	05 04	18 04	12 15	28 14	09 26	23 25	03 06	17 06
May	06 29	20 28	13 09	29 08	09 20	24 19	03 01	19 00	14 11	29 10	07 22	23 21	04 03	18 02	13 13	28 12	08 24	23 23	02 06	17 04
June	09 27	19 26	15 07	28 07	10 18	23 18	03 ♎ 29	18 28	16 09	28 09	10 20	22 20	04 01	17 00	12 11	27 11	07 22	22 22	01 03	16 02
July	05 26	19 25	17 06	28 05	11 17	23 16	06 28	18 27	13 08	28 07	08 19	22 18	02 ♌ 30	17 29	12 10	27 09	07 21	22 20	01 02 / 16 01	02 / 31 00
Aug.	06 24	18 23	18 04	27 03	10 15	22 14	08 26	17 25	14 06	27 05	07 17	21 16	01 28	16 27	11 08	26 07	06 19	21 18	15 ♊ 30	30 29
Sept.	09 22	17 22	15 03	26 02	12 14	21 13	01 24	16 24	13 05	26 04	05 16	20 15	16 26	30 25	11 07	25 06	04 18	20 17	14 28	29 27
Oct.	12 21	17 20	10 01	26 00	08 12	21 11	01 23	16 22	11 03	26 02	05 14	20 13	17 24	30 23	09 05	25 04	06 16	20 15	13 26	29 25
Nov.	01 19	16 19	10 ♏ 30	25 29	10 10	20 10	19 21	30 20	15 01	25 00	07 12	19 12	16 23	29 23	09 03	24 03	05 14	19 14	14 24	28 23
Dec.	01 18 / 17 17	31 16	12 28	25 27	15 09	20 08	20 19	30 18	10 ♍ 30	25 29	03 11	19 10	13 21	29 20	10 02	24 01	04 13	19 12	14 23	28 22

	1965		1966		1967		1968		1969		1970		1971		1972		1973		1974	
Jan.	12 ♊ 21	27 21	07 ♊ 02	22 02	02 ♉ 13	17 12	12 ♈ 23	27 23	06 ♈ 04	21 04	01 ♓ 15 / 15 14	31 14	11 ♒ 25	26 25	06 ♒ 06	21 06	15 ♑ 17	30 16	10 ♐ 27	25 27
Feb.	11 20	26 19	05 01	21 ♉ 30	01 12	16 11	12 22	26 21	06 03	20 02	16 13		11 24	25 23	06 05	20 04	14 15		08 26	24 25
Mar.	13 18	28 17	09 29	23 28	02 10	18 09	12 20	27 19	07 01	22 00	03 12	17 11	13 22	27 21	07 03	21 02	01 14 / 17 13	31 13	10 24	26 23
Apr.	14 17	27 16	08 28	22 27	04 09	17 08	14 19	26 18	06 ♓ 30	21 29	01 11	16 10	11 21	26 20	05 01	20 00	15 12	30 11	09 23	25 22
May	16 15	27 14	10 26	22 25	02 07	17 06	12 17	26 16	06 28	21 27	01 09 / 15 08	31 07	11 19	26 18	05 ♑ 30	20 29	16 10	30 09	11 21	25 20
June	17 13	26 13	08 24	21 24	01 05	15 05	12 15	25 15	06 26	20 26	18 07	30 06	13 17	25 17	03 28	19 28	13 09	29 08	09 19	24 19
July	14 12	26 11	10 23	21 22	01 04 / 18 03	31 02	14 14	25 13	07 25	20 24	19 05	30 04	12 16	25 15	04 27	19 26	15 07	29 06	08 18	24 17
Aug.	10 10	25 09	05 21	20 20	19 01	30 00	11 12	24 11	05 23	19 22	16 03	29 03	12 14	24 13	02 25	18 24	13 05	28 05	09 16	23 16
Sept.	15 09	24 08	03 20	19 19	14 ♈ 30	29 29	14 11	23 10	04 22	18 21	16 02	28 01	10 13	23 12	03 24	17 23	11 04	27 03	06 15	22 14
Oct.	17 07	24 06	05 18	19 17	20 28	29 27	13 09	23 08	07 20	18 19	18 00	28 ♒ 30	11 11	23 10	02 22	17 21	14 02	27 01	08 13	22 12
Nov.	07 06	23 05	09 16	18 16	21 27	28 26	08 08	22 07	04 18	17 18	15 29	27 28	10 10	22 09	01 20	16 20	12 00	26 ♐ 30	05 12	21 11
Dec.	09 04	23 03	11 15	18 14	17 25	28 24	06 06	22 05	06 17	17 16	16 27	27 26	07 08	22 07	01 19 / 17 18	31 17	12 29	26 28	07 10	21 09

	1975	1976	1977	1978	1979	1980	1981	1982	1983	1984
Jan.	05 ♐ 08	15 ♏ 19	09 ♎ 29	04 ♎ 10	14 ♍ 21	09 ♍ 01	03 ♌ 12	13 ♋ 23	08 ♋ 03	03 ♊ 14
	20 08	30 18	24 29	19 10	29 20	29 00	18 12	28 22	23 03	18 14
Feb.	03 07	13 17	08 28	04 09	14 19	08 ♌ 30	02 11	13 21	07 02	03 13
	19 06	29 16	23 27	18 08	28 18	23 29	17 10	27 20	22 01	17 12
Mar.	06 05	15 15	09 26	05 07	16 17	10 28	04 09	14 19	08 00	02 11
	21 04	30 15	25 25	20 06	30 17	24 27	19 08	29 19	24 ♊ 30	18 10
Apr.	06 04	17 14	11 25	04 06	15 16	07 27	05 08	12 18	08 29	03 10
	20 03	29 13	24 24	19 05	29 15	23 26	18 07	28 17	23 28	17 09
May	09 02	16 12	09 23	04 04	17 14	10 25	04 06	13 16	07 27	02 08
	20 01	29 11	24 22	19 03	29 13	23 24	18 05	28 15	23 26	17 07
June	04 00	18 11	11 22	06 02	12 13	08 24	05 04	13 15	07 26	01 06
	19 ♏ 30	28 10	23 21	18 02	28 12	22 23	17 04	27 14	22 25	16 06
July	04 29	14 09	09 20	08 01	15 11	07 22	03 03	12 13	09 24	01 05
										16 04
	19 28	28 08	23 19	18 00	28 10	22 21	17 02	27 12	22 23	31 03
Aug.	10 27	16 07	10 18	02 ♍ 29	14 09	11 20	01 01	11 11	05 22	15 03
							16 00			
	18 26	27 07	22 18	18 28	27 09	21 20	31 ♋ 30	26 11	21 22	30 02
Sept.	12 26	10 06	06 17	01 28	11 08	07 19	17 29	13 10	06 21	14 01
	17 25	26 05	21 16	16 27	26 07	20 18	30 28	25 09	20 20	29 00
Oct.	07 24	12 04	08 15	01 26	16 06	05 17	17 27	15 08	06 19	14 ♉ 29
	17 23	26 03	21 14	31 25	26 05	20 16	30 27	25 07	20 18	29 28
Nov.	01 22	09 03	16 14	18 24	10 05	08 16	18 26	09 07	04 18	13 28
	16 22	25 02	20 13	30 23	25 04	19 15	29 25	24 06	19 17	28 27
Dec.	01 21	11 01	17 12	16 22	12 03	09 14	14 24	10 05	05 16	13 26
	15 20									
	31 19	25 00	20 11	30 21	25 02	19 13	29 23	24 04	19 15	28 25

	1985	1986	1987	1988	1989	1990	1991	1992	1993	1994
Jan.	12 ♉ 25	07 ♉ 06	02 ♈ 16	12 ♓ 27	06 ♓ 08	01 ♒ 18	11 ♑ 29	06 ♑ 10	15 ♐ 20	10 ♐ 01
						15 18				
	27 24	22 05	17 16	27 26	21 07	31 17	26 28	21 09	30 19	25 ♏ 30
Feb.	11 23	06 04	01 15	12 25	05 06	16 16	10 27	06 08	14 28	08 29
	26 22	21 03	16 14	26 24	20 05		26 26	20 07		24 28
Mar.	13 21	07 02	02 13	12 23	08 04	03 16	13 25	07 06	01 17	11 27
									16 16	
	28 21	23 01	18 12	27 23	22 04	17 14	27 25	21 06	31 16	26 27
Apr.	14 20	09 00	04 12	12 22	08 03	01 14	13 24	05 05	15 15	09 26
	27 19	22 ♈ 30	17 11	26 21	21 02	16 13	26 23	20 04	30 14	25 25
May	14 18	07 29	02 10	14 20	10 01	01 12	10 22	06 03	15 13	11 24
						16 11				25 23
	27 17	22 28	17 09	26 19	21 00	31 10	26 21	20 02	30 13	
June	16 17	11 28	01 08	12 19	05 ♒ 30	17 10	12 21	03 01	15 12	08 23
	26 16	21 27	16 08	25 18	20 29	30 09	25 20	19 00	29 11	24 22
July	17 15	13 26	01 07	13 17	05 28	18 08	14 19	04 ♐ 30	15 10	09 21
			16 06							
	26 14	21 25	31 05	25 16	20 27	30 07	25 18	19 29	29 09	24 20
Aug.	10 13	05 24	18 05	10 15	04 26	19 07	11 17	02 28	14 09	09 19
	25 13	20 24	30 04	23 15	19 26	29 06	24 17	18 28	28 08	23 19
Sept.	10 12	04 23	19 03	11 14	05 25	15 05	09 16	03 27	11 07	06 18
	24 11	19 22	29 02	23 13	18 24	28 03	23 15	17 26	27 06	22 17
Oct.	12 10	04 21	16 01	12 12	04 23	16 03	08 14	02 25	13 05	07 16
	24 09	19 20	29 00	23 11	18 22	28 03	23 13	17 24	27 05	22 16
Nov.	14 09	08 20	13 ♓ 30	06 11	05 22	15 02	07 13	01 24	13 04	06 15
	23 08	18 19	28 29	22 10	17 21	27 01	22 12	16 23	26 03	21 14
Dec.	16 07	09 18	17 28	08 09	02 20	17 00	10 11	01 22	14 02	07 13
								18 21		
	23 06	18 17	28 27	22 08	17 19	27 ♑ 29	22 10	31 20	26 01	28 12

	1995	1996	1997	1998	1999	2000	2001	2002	2003	2004
Jan.	05 ♏ 12 20 11	15 ♎ 22 30 21	09 ♎ 03 24 02	04 ♍ 14 19 13	14 ♌ 24 29 23	09 ♌ 05 24 04	03 ♋ 16 18 15	13 ♊ 26 28 25	08 ♊ 07 23 06	03 ♉ 18 18 17
Feb.	03 10 19 09	15 20 29 19	08 01 23 00	04 12 18 11	12 22 28 21	09 03 23 02	02 14 17 13	13 24 27 23	07 05 22 04	03 16 17 15
Mar.	05 09 21 08	14 19 30 18	10 ♍ 30 25 29	06 10 20 10	16 21 30 20	10 01 24 00	04 12 19 12	15 23 29 22	11 03 24 03	05 14 18 14
Apr.	07 07 20 06	14 17 29 16	08 28 24 27	05 09 19 08	16 19 29 18	08 ♋ 30 23 29	06 11 18 10	15 21 28 20	08 02 23 01	02 13 17 12
May	06 05 20 04	13 15 29 15	09 26 24 25	03 07 19 06	17 17 29 17	10 28 23 27	04 09 18 08	14 19 28 19	11 00 23 ♉ 30	03 11 17 10
June	07 04 19 03	13 14 28 13	08 25 23 24	04 06 18 05	16 16 28 15	09 27 22 26	05 08 17 07	11 18 27 17	10 29 22 28	01 10 16 09
July	05 02 19 01	12 12 28 11	09 23 23 22	02 04 18 03	15 14 28 13	11 25 22 24	02 06 17 05	13 16 27 15	10 27 22 26	01 08 16 07 31 06
Aug.	12 00 18 ♎ 30	13 11 27 10	07 22 22 21	02 02 17 02	14 13 27 12	05 24 21 23	01 04 17 04 31 03	12 15 26 14	06 26 21 25	15 06 30 05
Sept.	08 29 17 28	13 09 26 08	07 20 21 19	01 01 16 00	16 11 26 10	08 22 20 21	18 02 30 01	14 13 25 12	09 24 20 23	15 04 29 03
Oct.	10 27 17 26	14 07 26 07	06 18 21 18	01 ♌ 29 17 28 31 28	10 09 26 09	11 20 20 20	17 00 30 ♊ 30	11 11 25 11	07 22 20 22	16 03 29 02
Nov.	01 26 16 25	12 06 25 05	06 17 20 16	18 27 30 26	12 08 25 07	13 19 19 18	18 29 29 28	14 10 24 09	08 21 19 20	15 01 28 00
Dec.	01 24 17 23 31 22	11 04 25 03	07 15 20 14	16 25 30 24	09 06 25 05	09 17 19 16	17 27 29 27	10 08 24 07	03 19 19 18	13 ♈ 30 28 29

	2005	2006	2007	2008	2009	2010	2011	2012	2013	2014
Jan.	12 ♈ 28 27 27	07 ♈ 09 22 08	02 ♓ 20 17 19	12 ♒ 30 27 29	06 ♒ 11 21 10	01 ♑ 22 16 21 31 20	11 ♑ 02 26 01	06 ♐ 13 21 12	15 ♏ 23 30 22	10 ♏ 04 25 03
Feb.	11 26 26 25	06 07 21 06	01 18 16 17	12 28 26 27	04 09 20 08	15 19	10 00 25 ♐ 30	05 11 20 10	13 21	08 02 24 01
Mar.	14 25 28 24	07 05 23 05	02 16 18 16	12 27 27 26	08 08 22 07	03 18 17 18	13 29 27 28	06 10 21 09	01 20 15 20 31 19	11 01 26 ♎ 30
Apr.	16 23 27 22	09 04 22 03	04 15 17 14	12 25 26 24	07 06 21 05	01 17 16 16	13 27 26 26	05 08 20 07	04 18 30 17	10 29 25 28
May	17 21 27 21	09 02 22 02	02 13 17 12	14 23 26 23	08 04 21 04	01 15 17 14 31 14	11 25 26 24	06 06 20 06	15 16 30 16	09 27 25 27
June	15 20 26 19	06 01 21 ♓ 30	01 12 16 11	10 22 25 21	07 03 20 02	11 13 30 12	11 24 25 23	03 05 19 04	16 15 29 14	08 26 24 25
July	17 18 26 17	06 29 21 28	01 10 18 09 31 08	12 20 25 19	09 01 20 00	18 11 30 11	12 22 25 21	04 03 19 02	15 13 29 13	10 24 24 23
Aug.	20 17 25 16	10 28 20 27	19 08 30 07	13 19 24 18	04 ♑ 30 19 29	21 10 29 09	11 21 24 20	02 02 18 01	14 12 28 11	07 23 23 22
Sept.	17 15 24 14	12 26 19 25	20 06 29 05	08 17 23 16	03 28 18 27	18 08 28 07	09 19 23 18	02 ♏ 30 17 29	13 10 27 09	07 21 22 20
Oct.	13 13 24 13	03 24 19 24	22 05 29 04	10 15 23 15	04 26 18 26	14 07 28 06	11 17 23 17	02 28 17 28	14 09 27 08	08 19 22 19
Nov.	15 12 23 11	05 23 18 22	23 03 28 02	15 14 22 13	04 25 17 24	15 05 27 04	06 16 22 15	01 27 16 26	12 07 26 06	07 18 21 17
Dec.	09 10 23 09	05 21 18 20	13 01 28 01	16 12 22 11	03 23 17 22	17 03 27 03	08 14 22 14	01 25 18 24 31 24	10 05 26 05	06 16 21 16

	2015		2016		2017		2018		2019		2020		2021		2022		2023		2024	
Jan.	05 ♎ 15		15 ♍ 25		09 ♍ 06		04 ♌ 17		14 ♋ 27		09 ♋ 08		03 ♊ 19		13 ♉ 29		08 ♉ 10		03 ♈ 21	
	20	14	30	24	24	05	19	16	29	26	24	07	18	18	28	28	23	09	18	20
Feb.	04	13	14	23	07	04	02	15	13	25	08	06	03	17	11	27	07	08	02	19
	19	12	29	22	23	03	18	14	28	24	23	05	17	16	27	27	22	07	17	18
Mar.	05	12	15	22	12	03	06	14	16	24	09	05	04	16	13	26	10	07	03	18
	21	11	30	21	25	02	20	13	30	23	24	04	19	15	29	25	24	06	18	17
Apr.	07	10	14	20	11	01	05	12	15	22	08	03	04	14	14	24	09	05	02	16
	20	09	29	19	24	00	19	11	29	21	23	02	18	13	28	23	23	04	17	15
May	05	08	16	19	09 ♌ 30		06	10	14	21	10	01	05	12	12	23	07	03	03	14
	20	08	29	18	24	29	19	10	29	20	23	00	18	12	28	22	23	03	17	14
June	03	07	13	17	12	28	04	09	14	19	07 ♊ 30		04	11	13	21	08	02	01	13
	19	06	28	16	23	27	18	08	28	18	22	29	17	10	27	20	22	01	16	12
July	05	05	15	15	11	26	06	07	15	17	06	28	05	09	12	19	07	00	01	11
																			16	10
	19	04	28	15	23	25	18	06	28	17	22	27	17	08	27	19	22 ♈ 30		31	10
Aug.	09	04	17	14	13	24	07	06	11	16	10	27	01	08	12	18	08	29	14	09
													15	07						
	18	03	27	13	22	24	17	05	27	15	24	26	31	06	26	17	21	28	30	08
Sept.	11	02	21	12	08	23	01	04	13	14	09	25	18	05	12	16	06	27	13	07
	17	01	26	11	21	22	16	03	26	13	20	24	30	04	25	15	20	26	29	06
Oct.	10	00	14	11	09	22	01	02	15	13	11	24	15	04	12	15	07	26	13	06
							17	02												
	17 ♍ 30		26	10	21	21	31	01	26	12	20	23	30	03	25	14	20	25	29	05
Nov.	01	29	09	09	14	20	18	00	10	11	04	22	16	02	14	13	04	24	14	04
	16	28	25	08	20	19	30 ♋ 29		25	10	19	21	29	01	24	12	19	23	28	03
Dec.	01	27	11	07	15	18	22	28	16	09	04	20	17	00	10	11	04	22	12	02
	16	26																		
	31	26	25	07	20	18	30	28	25	09	19	19	29 ♉ 30		24	11	19	22	28	02

	2025		2026		2027		2028		2029		2030		2031		2032		2033		2034	
Jan.	12 ♈ 01		07 ♓ 12		02 ♒ 23		12 ♒ 03		06 ♑ 14		01 ♐ 25		11 ♐ 05		06 ♏ 16		15 ♎ 26		10 ♎ 07	
											15	24								
	27	00	22	11	17	22	27	02	21	13	31	23	26	04	21	15	30	25	25	06
Feb.	11 ♓ 30		05	10	01	21	11	01	06	12	16	22	09	03	05	14	13	24	10	05
	26	29	21	09	16	20	26	00	20	11			25	03	20	13			24	05
Mar.	14	28	08	09	02	20	12 ♑ 30		07	11	03	22	12	02	06	13	01	24	11	04
																	15	23		
	28	27	23	08	18	19	27	29	22	10	17	21	27	01	21	12	31	22	26	03
Apr.	13	26	08	07	04	18	10	28	07	09	01	20	11	00	05	11	14	21	09	02
	27	25	22	06	17	17	26	27	21	08	16	19	26 ♏ 29		20	10	30	20	25	01
May	15	25	10	05	02	16	12	27	08	08	01	18	11	29	06	10	16	20	09	00
											16	18								
	27	24	22	05	17	16	26	26	21	07	31	17	26	28	20	09	30	19	25 ♍ 30	
June	13	23	10	04	01	15	09	25	07	06	17	16	10	27	03	08	14	18	08	29
	26	22	21	03	16	14	25	24	20	05	30	15	25	26	19	07	29	17	24	28
July	15	21	11	02	01	13	11	23	09	04	16	14	12	25	04	06	15	16	10	27
					16	13														
	26	21	21	02	31	12	25	23	20	04	30	14	25	25	19	06	29	16	24	27
Aug.	12	20	05	01	17	11	13	22	05	03	18	13	13	24	02	05	14	15	08	26
	25	19	20 ♒ 30		30	10	24	21	19	02	29	12	23	23	18	04	28	14	23	25
Sept.	14	18	04	29	19	09	15	20	06	01	15	11	11	22	03	03	12	13	07	24
	24	17	19	28	29	08	23	19	18	00	28	11	23	21	17	02	27	13	22	23
Oct.	13	17	04	28	18	08	16	19	03 ♐ 30		14	10	12	21	02	02	13	12	08	23
	24	16	19	27	29	07	23	18	18	29	28	09	23	20	17	01	27	11	22	22
Nov.	15	15	09	26	19	06	06	17	04	28	17	08	07	19	01 ♎ 30		14	10	05	21
	23	14	18	25	28	05	22	16	17	27	27	07	22	18	16	29	26	09	21	20
Dec.	09	13	10	24	17	05	08	15	06	26	18	07	11	17	01	28	12	09	07	20
															16	28				
	23	13	18	24	28	04	22	15	17	26	27	06	22	17	31	27	26	08	21	19

	2035		2036		2037		2038		2039		2040		2041		2042		2043		2044	
Jan.	05 ♍ 18		15 ♌ 28		09 ♌ 09		04 ♋ 20		14 ♋ 00		09 ♊ 11		03 ♉ 22		13 ♉ 02		08 ♈ 13		03 ♓ 24	
	20	17	30	27	24	08	19	19	29 ♊ 29		24	10	18	21	28	01	23	12	18	23
Feb.	03	16	13	26	08	07	04	18	14	28	09	09	02	20	12	00	06	11	03	22
	19	16	29	26	23	07	18	18	28	28	23	09	17	20	29 ♈ 30		22	11	17	22
Mar.	05	15	15	25	10	06	06	17	16	27	09	08	04	19	13	29	10	10	02	21
	21	14	30	24	25	05	20	16	30	26	24	07	19	18	29	28	24	09	18	20
Apr.	07	13	15	23	11	04	05	15	15	25	08	06	05	17	12	27	09	08	03	19
	20	12	29	22	24	03	19	14	29	24	23	05	18	16	28	27	23	07	17	18
May	06	12	16	22	11	03	04	14	15	24	07	05	04	16	13	26	08	07	02	18
	20	11	29	21	24	02	19	13	29	23	23	04	18	15	28	25	23	06	17	17
June	09	10	14	20	10	01	06	12	15	22	07	03	05	14	12	24	08	05	01	16
	19	09	28	19	23	00	18	11	28	21	22	02	17	13	27	23	22	04	16	15
July	04	08	16	19	08 ♋ 30		07	10	14	21	09	01	03	12	13	23	08	03	01	14
																			15	14
	19	08	28	18	23	29	18	10	28	20	22	00	17	12	27	22	22	03	31	13
Aug.	09	07	12	17	11	28	06	09	13	19	06 ♉ 30		01	11	12	21	07	02	14	12
													16	10						
	18	06	27	16	22	27	17	08	27	18	21	29	31	09	26	20	21	01	30	11
Sept.	10	05	10	15	05	26	01	07	11	17	06	28	17	08	11	19	08	00	15	10
	17	04	26	15	21	25	16	06	26	17	20	27	30	08	25	19	20 ♓ 30		29	10
Oct.	09	04	12	14	07	25	01	06	13	16	10	27	18	07	12	18	05	29	13	09
							17	05												
	17	03	26	13	21	24	31	04	26	15	20	26	30	06	25	17	20	28	29	08
Nov.	01	02	14	12	14	23	19	03	15	14	11	25	16	05	12	16	04	27	13	07
	16	01	25	11	20	22	30	02	25	13	19	24	29	04	24	15	19	26	28	06
Dec.	01	00	17	11	15	21	20	02	14	13	04	24	15	04	14	15	05	26	13	06
	15 ♌ 30																			
	31	29	25	10	20	21	30	01	25	12	19	23	29	03	24	14	19	25	28	05

	2045		2046		2047		2048		2049		2050		2051		2052		2053		2054	
Jan.	12 ♓ 04		07 ♒ 15		02 ♑ 26		12 ♑ 06		06 ♐ 17		01 ♏ 28		11 ♏ 08		06 ♎ 19		15 ♍ 29		10 ♍ 10	
											15	27								
	27	03	22	14	17	25	27	05	21	16	31	26	26	07	21	18	30	28	25	09
Feb.	10	02	06	13	01	24	11	05	05	15	15	26	10	07	06	17	14	28	08	09
	26	02	21	13	16	24	26	04	20	15			25	06	20	17			24	08
Mar.	15	01	07	12	02	23	12	03	08	14	03	25	13	05	07	16	01	27	11	07
																	16	26		
	28	00	23	11	18	22	27	02	22	13	17	24	27	04	21	15	31	25	26	06
Apr.	12 ♒ 29		09	10	04	21	12	01	08	12	01	23	13	03	05	14	14	24	09	05
	27	29	22	09	17	20	26	00	21	11	16	22	26	03	30	13	30	24	25	05
May	15	28	06	09	02	20	11 ♐ 30		07	11	01	22	10	02	06	13	16	23	11	04
											16	21								
	27	27	22	08	17	19	26	29	21	10	31	20	26	01	20	12	30	22	25	03
June	17	26	08	07	01	18	14	28	07	09	18	19	09	00	03	11	15	21	10	02
	26	25	21	06	17	17	25	27	20	08	30	18	25 ♎ 30		19	10	29	20	24	01
July	16	25	10	05	01	16	12	27	08	08	18	18	11	29	04	10	14	19	09	00
					17	16														
	26	24	21	05	31	15	25	26	20	07	30	17	25	28	19	09	29	19	24 ♌ 30	
Aug.	17	23	11	04	19	14	13	25	05	06	18	16	12	27	02	08	13	18	09	29
	25	22	20	03	30	13	24	24	19	05	29	15	24	26	18	07	28	17	23	28
Sept.	10	21	04	02	19	12	11	23	06	04	14	14	10	25	03	06	14	16	07	27
	24	21	19	02	29	12	23	23	18	04	28	14	23	25	17	06	27	16	22	27
Oct.	12	20	04	01	20	11	15	22	04	03	15	13	16	24	02	05	13	15	08	26
	24	19	19 ♑ 30		29	10	23	21	18	02	28	12	23	23	17	04	27	14	22	25
Nov.	09	18	09	29	19	09	17	20	05	01	18	11	10	22	01	03	10	13	06	24
	23	17	18	28	28	08	22	19	17	00	27	10	22	21	16	02	26	13	21	23
Dec.	08	17	11	28	20	08	12	19	02 ♏ 30		19	10	12	21	01	01	13	12	06	23
															20	00				
	23	16	18	27	28	07	22	18	17	29	27	09	22	20	31 ♍ 30		26	11	21	22

GLOSSARY

Angle: The Ascendant and Descendant are termed angles; the Midheaven and Fourth House cusp are also called angles, as these axes form a cross through the horoscope, indicating sensitive personal points. Other angles include the Vertex/Anti-Vertex. These represent key points in a horoscope—very personal points that require a time of birth to calculate.

Anti-Vertex: A point in the chart that is comparable to the Ascendant. See chapter 3.

Ascendant: The start of the First House; rules the demeanor and physical body.

Conjunction: A powerful aspect consisting of two bodies or points in the same sector of the zodiac, within a few degrees. Most powerful if they share the same degree.

Converse: Type of progression method useful for prediction. See chapter 9.

Descendant: The start of the Seventh House; represents other people.

Dragon's Head: The North Node. Also known as Rahu.

Dragon's Tail: The South Node. Also known as Ketu.

Ephemeris: A book or list that gives the planetary positions daily for long increments of time.

Fortuna: The Part of Fortune is also called Fortuna, representing a place of joy.

Fortune Planets: Jupiter, Venus, and the Sun.

IC: The Fourth House cusp. Also known as the Lower Heaven, or Imum Coeli.

Karma: Rewards for past deeds, whether positive or negative. Karma is an objective, impersonal balancing mechanism existing in the universal spirit.

Ketu: Vedic astrologers call the South Node Ketu.

Line of Advantage: An imaginary line through the Second and Eighth Houses of the horoscope that indicates specific advantages in life if the North Node is above the line. See chapter 2.

Mean Node: A way of measuring the position of the lunar nodes. See chapter 1.

Midheaven: The tiptop of the chart, signifying worldly recognition and status. The Midheaven is the start of the Tenth House. Also known as the MC or Medium Coeli.

Orb: The amount of leeway allowed from an exact aspect of 0, 60, 90, or 120 degrees for the conjunction, sextile, square, and trine aspects respectfully. The recommended orbs are given in each chapter and they vary, depending on the type of nodal connection that is being applied and is under discussion.

Part of Fortune: A point in the chart that shows where joy and fortune can be found.

Progression: The progression of our lives is reflected in our horoscope through a technique known as Secondary Progressions. See the start of chapter 9 for an explanation.

Rahu: Vedic astrologers call the North Node Rahu.

Retrograde: From our viewpoint on earth, planets other than the Sun and Moon appear to back up at certain times of the year. They aren't really moving backward, but appear to be moving backward in the zodiac from an earthly perspective.

Sextile: Two bodies or celestial points that are 60 degrees apart in the zodiac. A friendly relationship or aspect.

Square: Two bodies or celestial points that are 90 degrees apart in the zodiac. A stressful relationship or aspect.

Trine: Two bodies or celestial points that are 120 degrees apart in the zodiac. A friendly relationship or aspect.

True Node: A way of measuring the position of the lunar nodes. See chapter 1.

Vertex: A point in the chart that is comparable to the Descendant. See chapter 3.

BIBLIOGRAPHY

Braha, James T. *Ancient Hindu Astrology for the Modern Western Astrologer.* Hong Kong: Liang Yu Printing Factory, Ltd., 1993.

Goldstein-Jacobson, Ivy M. *The Way of Astrology.* Pasadena, CA: Pasadena Lithographers, 1967.

Koparker, Mohan. *Lunar Nodes.* Rochester, NY: Mohan Enterprises, 1977.

Schulman, Martin. *Karmic Astrology: The Moon's Nodes & Reincarnation.* New York, NY: Samuel Weiser, Inc., 1975.

Teal, Celeste. *Eclipses: Predicting World Events & Personal Transformation.* Woodbury, MN: Llewellyn Publications, 2006.

____. *Identifying Planetary Triggers.* St. Paul, MN: Llewellyn Publications, 2000.

____. *Predicting Events with Astrology.* St. Paul, MN: Llewellyn Publications, 1999.

Trivedi, Prash. *The Key of Life.* New Delhi: Sagar Printers & Publishers, 2002.

White, George. *The Moon's Nodes.* Tempe, AZ: American Federation of Astrologers, 1989.

WEBSITE RESOURCES

Following is a list of Internet astrology resources; several places where you can acquire either a free or fee-based copy of your horoscope just by entering your birth data, including date, time, and location. Along with the date and city of your birth, having an accurate birth time produces an accurate chart. If unsure of the birth time by even a few minutes, check your birth certificate. The last link below allows you to obtain an official U.S. birth certificate.

If you are unable to find your birth time due to a lack of records, but feeling determined about seeing your true horoscope, find a professional astrologer, competent in "rectification," to help you. Such an expert can find your birth time, working backward, based on a list of important events and dates that you provide. Not many astrologers do this work, and fewer are competent, so be sure to ask about their experience. Otherwise, if you've no idea, omit the time entirely. This will produce a sunrise chart for you and your Sun should appear on your First House cusp, the Ascendant. This produces a logical house sequence and planetary placements, whereas an inaccurate time only confuses things. This method will give you a workable chart, though less personal in nature than if you have your time of birth.

www.alphee.com	www.thenewage.com
www.alabe.com	www.astro.com
www.astro-horoscopes.com	www.astrology-search.com
www.astrologyhouse.com	www.astrologicalknowledge.com
www.astrodatabank.com	www.llewellyn.com
www.astrology-numerology.com	www.astrologers.com
www.stariq.com	www.mountainastrologer.com
www.moonvalleyastrologer.com	www.astrologysoftware.com
www.astrolog.org	www.mohanstars.com
www.cdc.gov/nchs/howto/w2w/w2welcom.htm	

The above sites have informative articles and links and some also provide free or fee-based software to download to create your own charts.

CHART DATA RESOURCE NOTES

Chapter One

Paula Abdul
BC/BR in hand (Rodden Rating: AA)
Reference: AstroDatabank
www.astrodatabank.com

Larry Flynt
G. Wolfsohn quotes B.C.
(Rodden Rating: AA)
Reference: AstroDatabank
www.astrodatabank.com

Al Pacino
BC in hand (Rodden Rating: AA)
Reference: AstroDataBank
www.astrodatabank.com

Chapter Two

JFK Jr.
Garth Allen quotes Jackie Onassis in
the press (Rodden Rating: A)
Reference: AstroDatabank
www.astrodatabank.com

Jim Morrison
BC/BR in hand (Rodden Rating: AA)
Reference: AstroDataBank
www.astrodatabank.com

Judy Garland
BC in hand (Rodden Rating: AA)
Reference: AstroDatabank
www.astrodatabank.com

RuPaul
John McKay-Clements quotes BC
(Rodden Rating: AA)
Reference: AstroDatabank
www.astrodatabank.com

Jason Alexander
BC/BR in hand (Rodden Rating: AA)
Reference: AstroDatabank
www.astrodatabank.com

Oprah Winfrey
From memory (Rodden Rating: A)
Reference: AstroDatabank
www.astrodatabank.com

Chapter Three

Ted Turner
BC/BR in hand
(Rodden Rating: AA)
Reference: AstroDatabank
www.astrodatabank.com

Angelina Jolie
Marc Penfield quotes BC
(Rodden Rating: AA)
Reference: AstroDatabank
www.astrodatabank.com

Patricia Krenwinkel
Contemporary American
    Horoscopes quotes BC
(Rodden Rating: AA)
Reference: AstroDatabank
www.astrodatabank.com

Pablo Picasso
Filipe Ferreira quotes BC
(Rodden Rating: AA)
Reference: AstroDatabank
www.astrodatabank.com

Neil Armstrong
BC in hand (Rodden Rating: AA)
Reference: AstroDatabank
www.astrodatabank.com

Althea Flynt
BC/BR in hand
(Rodden Rating: AA)
Reference: AstroDataBank
www.astrodatabank.com

Princess Alice
Sandra Rozhon quotes official
    announcement
(Rodden Rating: AA)
Reference: AstroDataBank
www.astrodatabank.com

Chapter Seven

Donald Trump
From memory (Rodden Rating: A)
Reference: AstroDatabank
www.astrodatabank.com

Robin Williams
BC/BR in hand
(Rodden Rating: AA)
Reference: AstroDatabank
www.astrodatabank.com

Nicolas Cage
BC/BR in hand
(Rodden Rating: AA)
Reference: AstroDatabank
www.astrodatabank.com

Cameron Diaz
Frank C. Clifford quotes BC
(Rodden Rating: AA)
Reference: AstroDatabank
www.astrodatabank.com

Karen Carpenter
Steinbreacher quotes BR
(Rodden Rating: AA)
Reference: AstroDatabank
www.astrodatabank.com

Chapter Eight

James Van Praagh
From memory (Rodden Rating: A)
Reference: AstroDataBank
www.astrodatabank.com

Timothy McVeigh
Quotes BC/BR
(Rodden Rating: AA)
Reference: AstroDataBank
www.astrodatabank.com

Alicia Silverstone
Frank C. Clifford quotes BC in
    hand (Rodden Rating: AA)
Reference: AstroDataBank
www.astrodatabank.com

Michael Moore
Quotes BC (Rodden Rating: AA)
Reference: AstroDatabank
www.astrodatabank.com

Leonardo DiCaprio
BC/BR in hand
(Rodden Rating: AA)
Reference: AstroDatabank
www.astrodatabank.com

George Clooney
Quotes BC (Rodden Rating: AA)
Reference: AstroDatabank
www.astrodatabank.com

Jennifer Aniston
Marc Penfield quotes BC
Reference: AstroDatabank
www.astrodatabank.com

Chapter Nine

Ron Howard
Contemporary American
    Horoscopes quotes BC
(Rodden Rating: AA)
Reference: AstroDatabank
www.astrodatabank.com

Sonny Bono
Contemporary American
    Horoscopes quotes B.C.
(Rodden Rating: AA)
Reference: AstroDataBank
www.astrodatabank.com

Seung-Hui Cho
No known birth time
Birth Date Reference: Wikipedia,
http://www.vtreviewpanel.org/re-
port/report/11_CHAPTER_IV

Chapter Twelve

Paula Abdul's Solar Return
Patricia Krenwinkel's Solar Return

INDEX